**Longman Exam Guides
Business Communication**

WITHDRAWN
WITHDRAWN
WITHDRAWN

Longman Exam Guides

Series Editors: Stuart Wall and David Weigall

Titles available:

Accounting Standards
Biology
Bookkeeping and Accounting
British Government and Politics
Business Communication
Business Law
Commerce and Background to Business
Economics
Elements of Banking
English as a Foreign Language: Preliminary Examinations
English as a Foreign Language: Intermediate Examinations
English Literature
General Principles of Law
General Studies
Monetary Economics
Office Practice and
     Secretarial Administration
Pure Mathematics
Secretarial Skills

Forthcoming:

Accounting: Financial
Applied Mathematics
Business Studies
Chemistry
Company Law
Computer Science
Cost and Management Accounting
Electronics
English as a Foreign Language: Advanced
French
Geography
Investment
Modern British History
Physics
Sociology
Statistics
Taxation

Longman Exam Guides

BUSINESS COMMUNICATION

Elizabeth Kenrick
with
Sylvia Griffiths
Gillian Parata

LONGMAN
London and New York

Longman Group UK Limited
Longman House, Burnt Mill, Harlow
Essex CM20 2JE, England
Associated companies throughout the world

*Published in the United States of America
by Longman Inc., New York*

First published 1987

British Library Cataloguing in Publication Data
Kenrick, Elizabeth
   Business communication. – (Longman exam
guides)
1. Communication 2. Communication in
management
I. Title II. Griffiths, Sylvia H.
001.51′024658 P90

ISBN 0-582-29680-3

Library of Congress Cataloging in Publication Data
Kenrick, Elizabeth, 1937–
   Business communication.
   (Longman exam guides)
   Bibliography: p.
   Includes index.
   1. Communication in management. I. Griffiths,
Sylvia H., 1946– . II. Parata, Gillian, 1947– .
III. Title. IV. Series.
HF5718.K46 1987   001.51′02465   86-14768
ISBN 0-582-29680-3

Produced by Longman Singapore Publishers (Pte) Ltd.
Printed in Singapore

Contents

Editors' preface

Much has been said in recent years about declining standards and disappointing examination results. While this may be somewhat exaggerated, examiners are well aware that the performance of many candidates falls well short of their potential. Longman Exam Guides are written by experienced examiners and teachers, and aim to give you the best possible foundation for examination success. There is no attempt to cut corners. The books encourage thorough study and a full understanding of the concepts involved and should be seen as course companions and study guides to be used throughout the year. Examiners are in no doubt that a structured approach in preparing for and taking examinations can, together with hard work and diligent application, substantially improve performance.

The largely self-contained nature of each chapter gives the book a useful degree of flexibility. After starting with Chapters 1 and 2, all other chapters can be read selectively, in any order appropriate to the stage you have reached in your course. We believe that this book, and the series as a whole, will help you establish a solid platform of basic knowledge and examination technique on which to build.

Stuart Wall and David Weigall

Acknowledgements

The authors would like to thank John Fletcher of Slough College of Higher Education for supplying helpful materials.

We are grateful to the following for permission to reproduce copyright material:

British Association for Commercial and Industrial Education for fig. 12.7; British Telecommunications plc for the British Telecom Logo; Burton Daily Mail Ltd for part of fig 13.9; Cambridge City Council for figs 11.2 and 13.1; Cambridge Communication Ltd for fig 10.13 from USS Pension Scheme Booklet; Cambridge Evening News for fig 12.6; Cambridgeshire Community Council for fig 4.8; Cambridgeshire Constabulary for fig 7.6; Dalgety UK Ltd for 'The Flour Grader'; Dun & Bradstreet Ltd for fig 13.10 from *D&B Update*; Endsleigh Insurance Services Ltd for fig 11.1; FBC Ltd for an extract from *Action*, Fisons House Magazine; Financial Times for an extract from the article 'Giving employees something to chew on' by Arnold Kransdorff in *Financial Times* 24/9/80; the author, Tony Hathway for figs 3.5 and 3.6(c) Bristol Polytechnic 1981; William Heinemann Ltd for an extract from *Effective Communication Made Simple* by E.C. Eyre; the Controller of Her Majesty's Stationery Office for fig 13.5 Crown Copyright; IBM United Kingdom Ltd for the IBM Logo; Kellogg Company of Great Britain Ltd for figs 3.7, 5.7 and 5.8; Mast (Cambridge) for fig 10.11; National Consumer Council for fig 13.8; Northampton Chronicle and Echo for part of fig 13.9; Rowntree Mackintosh plc for fig 10.12 from their *Employee Report 1984*; W.H. Smith & Son Ltd for the WHS Logo; The Sports Council for fig 4.5; Surveyors Technical Services for fig 8.8(c) RICS October 1984; Ultimate Office Equipment Ltd for figs 5.5 and 5.6; Wilkinson Sword Ltd for fig 13.7;

and the following examination boards for permission to reproduce past examination questions: Association of Accounting Technicians; The Institute of Chartered Secretaries and Administrators; The London Chamber of Commerce and Industry; The Royal Society of Arts Examination Board; the Scottish Vocational Educational Council.

Any answers or hints on answers are the sole responsibility of the authors and have not been provided or approved by the examination boards. The examination boards accept no responsibility for the accuracy or method of working in any of the answers.

How to use this book

Communication, as distinct from English language or office skills, is a relatively new examination subject which has been introduced in response to the growing importance of communication skills in business and professional life. It is not a subject which can be neatly divided into distinct topics, so you should be constantly aware of the relevance of material in chapters other than the one you are currently revising. You will find that we often jog your memory with cross-references. You are strongly advised to follow these up, even if they refer to chapters not strictly relevant to your syllabus, because they point to a stimulating way of gleaning useful background information. For example, the passage set for a Summary question in Chapter 6 concerning the communication policy of a large company is brought to life by the extracts from that company's publications shown in Chapter 4.

The order in which the topics are presented corresponds roughly with the usual order in which they are covered in a college course. Thus letter-writing is usually studied before the realistic and professional presentation of other means of communication; while practice at comprehension and summary is essential before tackling reports.

We have assumed that you are also following one of the current textbooks referred to in the bibliographies at the end of each chapter. A home-based student might just be able to pass an exam by reading the book from cover to cover, but it is primarily designed to help you with your revision and to give practical advice on how to tackle a wide range of exam questions.

Section A of each chapter sets the topic in context and outlines what you will need to know.

Section B gives you a summary of the material most frequently examined, and takes you through a representative selection of practical tasks.

Section C provides examples of documents and extracts from publications. Wherever possible we have used actual rather than fictitious examples in order to give a realistic flavour. We hope that this material will be useful to teachers as well as to students, and that it will encourage readers to collect further examples.

Section D presents a selection of questions from recent examination papers. Communication exams present a particular problem because of the increasing tendency to set 'case study' papers rather than self-contained questions. We show one complete paper in Chapter 1. We have also extracted as many examples as is practicable from such papers without reproducing them in their entirety. You should always try the questions yourself before looking at the answers. Do not confine yourself to questions from your own particular exam, and do at least look at questions outside your syllabus because the answers often contain useful background information.

Section E discusses the problems raised by each question and presents an outline on which you could build a successful answer and/or a full 'tutor's answer'.

Section F gives you practical advice on how to pursue the topic further, and a list of useful publications and films.

You will notice that we place a strong emphasis on language skills. Communication students – particularly secretarial students – are often dismayed at first by all the red marks under the incorrect punctuation and the sloppy phrasing, much of which may previously have gone without comment in subject essays at school. Communication teachers have to be rigorous about details, because they have to prepare you for jobs which demand a professional use of language in a business context. If you are concerned about your written style you should consult the bibliographies at the end of Chapters 3 and 5.

(In order to avoid cumbersome instructions we have had to use 'he', 'him' and 'his' throughout while being uncomfortably aware that the majority of readers are likely to be female.)

The table overleaf will help in locating the chapters of this book relevant to particular courses.

Many of the chapters will also be useful to students studying other subjects which include communications. Examples of these are RSA Secretarial Duties, the Institute of Industrial Management, LCCI Private Secretary's Certificate (Structure of Business), RSA Background to Business, GCE A level (AEB) Business Studies, as well as many other professional examinations. Teachers studying for the RSA Teacher's Certificate in the Teaching of Communication Skills and the City and Guilds Teacher's Certificate 730 will also find most of the book relevant to their course. Modules at B/TEC HND level which include communications will find all the chapters useful in supporting business assignments.

Examining body	London Chamber of Commerce and Industry					
Examination	English for Commerce			Comm. – Use of English.	Comm. – Use of English.	Comm. – Use of English.
Level	Elem.	Int.	Higher	Sec. Studies Cert.	P.S.C.	P & E Sec. Dip.
Chapter						
3. Principles and practice of business communication						
4. Letters	√	√	√	√	√	√
5. Internal written communication	√	√	√	√	√	√
6. Comprehension and summaries	√	√	√	√	√	√
7. Reports			√	√	√	
8. Meetings				√	√	√
9. Oral communication			√	√	√	√
10. Visual communication						√
11. Forms and questionnaires						
12. Job applications and interviews				√	√	
13. Public relations					√	

Topics and examinations

Examining body	AAT	B/TEC	SCOTVEC			GCE: AEB		
Examination	Comm.	People in Org.	Comm.			Comm. Studies		English Lang. (Prof. Bus.)
Level	—	Nat.	I	II	III	Adv.	O/A	O/A
Chapter								
3. Principles and practice of business communication	√	√			√	√	√	
4. Letters	√	√	√	√	√	√	√	√
5. Internal written communication	√	√		√	√	√	√	√
6. Comprehension and summaries		√	√	√	√			√
7. Reports	√	√		√	√	√	√	√
8. Meetings	√	√		√	√	√	√	√
9. Oral communication		√	√	√	√	√	√	√
10. Visual communication		√		√	√	√	√	√
11. Forms and questionnaires	√	√		√	√	√	√	√
12. Job applications and interviews		√		√		√	√	√
13. Public relations		√			√	√	√	

Royal Society of Arts				Pitman Examinations Institute						AMSPAR	IoB
Communication in Business			Comm.	Eng. for Bus. Comm.			Eng. for Office Skills		Eng. for the Sec.	English	Bus. Comm.
I	II	III	D P A	EI	Int.	Adv.	EI	Int.	Adv.		Prelim. Cert.
	√	√		√							
√	√	√	√	√	√	√			√	√	√
√	√	√	√	√	√	√			√	√	√
			√				√	√	√	√	√
	√	√	√		√	√			√	√	
	√	√	√						√	√	
√	√	√	√							√	
√	√	√	√								
√	√	√	√							√	√
√	√	√	√								
	√	√	√								

Chapter 1

The examinations

Communication is an ever-changing subject, so the examiners have to respond by introducing new material and by devising new ways of testing candidates, both in writing and orally. There is also an increasing emphasis on visual and electronic means of communication. It is therefore important to keep abreast of current trends by getting the latest syllabus, copies of the last two years' examination papers, and recent examiners' reports, where available (see p. 51). You should also try to be familiar with current developments in business, such as the changing relationship between manufacturing, servicing and 'high tech' industries, or the new applications of information technology within organisations. The business pages of the national and local newspapers will help in this respect. Familiarity with current developments in business will help you place the various techniques of business communication in a contemporary setting. It will also help you understand and use an appropriate vocabulary in answering questions.

General management/professional and business studies

In this type of examination you will be expected to be aware of the principles of communication, the implications of the different modes of communication for the enterprise, and the various ways each mode can be applied. This means that you must be able to write *about* communication, and to *apply* your knowledge by producing the required documents for a given situation. Advanced candidates will also be required to read, understand and select from long and detailed texts, and to use sophisticated vocabulary and terminology from business or related subjects, such as law. These exams sometimes involve multi-choice questions which test your knowledge of basic principles and their application. The final examination includes marks for continuous assessment and compulsory assignments undertaken during the course.

Secretarial/clerical

This type of exam may include:

(a)   Practical questions involving letters, memos, minutes, etc. to test your knowledge of, and accuracy in, standard office procedures.

1

(b) Questions involving summaries, comprehension, etc. to test your understanding and use of language in a business context.

(c) Exercises in which you have to put yourself into a role, read and understand some lengthy and difficult background material and reproduce selected information from it in the appropriate style, register and format, e.g. circular memos, reports, etc. Sometimes you are asked to untangle some jumbled notes and convert them into documents.

Practical and general

N.B. **Many examinations now follow a *case study* format. All the questions from the following example are answered in outline and/or in full in the appropriate chapters. In each case there is a reference back to this complete paper.**

THE ROYAL SOCIETY OF ARTS EXAMINATIONS BOARD
SINGLE-SUBJECT EXAMINATIONS

**COMMUNICATIONS IN BUSINESS STAGE II (Intermediate)
WEDNESDAY, 20th JUNE, 1984
(TWO AND A HALF HOURS ALLOWED).**

You have TEN *minutes to read through this paper before the start of the examination.*
ALL *questions are to be attempted. They should be answered in the order in which they appear. Begin each answer on a new page.*
The mark allocation for each question is given. You are advised to take this into account in planning your work.
Answers will be assessed on layout, content, use of English and effectiveness in the given situation.

GENERAL INFORMATION APPLICABLE TO ALL QUESTIONS
(Information obtained from one question can be used in answering another)

You are employed as a secretary/personal assistant to Mark Grant who is Managing Director of Eastview Nurseries, a large garden centre situated in the outskirts of the town of Glanton. The garden centre was established by Mr Grant and three partners some fifteen years ago and now it is the major supplier of trees, plants and garden equipment in the Glanton area, although there are a number of competitors.

The four partners are directors of the private company, Eastview Nurseries Ltd., which owns the garden centre, and each have particular jobs within the organisation. Mr Grant is Managing Director and although he is not an expert on the subject of trees and plants, he has a shrewd business mind and has been a major part of the Nurseries' success.

Last year the centre held a very successful Dutch bulb festival which boosted sales of bulbs tremendously, and the partners are now considering holding a similar event as part of a national shrub week which will be taking place in the week beginning 21st July.

At the last meeting of the partners on 18th June it was decided that there will be an Eastview Shrub Week starting on Saturday 21st July, at which there will be special events to promote the sale of shrubs. It will begin with a well publicised day on the Saturday at which there will be demonstrations, special offers on shrubs, competitions and free gifts.

1.   *Writing a letter of reply*

SITUATION

While preparations for the shrub event are going ahead, Mr Grant receives a letter from Ted Eden, a famous gardening expert who has written many books on the subject and who appears on television regularly. Mr Eden, of "Appledore", Chatsworth Lane, Midwich, Derbyshire has recently published a book *The Complete Shrub Gardener* and wishes to promote sales of the book by appearing at garden centres. Mr Grant and the partners feel it would be a good idea to ask him to perform some kind of official opening of the week on the Saturday afternoon before he sells autographed copies of his book.

ASSIGNMENT

Draft a letter for Mr Grant's signature to Mr Eden, bearing in mind Mr Grant's instructions which were:

> "Write to him please − tell him about our shrub event. Tell him he can sell his books − we will provide him with a table in the main sales area, or he may want to be outside if the weather's OK. Ask him if he would mind saying a few words to open the thing. All he has to do is to say what a great idea it is and how lovely shrubs are − that sort of thing. Tell him if he'll open the event for us, we won't charge him to sell his books. If he won't then we'll have to ask for a percentage of sales, say 15%. Tell him to come to the office entrance at 1.45 p.m. (not the main entrance, there'll be crowds there) and he can open the show or start selling at 2.00 p.m. Ask him what time he plans to leave − we don't close until 9.00 p.m., but I'm sure he'll have to go before then. See if you can find out if he has plans for tea or should we lay it on for him."

(*Note*: You can assume you will use the company's headed notepaper, but you should prepare a complete letter using an appropriate format. A suitable answer will probably use about 200 words).   (20 marks)

2.   *Writing a report*

SITUATION

The wife of one of the partners is a member of the management committee of the St Jude's Trust, a charitable organisation which provides residential facilities for the elderly. The Trust has just completed a new home in Glanton which is soon to be opened. The partners have been approached to make a donation of shrubs to the Trust and this was readily agreed. It will be good publicity and it is a worthy cause.

The Trust has requested twenty shrubs, ten for each side of the main entrance path, but has left it to the Company as to what species of shrubs they should be. The matron of the home has requested that the twenty shrubs be of the same species, and there will be a plaque to indicate they were donated by Eastview Nurseries. Mr Grant has asked his Chief Gardener, Jack Holder, to suggest a number of possible shrubs and has received the following notes from Mr Holder.

"Possible shrubs:

Hydrangea — my favourite — beautiful flower but needs sheltered site. Flowers in August/September and some species can grow up to thirteen feet. Perhaps not so reliable out of doors as inside.

Fuchsia — very popular — there's a lot of them in Glanton. Grows up to two to four feet tall. Flowers during the summer but dies off completely in the winter and grows again in the spring.

Forsythia — Early flowering (spring) very attractive yellow flower. Trees can grow to fifteen feet. Don't need much attention — very vigorous.

Skimmias — not very well known, but a very attractive small shrub — grows up to about three feet. Produces berries and flowers. Grows easily in all soils. Often flowers are highly scented.

Camelia — lovely shrub. Very popular with old people. Hundreds of varieties available, beautiful flowers, usually pink or crimson. Flowers all through summer — different varieties are different sizes. Takes a bit of growing — can be affected by winds and need protection from frost.

Chamaecyparis — a coniferous evergreen. Doesn't flower, but attractive greenery all year round. Most varieties are like small trees and you get a nice hedge effect. Doesn't need much attention.

Buddleia — grows up to ten feet — flowers from June onwards — often lilac coloured flowers. Doesn't grow so well in alkaline soil.

Viburnums — very easily grown and showy — usually white flowers — can grow up to ten feet. Not very well known plant but often attractive leaves. Summer flowerer. old species.

Hydrangea, fuchsia, forsythia and buddleia are deciduous plants (they flower in summer and there is nothing to see in winter). Skimmia, camellia and viburnums are flowering evergreens — (remember to plant both males and females if you want berries and flowers) and chamaecyparis is a coniferous evergreen — no flowers. I haven't included rhododendrons — there's so many of those these days. All the ones I've mentioned cost about the same amount."

ASSIGNMENT

Using these notes, write a report on the possible shrubs that could be donated to the St Jude's Trust, to be tabled by Mr Grant at the next partners' meeting. you are not asked to make specific recommendations, but your report should help the partners in deciding which shrub to donate. You should use any suitable format and a suitable answer would probably include about 200 words. (20 marks)

3. *Producing a leaflet*

SITUATION

The shrub event will be publicised locally and nationally and part of the campaign will be the distribution of leaflets in the town, especially in areas where the houses have good sized gardens.

Mr Grant want a leaflet that is eye catching and attractive as well as informative. It should point out that the event is part of a national shrub week and that many new varieties will be on sale. It should point out that the event goes on all week, but Ted Eden will open it on Saturday 21st July. It should remind readers that the garden centre will still be selling its full range of plants, trees and equipment — and still has good car parking, a restaurant and a children's play area.

ASSIGNMENT

Design the leaflet for the printers. You should aim for careful selection of information from the paper, good balance and layout, and general good communication. No detailed art-work is required but you should indicate where illustrations (if required) should be placed. Use the whole of one or two sides of your answer book; you may ignore the margins for this question only. (20 marks)

4. *Preparing a notice of meeting and writing an agenda*

SITUATION

The last partners' meeting before the shrub event is to take place in Mr Grant's office on 4th July at 10.00 a.m. You have been asked to prepare the agenda; you have asked the partners what they wish to include.

Mr Grant wants the final arrangements for the shrub week to be on the agenda, including Mr Eden's opening. He also wants the donation to the St Jude's Trust to be included and wants to consider the next season's Christmas tree order.

David Lewis (Chief Acccountant) wants to discuss the renewal of the Van der Geesingen bulb contract and also the outstanding debts from 1981–82.

Andrew Newman (Personnel Director) wants to discuss temporary staff appointments during shrub week.

Christopher Davidson (Sales and Marketing Director) send his apologies for absence (he will be at the Norwegian Conifer Convention in Trondheim) but wishes to table his report on the possibility of selling garden barbecue equipment at the centre.

ASSIGNMENT

Write the notice of the meeting and the agenda. The appropriate standard agenda items should be included as well as the above items.

(*notice*: 5 marks)

(*agenda*: 15 marks)

Chapter 2

How to tackle your examination

PREPARATION

Because of the range of skills tested and the difference in emphasis between examining bodies there can be no single method of preparation that will suit all exams. A *written* exam is usually the most important element in the final assessment, so you must train yourself in the techniques needed for a one-off performance within a time limit. You should practise answering recent questions within the allotted time and without reference to your notes or books.

Check that you are totally familiar with the conventions of layout of business documents; it is quite unnecessary to lose marks for slips such as using 'Yours faithfully' after 'Dear Mr Name', or putting the date on the left in a semi-blocked letter, or forgetting that press releases should be double spaced.

TAKING THE EXAM

Many candidates fail by not following the *rubric* of the question, i.e. the instructions. For example, many marks can be lost for *exceeding* the maximum length of a summary question. Note that an instruction to *Draft* really means *Write*.

UNDERSTANDING THE QUESTION

This is particularly important in communication exams as the question often contains the answer, especially in exams which ask you to assume a role. The information given in the background material should be thoroughly absorbed; you can safely bet that every detail is going to be relevant. The account of the circumstances surrounding your role are usually a necessary part of your answer as they indicate the appropriate style and tone to be used. The sort of questions which start 'You are so and so' ..., and proceed to describe awkward people and situations to which you have to respond by writing a letter, memo, etc. are peppered with clues. Assess the situation thoroughly, and imagine yourself into the role, even if it is outside your experience. Draw upon the knowledge you have gained from other subjects in your course, e.g. law, personnel, office skills, or from your work experience, however slight.

Many exams are now adopting the 'case study' format, where all the questions are centred on *one role* within a particular organisation; so you need to read *all* the background material and *all* the questions before you even attempt your first answer. (See example Ch. 1 pp. 2–5.)

DECIDING ON THE TIME AND LENGTH OF ANSWER

Some exams give you 10 minutes to read through the whole paper before the stop-watch starts ticking. A useful first step is to tot up the allocation of marks for *all* the questions: this will give an indication of how much time to spend on each question. For example: Total time 3 hours = 180 minutes, in which to answer 6 questions; so 10 marks = 18 minutes; 20 marks = 36 minutes; 25 marks = 45 minutes. Since most questions give you the *mark* allocation, you can now work out exactly *how long* you should spend on each question.

The mark allocation also indicates the length of the answer. For example, a comprehension question worth 6 marks indicates that more than one point is required — perhaps 3 points carrying 2 marks each. A question giving 2 marks for an explanation/translation of a phrase might imply roughly ½ a mark per word. You have to be mercenary about marks; the odd 2 or 3 marks might make all the difference between pass or fail, or between pass and distinction. But do not spend *too much* time on a 1–2 mark 'quickie' question, either in worrying about what to write, or in writing more than is needed.

It will be helpful if you have calculated *before* the examination roughly how many words you usually write per line and per page. This will help you in answering longer questions, e.g. those asking for 'about' or 'not more than' 200 words. If you are well trained you should also be able to make allowances for lines with a brief heading, indentation or a crossing-out. If you are really well trained, there will not be any crossings-out! You need not state the number of words at the end of your answer — it is up to the examiners to check (except for certain summary questions).

PRESENTATION OF ANSWER

Examiners work from marking schemes indicating what proportion of marks to allocate to presentation, style, appreciation of problem set, etc. There will usually be generous allocation of marks for:

● *Correct format and conventions*: The position in which you place dates, references, subject headings, numberings, etc.
● *Clear and attractive layout*: Use a fresh page for each question; leave a left-hand margin of about an inch and a right-hand margin of about ½ an inch; allow for double line spaces at the tops and

bottoms of answers, and single line spaces between paragraphs. It is better to overdo the spacing than to skimp or cramp, but do not let indentation push you into too narrow a shape, such as one only leaving room for about five words per line.

Use capitals or underlinings where appropriate, but do not overdo them. You may add one extra colour, but preferably not red or green, which the examiners use for marking.

- *Handwriting*: Remember that an examiner may have about 500 scripts to mark — and your script may be the 456th and be marked late at night. Your paper will therefore have a better chance if it is clearly legible.

Make sure you have not slipped into bad habits such as running letters together so that they look like spelling mistakes, e.g. '*accountable*', or *dd or at of date*. And do try to dot your i's and cross your t's! Secretarial students who have become used to the neat and efficient appearance of typed work should practise *handwritten* exercises. The procedures learnt in typing will help to improve your handwritten presentation, as in spacing, in the use of capitals, in underlinings, etc.

- *Accuracy in spelling and punctuation*: Many marks are lost for careless slips between brain and pen. Even if you are shaky on commonly misspelt words like *correspondence*, or in the use of the semicolon, you should check — slowly and carefully — for the silly mistakes you might have made under pressure, e.g. confusing *their* and *there*, *Companies* and *Company's*.

N.B. Do remember to take an all-purpose kit:

(a)   Two writing pens you feel comfortable with;
(b)   a fine-tip for insertions and corrections;
(c)   two medium to thick fibre tips for logos, letterheads and diagrams;
(d)   a ruler, compasses and protractor for diagrams;
(e)   two sharp pencils and a rubber for rough work and diagrams; and perhaps some Tippex for emergencies;
(f)   a dictionary and a calculator (if allowed).

Finally: Do observe the idiosyncracies of the examiners. If *they* use a particular form of writing the date, you should copy it. If *they* refer to 'the Chairman', then swallow your feminism or modernity and follow suit. Do not underestimate the importance of what might seem to you to be minor details.

For a discussion of the techniques useful in preparing for and taking *oral* and *telephone* examinations, see Chapter 9.

Chapter 3

Principles and practice of Business Communication

A. GETTING STARTED

'A breakdown in communication' seems to have replaced 'circumstances beyond our control' as the standard reason − or excuse? − for disputes and mismanagement in business and public life. Behind this well-worn phrase lies an increasing awareness that good communication is the key to acceptance and trust, and therefore to higher productivity and profits; whereas bad communciation leads to poor results. So, managers and trade union officials get sent on courses to learn how to be good communicators; companies call in firms of communication consultants and hire training films and videos. Meanwhile, the examining bodies reflect the trend − and set the pace − by asking questions which test background knowledge of how information is exchanged in business and public administration.

You need to be aware of recent changes in attitudes to communication. People now expect swifter, clearer and more democratic communication than they used to even ten years ago. They are less prepared to take things on trust, more impatient and resentful about being 'left in the dark'. Voters expect more information and slicker presentation from politicians. Citizens expect to be consulted and informed about proposals which affect them, such as road-widening schemes or school closures. Shareholders expect a snappy presentation of the financial picture before voting for a merger or take-over. Employees expect to be consulted and informed about company policy and changes in working conditions − management can no longer just stick up a notice and expect the message to get through and have the desired effect.

You should also be aware of how modern technology has vastly increased the speed, range and variety of the means and methods of communication. We now take for granted a host of electronic devices such as satellite television pictures, video, radio-paging, etc. Computer graphics and word processors allow for more sophisticated forms of visual and written communication, e.g. colourful explanatory rate-demand leaflets from local councils, and all those mass produced 'personalised' salesletters we love to hate.

This chapter gives an outline of the patterns and problems of communication, and of the various channels and means used to communicate both *within* organisations and *between* organisations and the public. It is designed to help you answer general 'quiz' type questions, and to give a useful background for answering practical and 'case study' questions.

B. ESSENTIAL PRINCIPLES

Communication as an examinable subject in its own right is relatively new. It contains elements from subjects such as English language, media studies, psychology and business studies. Although most of the exams covered in this book are concerned with the context and practical application of communication in business, you will be better able to appreciate communication patterns and problems in organisations if you have a grasp of the basic process or cycle of communication (see Fig. 3.1).

Fig. 3.1 The communication cycle

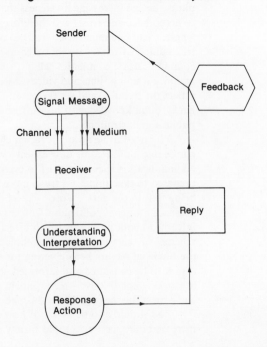

In order to be effective, communication must be two-way. A blockage or breakdown at any stage will disrupt the cycle, causing delay and/or misunderstanding, thereby frustrating the purpose of the message.

Sender

The SENDER must be clear about:

- The purpose: *Why* send the message? What action/response is needed? Is it urgent? Is it really necessary?
- The receiver: *Who* should it be sent to? An individual? Several people? A group? Everybody? Persons known or unknown?
- The content: *What* does he want to say? Is it short or long; simple of complex? How important is it?
- The channel: *What* route should it take? Via line management? Unions? Is there an acceptable short-cut?
- The medium: *How* should it be sent? In writing? Orally? In pictures? In one or more ways? In some other way?

Signal Message

The SIGNAL/MESSAGE must be clear in both intention and content. The receiver should be able to recognise its purpose and to understand quickly what it is about.

Channel

The CHANNEL should be acceptable. In a small office with just a few people working closely together, communication can be quick and informal, but as an organisation grows its channels of communication grow longer and more formalised. Most large organisations have agreed lines of *vertical communication* (see Fig. 3.2). Short-cuts upwards or downwards might leave someone in the middle feeling resentful at having been bypassed.

The danger is that vertical communication becomes too much of a one-way process, from the top downwards. It is important to encourage upwards communciation and feedback from junior levels by providing appropriate channels. Many organisations have **consultative committees** consisting of elected representatives from all levels. These are distinct from the trade union/management channels of negotiation on pay and conditions, and deal with subjects such as training, pensions, amenities and welfare, catering, etc. **Health and safety committees** also draw together representatives from all departments.

Suggestion schemes are useful for tapping ideas from all levels of the organisation. Prizes are offered for the best suggestions, and the results published in newsletters and house magazines (see Ch. 5).

There should also be constant communication *within* departments and *between* departments. Usually there are frequent meetings between departmental heads at the top levels of the organisation, but lower down there is a tendency for people to work in isolated compartments. It is good communication policy to break down barriers *between* departments wherever possible by setting up working groups and by inviting representatives of other departments to regular briefings. The variety of horizontal and diagonal channels of communication necessary to the

Fig. 3.2 Vertical communication in a large company

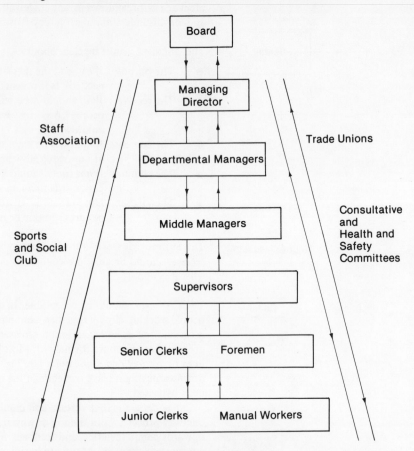

smooth running of a department is well illustrated by Fig. 3.3, taking a typical local authority department for illustration.

All too often there will be one or two awkward characters in a department or office who cause communication problems. This usually results in everyone else finding ways and means of avoiding direct communication with them, with a consequent loss of efficiency. If the offending party holds a relatively senior post, the problem may become still more serious. The responsibility for sorting out such situations lies with the head of department, perhaps with the help of the PERSONNEL Officer.

The MEDIUM must be appropriate. The choice of *how* to send the message will depend on the **purpose**, the **channel** and the **receiver**(s). A safety officer who has just completed a survey of all the electrical wiring in the workshop would be expected to write a technical report, rather than just give the production manager a ring. A shop steward involved in

Fig. 3.3 Horizontal, diagonal and vertical communication within a local authority department

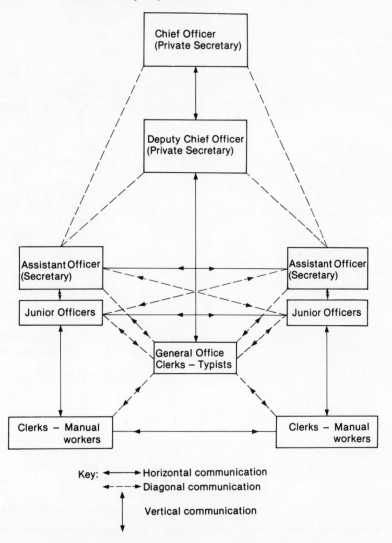

Key:
⟵⟶ Horizontal communication
⟵- - -⟶ Diagonal communication
↕ Vertical communication

pay negotiations would call a meeting of his members where he could gauge reactions and answer questions; if he put up a notice announcing the results, he would get short shrift.

The basic choice is between **written, spoken** and **visual** forms of communication, or a combination of these. The message may then be sent by conventional means, e.g. the internal post, or by electronic or computerised link-ups (see Fig. 3.4.). Most of these means of communication are considered in detail elsewhere in the book. Here we merely summarise the main characteristics of each.

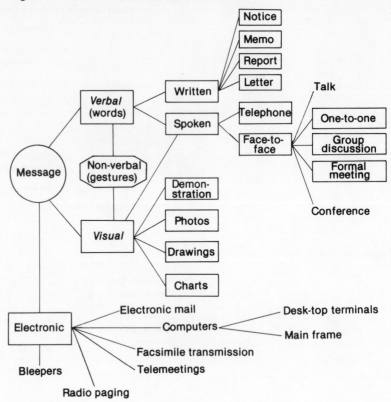

Fig. 3.4 Means of internal communication

Written	
	● The sender can consider all aspects and details of the message and produce a precise and polished document.
	● The receiver can scan the message, then study it in detail when he chooses.
	● A permanent record is provided.
	But − it can be slow; the receiver may lack the ability to read or interpret the message adequately; no immediate feedback is possible.
Spoken	
	● The sender saves time on preparation and polishing.
	● Feedback is immediate − the receiver can grasp the message immediately, ask questions where necessary, and give his response.
	● Communication is more personal, reinforced by gesture and expression.
	● Many people find reading and writing laborious.
	But − the message may not be thoroughly absorbed; the receiver may forget all or part; no written record exists as reminder of confirmation.

Visual	• Pictures have more immediate impact than words.
	• Pictures are more easily understood by a wide audience.
	• Statistical information is clarified.
	But — complex information will need some explanatory text.
Electronic	• Instant transmission, e.g. of facsimile pictures, saves time in communicating over distances.
	• Storage and retrieval of information on computers reduces paperwork and saves labour.
	• Information technology allows speedy links between input and output, e.g. photocopiers linked to computers give immediate print-out and duplicating.
	• People can be contacted immediately by bleeper or radio-paging — useful for emergencies and when people are out of their offices.
	But — it is impersonal; it demands precision and expertise; and it is difficult to unscramble mistakes. (See *Exam Guide to Office Practice and Secretarial Administration*, Ch. 11 for details of the electronic office.)

Receiver

The RECEIVER/S should always be in the forefront of the mind of the sender. Before deciding on the appropriate medium, the sender needs to consider the personality, position, ability and expertise of the receiver. There would be no point in sending a detailed technical report to a manager who would not understand the jargon and symbols used. Close colleagues in neighbouring offices would not usually expect to exchange formal memos; they would speak face to face and perhaps jot down a reminder note.

Understanding Interpretation

UNDERSTANDING/INTERPRETATION The sender needs to take care that his message is not couched in complex or technical language unfamiliar to the receiver. Figures may often need clarifying by diagrams and explanatory text. The tone must be appropriate, to avoid causing offence or misinterpretation. The wrong choice of medium, 'talking down' to people, tactless gestures or expressions could distort the feedback.

Response Action

RESPONSE/ACTION The receiver reacts to the message favourably or unfavourably depending on its context and the means and manner of communication. He will then either take the appropriate action, or fail/refuse to do so.

Reply

REPLY The receiver now becomes the sender. He must decide whether the message needs an immediate reply, and choose the appropriate channel and medium.

Feedback

FEEDBACK The sender should be satisfied that the message has been received, understood and correctly interpreted, and that the appropriate action has been taken. He may also need to know about the receiver's reaction and whether he is ready for the follow-up.

INFORMAL COMMUNICATION

Of course a great deal of communication at work is spontaneous and informal. People bump into each other in the corridors, pop in and out of each others' offices, call each other on the internal telephone, or chat in the canteen. News, instructions and opinions are quickly passed on by word of mouth or by brief notes on scraps of paper. Problems which may have loomed large during a formal meeting can often be sorted out by a five-minute chat afterwards.

RUMOUR DEPARTMENT

Management have long been aware that staff spend too much time transmitting and discussing rumours regarding our business, which is counter-productive and leads to duplication of effort. It has been decided to centralise the activity on a Group basis to ensure this important sphere of activity is conducted on a planned and cost effective basis.

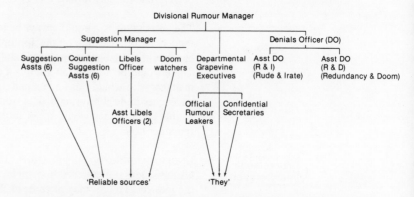

The departmental structure is outlined below. Official Rumour Prefixes (ORPs) are also indicated which *must* be used for the dissipation of all Approved Rumours. These must be selected on the basis of the source of the rumour and its Incredibility Rating (IR number).

OR Prefixes:
IR 1 I hear from a reliable source that . . . .
2 I was surprised to hear that . . .
3 I learnt only yesterday that . . . .
4 It's been suggested that . . . .
5 I think you'll find that . . . .

OR Prefixes:
IR 1 'They' say that . . . .
2 Did you know that . . . .
3 Hey – guess what . . . .
4 Don't pass this on but . . . .
There's a story going the rounds that . . . .

OR Prefixes:
IR 1 There's no truth in the rumour that . . . .
2 My contact on the middle floor tells me . . . .

NB This must only be used when speaking to employees on a lower grade than yourself.

(Source: Reproduced with kind permission of FBC Limited.)

16

The informal exchange of information and ideas is a healthy sign; evidence that people trust each other and want to get on with the job as quickly as possible. However, if the formal channels of communication are inadequate, there is a danger that some of the messages informally passed down the line will get distorted. No news is invariably seen as bad news. Half-truths are twisted into misinformation and gossip. Rumours creep through the shop-floor, the offices, the lifts and the canteen, and within no time half the workforce believes they are about to be transferred or even made redundant.

This negative form of communication is known as the **grapevine**. Once it is allowed to take root it spreads at an alarming rate, smothering truth and trust, and sapping morale. Denials by management usually confirm rather than dispel people's fears. The grapevine flourishes in a climate of distrust and ignorance; it is a sure sign that management has neglected the downwards channels of communication.

See question 1 Chapter 6 for an account of how Kellogg's UK nipped the grapevine in the bud. Figure 5.8 on page 68 shows an extract from the staff bulletin – cheekily called *Grapevine* – whilst the extract on the previous page takes a light-hearted look at rumour.

C. USEFUL APPLIED MATERIALS

In 1981 British Telecom commissioned a report on communication in local government, based on research into two district councils (Kingswood and Mendip) (Figs 3.5 and 3.6). Staff estimated that they spent 74% of their time communicating, both within the organisation and externally. The same report provides useful detail on the methods of communication used by the two district councils (see Fig. 3.6).

Fig. 3.5 Local government staff time spent on communication

A great deal of staff time is spent communicating. When asked to estimate how their working day was divided, the responses from both authorities were very similar. Staff estimated that they spent ...

15% in meetings and discussion
35% in reading and writing
14% in making telephone calls
10% in other kinds of communicating
26% in non-communicating work

The reading and writing category may include varying degrees of communication, but it would be fair to say that staff believe they spend at least two-thirds of their time communicating in some way.

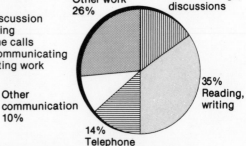

(Source: *Communication Patterns in Local Authorities.* A report by Tony Hathway, Bristol Polytechnic 1981.)

Fig. 3.6 Methods of communication in local authorities

Methods of communication
Communications *outwards* from the local
authorities appear to employ the common
methods fairly equally, with a slight preference
towards written contact.

Face-to-face	30%
Written	36%
Telephone	27%
Other	6%

Face-to-face contacts are much the same in both
authorities, but the figures mask a much higher
rate of telephone use at Kingswood than at
Mendip.

Inwards communications show a different
pattern.

Face-to-face	37%
Written	23%
Telephone	37%
Other	3%

Visits and telephone calls are definitely preferred
when making contact with the authority. This
pattern was similar in both Kingswood and
Mendip.

Received by L.A. staff   **Sent by L.A. staff**

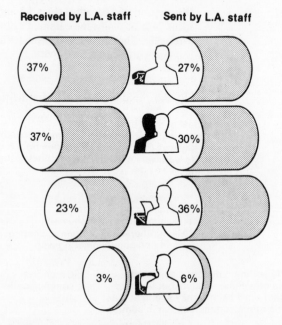

(Source: *Communication Patterns in Local Authorities.*
A report by Tony Hathway, Bristol Polytechnic 1981).

Some large organisations arrange one-day conferences for all staff at an outside venue. The idea behind such major, and presumably costly, exercises, is that staff will be more in a mood to accept and absorb management information and policy in a social setting (see Fig. 3.7).

Fig. 3.7   Report in Kellogg's News of an employee conference

AT THE time of going to press, final arrangements were being made for the 1985 conference programme.

Once again, every employee of the company was invited to one of a series of six conferences.

The theme this year was 'Kellogg's 1985 — Leader of the Packs', with the emphasis on high quality and low costs.

Corporate Training Manager, David Moores, told "Kellogg's News" that the series of conferences presented plenty of challenges themselves in terms of organisation and planning.

Logistics

This year, for example, the total work force of the Manchester factory attended one conference at the Free Trade Hall and were then taken by bus to 'Quaffers' in Stockport for an after-conference lunch.

The fleet of buses to ferry the 1,900-strong audience from Manchester's city centre to Quaffers was a major logistics exercise in its own right.

Well known radio and TV personality and 'DJ' Dave Lee Travis was the link man at the conferences. The ambitious presentations involved the use of special sets and nine projectors, with a standard format being tailored to the needs of each location.

The conferences are seen as a very important part of the communication of the Company's performance in 1984, and of plans for 1985 and beyond. We plan to give details of the presentations in our next issue.

(Source: © 1985 Kellogg Company)

The following question describes some of the communication problems which often result from the commercial success and expansion of a small firm. Your answer should draw upon the background knowledge of industrial relations you have gained from your course or from following current events in the media. The fact that Mr Palmer once worked 'on the bench' indicates a manufacturing concern.

Question 1 Discuss what you feel as *significant in terms of communication* in the following situation.

Harry Palmer was a hurt and bewildered man. He had just been informed that his staff wished to join a union. Not that this upset him too much, although he did feel that he had always treated his staff very well, they had good pay and conditions of work and he was always ready to listen to any member of his staff. What did upset him was the fact that it was completely unexpected. He had prided himself on being completely aware of what his staff were thinking, what they were like personally, and even about their family circumstances and problems. He still employed twenty of the staff he had started out with seven years ago and he had always had good relations with them. It was true that he knew less about the thirty or so other members of staff who had joined the firm over the past three years of its very rapid expansion. But his door was always open to them, and he was continually making this clear to them. When he remembered the early days, when he worked on the bench side by side with the people he had started with, he began to have slightly bitter thoughts about the original staff who were still with him. How could they keep him in the dark about what had obviously been going on? Why didn't they tell him they were dissatisfied? He was particularly annoyed about the claim which had been made that the workforce were told very little about what was happening to the firm. They must know how busy he had been chasing up the orders which had led to the recent growth in the firm, the very growth to which more than half of them owed their jobs. Well, if that was the way they wanted to play it, boss versus workers, so be it. He could be difficult too.

(Scottish HND in Secretarial Studies: Communication III, 1984)

(25 marks)

Question 2

Here is a question which spells out the problem mentioned on page 12 – the awkward character who causes breakdowns and blockages in communication. You are given a brief but all too recognisable picture of the irritable Mr Blunt. Because you appear to get on reasonably well with him, he uses you as a channel between himself and the office juniors.

The situation:

- You are employed as Senior Accounts Clerk in the Accounts Department of the Brunswick Trading Company Plc, Wolverhampton, West Midlands.

- There are 12 people working in the office altogether:
  The Accounts Office Manager, Mr Blunt
  His secretary
  2 clerk/typists
  2 filing clerks
  5 Accounts Clerks
  1 Senior Accounts Clerk (yourself)

- Your company operates as suppliers of office equipment and supplies.

- Your superior, Mr Blunt, the Accounts Office Manager, is a very busy man, known to be short-tempered but fair in his treatment of staff. He does pride himself on his discipline/efficiency and expects the same from everyone else. He seems to be, however, unsure of himself in some ways and does not seem to relate easily to people. He is surprisingly poor at making conversation and making decisions. Over the 18 months in which you have been in your present position, he has come to depend on you in some respects and values your views on some matters. He respects your honesty and integrity.

● He is inclined to be somewhat abrupt and even rude with junior staff, and in the past young office trainees tend to leave on this account.

You have an appointment with Mr Blunt tomorrow to assist him to work out some problems of communication in the office at the moment: he has mentioned the problems to you, as listed:

1. The office is to introduce a new system of computerised documentation from August 1st. What would be the most effective means of explaining to staff the methods, procedures and purposes of the new system?
2. As a result of the new system, at least two of the Accounts Clerks will be made redundant, and at least one filing clerk. What would be the most effective way of communicating news of redundancy in the office?
3. In the office, there is now no backlog of work outstanding compared to 6 months ago, and orders and enquiries are dealt with efficiently. Mr Blunt is apparently genuinely appreciative of this change for the better, but wonders if he should do something about it. Should he show his appreciation? What would be the most effective way to do so?

Task: Prepare yourself for the meeting by making out useful **notes** on each problem, mentioning **reasons** for your views.

(AAT specimen paper, 1985)

(30 marks)

Question 3 Discuss the circumstances in which it is advisable to communicate in writing, entirely or in part.

(Scottish HND in Secretarial Studies, 1984)

(10 marks)

E. OUTLINE AND TUTOR'S ANSWERS

Outline answer 1

(a) Palmer obviously runs business as a 'one-man band'. Inadequate management structure. With 50 employees there should by now be more delegation.

(b) Unrealistic to expect long-standing employees to approach him as they used to. He is often away or unavailable, and usually in a hurry. He should have made more effort to communicate with them, e.g. by regular briefings and occasional informal meetings for all staff. He is taken by surprise because he has not created channels for feedback. Grapevine has been allowed to develop.

(c) Inevitable that old hands will gradually identify more with new recruits than with him because they share similar tasks and work conditions.

(d) Wish to join trade union not necessarily a bad sign. Union could provide useful channel of communication with workforce as a whole rather than as individuals. Palmer's threat to 'be difficult too' indicates a period of conflict ahead.

Remember that these notes are for your own reference, not for Mr Blunt. You have to think both about the practical problems involved, and about the problem presented by Mr Blunt's inadequacies as a communicator. You have been cast in the role of 'go-between' and will need to be tactful when you meet him.

1. (a) <u>Methods</u>. Arrange a demonstration. Suggest calling in an outsider to explain equipment and methods – training officer? supplier's rep? Staff should have chance of 'hands-on' practice.

   Problems/Action
   If Mr B insists on doing it himself, advise him to brief you and his secretary.

   (b) <u>Procedures</u>. Advise Mr B to clarify procedures with his secretary so that she can help him show the rest of the staff. Flowchart would be helpful.

   Some of older staff might be resistant to change.

   (c) <u>Purposes</u>. Explain how new system fits in with rest of organisation. Prepare wall chart.

   If Mr B too busy offer to do chart.

2. Informal consultative meeting of section to explain the problem. Memos at this stage would be too impersonal. Presumably principle of 'last in, first out' will apply. Inform individuals as soon as he receives confirmation.

   Is Mr B going to try to persuade management to stop at three? Might anyone accept early retirement?

3. Good principle to express appreciation for good work. Best means is to send *circular memo* to each member of the team informing them of improvement and thanking them for special effort. Add more personal touch by speaking to all or some of staff.

   Staff will be upset by recent events – extra tact needed.

(Another question from this paper is covered in Chapter 5.)

This is a general question which can be answered in outline from material in this chapter. You should then apply some specific examples drawn from Chapters 4, 5, 7, 8 and 10.

(a) Detailed information, e.g. reports.
(b) Formal communication – record for file – required by law.
(c) Confirmation of oral.
(d) Reinforcement of oral.
(e) Particular formats, e.g. questionnaires.

Tutor's answer 3

It is advisable to communicate in writing in the following circumstances:

(a) When it is essential for the receiver to study detailed information, e.g. in a report, and to keep documents for future reference.

(b) In formal situations when a record should be filed for reference, e.g. tendering for a contract, confirming an order, or when required by law, e.g. notice of company AGM.

(c) As a confirmation and reminder of an oral message, e.g. a memo or letter following a telephone call.

(d) To reinforce an oral message, e.g. written instructions to accompany a demonstration of equipment.

(e) When the receiver is expected to use a particular written format in reply, e.g. a form or questionnaire.

(These are only the most obvious points, but should be enough for a 10-mark question. It is better to 'discuss' five circumstances than to give a long checklist without examples or reasons.)

F. A STEP FURTHER

General textbooks

The following contain useful chapters which set the principles of communication in a business context:

People and Communication, Evans D W. Pitman 1984. Chapter 1 discusses communication in organisations, while Chapter 2 provides a clear summary of recent developments in information technology.

Communication at Work, Evans D W. Pitman 1982.

Mastering Business Communication, Woolcott L A and Unwin W R. Macmillan 1983. Chapters 16, 17 and 18 cover general principles and information technology.

Communication in Business, Little P. Pitman 1983. Chapters 1 and 2 give a brief outline of the principles.

Effective Communication Made Simple, Eyre E C. Heinemann 1980. The first half of the book is devoted to a methodical summary of general aspects of internal and external communication.

More than words: An Introduction to Communication, Dimbleby, R. and Burton, G. Methuen 1986.

Books for managers

Communication at Work, Maude B. Business Books 1982.
Training for Communication, Adair J. Gower 1984.

Industrial Society booklet

The Manager's Responsibility for Communication Consultation

Specialist magazines

Management Today. Business Systems and Equipment.

Films

Video Arts: The Grapevine. The Secretary and her Boss, Parts I and II.

These films come with lively and instructive booklets which can be ordered separately.

Chapter 4   Letters

A. GETTING STARTED

When you write letters to friends or relatives your first concern is to write more or less what you would say face-to-face, without fussing over details of style and presentation. But when you have to write a formal letter, you have only a vague picture of the 'faceless' organisation or individual at the other end. You must therefore take more care to express yourself clearly and correctly, and to make your message look neat and attractive.

When you receive a reply you might form a more distinct impression. You notice the quality and design of the headed paper, the appearance of the typeface, the layout of the page, and the style and tone of the message. If any of these strike you as substandard, the letter will fail to project the positive and professional image that was intended. The most de luxe embossed stationery and the very latest electronic typewriter will never make up for the manager who cannot write good English, or the typist who has not learned to spell and punctuate correctly.

You should train yourself to become a critical reader of any non-personal letters you receive. Collect as many examples as possible; answers to enquiries or complaints, letters from officials, circulars from public services such as the Gas and Electricity Boards – even all those uninvited salesletters delivered door to door. If you are attending college, take them into class and use them to spark off critical discussion. Textbook examples are useful for illustrating particular points of presentation and style, but actual letters add life and reality to the subject – and often provide an unintended source of amusement.

Letters are the most generally used form of written communciation between organisations, and between organisations and individuals, so they feature in all examinations. Very few candidates will escape the question which ends with the instruction: 'Write a letter to ...' Most communication courses take business letters as a 'way in' to longer practical exercises in formal writing, such as reports. But although letters are closer to everyday experience, they are not necessarily easier to write than less familiar but more strictly conventional forms of written communication. This is because composing a letter is a 'one-off' exercise, and it is harder to predict what sort of questions to expect. You have to be able to adapt quickly to the format, style and tone appropriate to a wide range of situations. You should sound natural, yet you cannot write 'off the top of your head' as you might to a friend, since even the most routine formal letters need a clearly planned approach.

The opposite, and more common, fault is to assume that 'business' letters require a special style and vocabulary far removed from the informality of speech or letters to friends. Many students seize up when confronted by quite simple exercises, and produce letters which sound stiff and stilted. They are afraid of seeming amateur, so they clutch at words they would never normally use like 'commencement' and 'remittance', and dig out pompous phrases such as 'trusting this meets with your satisfaction'. The worst culprits can be those attending part-time courses, who seem to pick up these rusty conventions at their places of work and assume they are essential to a proper 'house style'.

Secretarial examining bodies have been in the forefront of the campaign for a simpler, more modern approach to business writing. Secretaries have an important contribution to make to an organisation's image, since they have a responsibility for sending letters out in a presentable and polished form. Far too many managers rely on their secretaries to decode their cryptic notes and reorganise their rambling dictations. This is why secretarial students get much more practice at letter-writing than those on other courses. Also, their examiners pay particular attention to details of style, and issue annual reports on the strengths and weaknesses of the answers which are a gold-mine of useful tips and warnings. General and management candidates can also learn a lot of useful detail by consulting textbooks aimed primarily at secretarial students.

Letter questions allow scope for subtlety and individuality, and therefore give stronger candidates a chance to shine, unlike more rigid exercises such as Minutes where the sentences more or less write themselves within a conventional format.

B. ESSENTIAL PRINCIPLES

We send fewer personal letters than we did twenty years ago. We prefer to talk to our friends and relatives on the telephone because it is quicker than writing letters, takes less effort, feels more natural and gets an immediate response. But in business life the volume of postal correspondence is increasing, particularly since the invention of the word processor, which has reduced the time, effort and expense involved.

Advantages of letters

What then are the advantages of letters over other forms of communication?

(a) Economy	Over long distances and across language barriers letters are cheaper than telephone calls, much cheaper than telex, and a fraction of the cost of travelling to meet people. (The new instant electronic post is surprisingly cheap.)
(b) Convenience	Letters can be drafted and typed at a time chosen by the sender. They can be amended right up to the last moment. The writer can concentrate on the whole message, without getting side-tracked by immediate reactions to particular points, as in conversation. The reader can focus his attention on a letter at a chosen moment, whereas telephone calls often catch him when he is distracted.
(c) Accuracy	The writer has time to make sure the message is clear and complete; the reader has time to absorb and check complex information.
(d) Filing	Letters provide a complete and accurate record of transactions. In some cases, e.g. contracts, they count as legally binding evidence.
(e) Image	It is often said that letters are 'ambassadors' because they provide the opportunity to project a favourable impression of the organisation or individual.

Disadvantages

Letters have corresponding *disadvantages* over other means of communication: over short distances they can be more expensive; they are slower (an exchange takes at least two days); they are less personal; and there is no immediate feedback.

PREPARATION

To prepare yourself for writing effective letters you need to master three main aspects:

1. **Format:** layout and appearance – standard pre-printed, individually typed, handwritten.
2. **Content:** structure and details of the message.
3. **Language:** style and tone.

A typical examiners' mark-scheme would allocate a proportion of marks to each of these aspects, usually allowing about 25, 35 and 40% respectively.

1. Format

If you are writing a letter from an organisation you will need a suitable letterhead (see Fig 4.1). The question may give you all the details, in which case reproduce them faithfully. If you are told only that you are writing on behalf of 'a small manufacturing company' or 'your local sports club' you will have to invent the products or the sports and the name and address. Base your design on real examples and make sure it looks clear and distinctive. Do not waste time on fancy artwork – one colour will do – and do not add a trademark or logo unless it is simple enough to draw in less than a minute.

What you do next will depend on whether you are typing or handwriting. If you are *typing* you should use the fully blocked or blocked format; if you are *handwriting* you should use the blocked or semi-blocked format. For blocked use 'open' punctuation, i.e. punctuate only the 'body' of the letter; for semi-blocked use 'closed' punctuation, i.e. also punctuate the address, etc. (see Fig. 4.4).

It is important to visualise the *shape* of your letter in advance, especially if you have untidy or eccentric writing. Remember that easy marks can be gained by correct and attractive layout.

● Make sure your lines of writing are evenly spaced over the page.
● Do not sprawl over the top part or squeeze the bottom part. If you reach a point where you have one or two sentences left to write and insufficient space left on the page, it is better to play safe and start a new page.
● Leave a clear extra space between paragraphs.
● Stop yourself writing up to the right-hand edge of the page by pencilling a faint margin which you can later rub out. A one-page

Fig. 4.1 Letter components *Organisation to individual in another organisation* (blocked).

ENAMELLON PRODUCTS LIMITED

198 Surrey Road Exwell London EW3 6SR

Telephone 01 546 9878   Telex ENPRO

```
Our Ref. WTR/jk                            25 November 1987


W.B. Johnson
Manager
Seaview Hotel
Western Avenue
Mereport
Wessex WLP 3RT


Dear Mr Johnson,
                        Subject-heading

                        Body of letter

                            Yours sincerely,



                            W.D.Lewis

                            W. D. Lewis.
                            Sales Manager.

enc.
c.c.
```

letter should look like a printed picture in a white frame, i.e. with reasonable even margins all around.

- Avoid splitting words at the right-hand edge, with is usually unnec-essary ————————————————————— and always un-attractive.
- Make sure you know all the main components of a formal letter in their usual forms and correct positions. (See Fig. 4.1).

Letterhead   Organisation's name, address, telephone and telex numbers, logo.

References   Author's and typist's initials, sometimes followed by a filing code: e.g.
Our ref. WTR/JK/C257
Your ref. HT/WLM

Date   Day, month, year: 26 November 1987

Recipient   Name, position, organisation:
     W. B. Johnson
     Manager
     Seaview Hotel

Recipient's address   Street, town, county, post-code:
     Western Avenue
     Mereport
     Wessex WLP 3RT

Salutation   Dear X,
NB If you do not know the name use Dear Sir, Dear Sirs, or Dear Madam. If you know the name use it.

Subject heading   Announcement of topic: e.g. <u>Delivery of bulk orders.</u>

Message   The body of the letter arranged into paragraphs.

Complimentary close   Dear Sir, ... Yours faithfully,
Dear Mr Jones ... ... Yours sincerely,
Dear John, ... Sincerely, kind regards, etc.

Signature   *W.D. Lewis*

Identification   Legible version of signature, job title. Women should specify Mrs, Miss, Ms – a Christian name only is not enough. Initials only will be assumed to be male.

Enclosure   Additional papers enclosed. Enc.

Copy reference   Note of recipient(s) of copy. c.c. ...

2. Content

(a) Structure

An effective letter must get its message across at a first quick reading. Busy managers do not have time to waste on letters whose purpose is unclear or which make heavy weather of straightforward matters. The hard work should be done by the writer, not the reader. Only very short simple letters can be written or dictated straight off; the sort commonly set in exams will need mapping out in advance. So before you start:

- Remind yourself of the *reason* for the letter by reviewing the background, e.g. a request or complaint.
- Decide exactly *what* you want to say and jot down a list of all relevant points.
- Group your points into *themes* within a logical sequence of paragraphs, perhaps following the order of the letter to which you are replying.

Even the most confident and fluent candidates should spend at least five minutes on the planning stage (see Fig. 4.3).

The subject heading	A clearly defined subject heading makes correspondence more efficient: clerical staff can quickly sort incoming mail; readers can immediately identify the subject; writers can shorten their introductory paragraph. A subject heading should always be used:

- when replying to a letter which used one;
- when writing the first of a sequence of letters on the same subject;
- if the subject is easily identifiable, e.g. an order, or a reference for a candidate for interview.

A heading more than a few words long is clumsy and probably pointless; some subjects cannot be distilled into a single heading. In letters with a personal touch a heading may strike the wrong note.

The opening paragraph	If you are replying to a letter you must first acknowledge it and refer to the date on which it was sent. Then you should introduce the main subject, without repeating the words of the subject heading if you have

Fig. 4.2 The structure of a typical letter

(1)   Subject heading (optional)

(2)   Opening paragraph stating the reason for writing and the subject-matter . . . .

(3)   Middle paragraph(s) containing further information, ideas, arguments . . . . questions . . . . . . etc. . . . .
. . . . Further points . . . . supporting detail . . . . etc. . . . .

(4)   Closing paragraph summarising outcome . . . . action proposed . . . . . .
Closing courtesies . . . . . .

used one, and briefly remind the reader of any relevant background. If you are starting the correspondence you will obviously have to give more detail than if you are replying. First paragraphs should be short and to the point, sometimes consisting of only one sentence.

The body of the letter	Your subsequent points should be arranged into clearly defined paragraphs. Keep them short − not more than a third of a page each. If a point or series of points looks like running on too long, find a suitable break in the flow. Unbroken chunks of prose look indigestible and important points may get buried. Give the reader small and medium-sized 'bites' to digest. But do not use too many very short paragraphs or your letter will sound breathless, like the popular press or hard-sell salesletters. If you are asked to write a letter of more than about 200 words, which covers two or more separate subjects, it is advisable to use **subheadings**.
The closing paragraph	The final paragraph usually consists of a summing-up, re-emphasising earlier points, and/or any instructions as to the response required − and by when − rounded off by some sort of closing comment and/or courtesy. In reality many letters do not really need a special closing paragraph, but the body of the letter can look rather naked without one and most examiners expect them because they indicate your grasp of structure, and of practical essentials like deadlines. P.S. Afterthoughts tacked on to the end of a letter will usually be discounted. Minor amendments and additions should be inserted into the text − which is why the importance of wide line spacing is emphasised in Chapter 2. P.P.S. Careful planning cuts out afterthoughts. Make use of your rough paper, pencil and rubber.
(b) Classification of letters	Letters can first be classified according to **how they are produced**; the most obvious general distinction is between letters which are *individually produced* and those which are *mass produced*. However, even one-off letters sent to only one person may now contain standard paragraphs which have been stored in a computer's memory bank.

- **One-off letters** written to a particular organisation or individual for a particular purpose. Drafted or dictated by an individual and typed either by the author or by a personal secretary or by a typist (see Fig. 4.5).
- **Standard or form letters** run off in large quantities and sent out as and when required. They contain messages which recur frequently, with blank spaces for the insertion of variables such as figures. Most still start 'Dear Sir/Madam', though more effort is now made to personalise them by using the actual name.
- **Circular letters** specially written to suit a particular purpose of occasion, e.g. to confirm conference arrangements, to inform customers of delivery arrangements, etc. They are reproduced in quantity and sent to a number of people simultaneously. Everyone receives the same message but with appropriate variations in the

style of address. Again, 'Dear Sir/Madam' is going out of favour, as is the rather sinister 'To whom it may concern'. An appropriate greeting such as 'Dear Member', 'Dear Customer' or 'Dear Resident' is used; or individual names are inserted (see Fig. 4.6). *NB* Circular letters requiring a reply or likely to prompt enquiries should always include the name of the person dealing with the matter, and, if necessary, an extension number.

- **Salesletters** are multiplying fast in the scramble to advertise goods and services. They may be 'targeted' at a small selected consumer group or locality, e.g. 'our double-glazing experts will be visiting your street next week', or they may be scattered by the thousand in a massive mail-drop. Names and addresses are culled from telephone directories, electoral registers and computerised records, and artfully inserted to give a 'personal' impression. They often include free offers, competitions and other sales gimmicks (see Fig 4.7).

- **Newsletters** are sent regularly by a range of organisations such as professional institutes, charities, residents' associations, to keep members informed, collect subscriptions, ask for donations, etc. include free offers, competitions and other sales gimmicks (see Fig. 4.8).

Letters can be further classified according to their **purpose**.

Classification of letters by purpose

Purpose	Classification/example
To seek information	Query
To give information	Acknowledgement
	Newsletter
To state an argument	Letter to press
To reply to an argument	Rejoinder letter to press
To make a complaint/claim	Complaint
To answer a complaint/claim	Adjustment
To apply for a job	Application
To resign from a job	Resignation
To seek/supply references	Reference
To place an order	Order
To accept an order/estimate/tender	Acceptance
To confirm an order	Confirmation
To submit an estimate/tender	Estimate
To sell/advertise something	Salesletter
To seek payment of debt	Collection (The first mild, the second stronger, the third an ultimatum)
To check credit-worthiness	Credit reference
To authorise credit	Authorisation

(c) The message

Of course some of the categories listed above are very broad, and many letters do not fall neatly into pairs or groups, e.g. personal messages such as congratulations or condolences. There are also many letters which require special tact, e.g. advising an employee to take early retirement or to accept demotion. Even the simplest letters pose problems of structure, and the examiners try to invent situations which demand a non-routine type of answer. So how should you order your points? Is it better to plunge straight in with your main point, or lead up to it gradually? Your approach will depend on the nature of the message and the likely reaction of the reader.

Nature of message

Positive

You announce good news, agree to do or send something, e.g. announce promotion, accept invitation, offer refund, write good reference. Straightforward to write.

Neutral

You report facts, make arrangements, request goods, services or information, e.g. announce conference, place order, query detail of brochure. Usually easy to write.

Suggested Structure

A Main point

B Factual details
    Further information/queries

C Next step(s)
    Offer help/further information
    Final message/question
    Positive friendly close

Negative

You announce bad news, decline to do or send something, criticise someone, e.g. notify unsuccessful applicant, refuse refund, give poor reference. Difficult to write.

Persuasive

You try to sell a product/service/idea, answer an accusation, answer a case, correct a false argument; e.g. salesletter, unsolicited request/suggestion request for donation or loan, letter to the press. Challenging to write.

Suggested Structure

A Neutral opening

B Facts/reasons/argument

C Unwelcome message/

D Soften blow/express hope/suggest follow-up

Most of the letters you will be asked to write in exams will arise from an outline situation, and/or a jumble of notes from a superior. Increasingly, the letter question is one step within a general situation applicable to all questions, so helpful guidance and information may be gleaned from a quick scan of the whole paper. However, it is good practice to think through the content of some of the common types of letters. So we now show a more detailed breakdown of the outlines suggested above.

Common types of letter: by nature of message

Positive

You accept an invitation to speak at a meeting/conference.

A Thank for invitation . . . say you will speak and what about . . .
B Give title of talk . . . indicate outline content . . . length . . . check on arrangements . . . room . . . audio-visual aids . . ., etc. . . .

	C Ask for confirmation that your proposals are acceptable ... look forward to event ...
Neutral	You invite someone to attend/speak at a meeting/conference.
	A Announce meeting/conference ... dates ... place ... subject(s) ... B Details of subject(s) .. outline programme (enclosed) ... description of venue ... catering/accommodation/entertainment (enclosed) C Express hope/reason for attendance ... request reply by specified date ...
Negative	You are refusing a request for financial support for an organisation/project/event.
	A Thank for letter ... interesting proposal ... B Express support for/reservations about proposal ... with reasons ... C Tell applicant that you cannot offer money ... give acceptable/plausible reason, e.g. year's budget already spent ... D Advise to apply again/suggest alternative source(s) of finance ... express confidence/hope/good luck ...
Persuasive	You are seeking financial support for an organisation/project/event ...
	A Say you have heard that the company might be interested in supporting the arts/sports/community welfare ... B Describe organistion/project/event ... premises ... activities ..., e.g. sponsored run, community centre ... C Give financial picture ... money already raised ... further needs ... D Re-emphasise need ... express hope of favourable response ...

Structure checklist

- Make your purpose clear straight away in a subject heading and/or opening sentence.
- Group your points in logical order, starting a new paragraph for each main point.
- End by indicating the next step, or by politely bringing the matter to a conclusion.

The details of the message

There are three main types of letter which you may be asked to write in an exam.

1. Those which give a *general instruction*, e.g. 'Write a letter to your local council complaining about the lack of sports facilities in your area'. (Often set in O and AO level, and some professional exams.)
2. Those which give you a *background situation* and ask you to write a familiar type of letter arising from it. (Often set in O and AO level, B/TEC assignments and some professional exams.)
3. Those which give you a *background situation and a set of notes from a colleague/superior* telling you roughly what to say — usually in jumbled order. (Often set in secretarial exams.)

Types (2) and (3) are often set as *part* of a paper based on a general situation applicable to all questions.

In a straightforward exchange of correspondence, for example between a customer and a supplier, the necessary details are usually obvious: the product required and for what purpose, the specifications, quantity, price, discount, delivery dates, etc. Yet even this sort of letter can be bungled, e.g. if a carpet supplier fails to warn a hotel manager of a delay in delivery of a particular colour it could throw a whole redecoration scheme out of gear.

Examiners usually give you situations which are not so straightforward, e.g. answering a complaint, or describing arrangements for an event/conference. They try to strike a balance between giving very little detail — thus forcing the candidate to spend as much time on invention as on writing — and giving so much detail that no scope is left for imagination or common sense. They often leave deliberate gaps in the information to test your practical grasp of the situation, e.g. if the chairman plans to visit a branch 'next week' you should supply the date and time; if you are arranging a day trip you should fix a practical timetable.

Whatever details you are given must be used sensibly and correctly, e.g. if you are setting up a meeting or visit on 24 June do not date your letter 20 June, even if it happens to be the day of your exam. Invented details must be plausible. If you are answering a complaint it is not a good idea to blame everything on some hapless junior who has since been given the sack, or to resort to standard excuses like strikes, computer breakdowns, bad weather, etc. Avoid the temptation to think up witty names and far-fetched events — that is the examiners' privilege.

3. Language

The hardest part of letter-writing is finding the right words. You may be quite fluent in conversation yet tie yourself into dreadful knots over writing a letter. Your correct format and careful structure can be spoiled by the wrong tone, clumsy wording, or mistakes in spelling and punctuation. The best cure is to read your letter assignments aloud and imagine yourself in the place of the reader; this should show up any words which sound awkward or tactless, and sentences which even you cannot understand. Your use of language should be:

- **Clear:** Choose the right words to convey your meaning.
- **Concise:** Cut out unnecessary words.
- **Fluent:** Link your words smoothly into sentences and paragraphs.
- **Natural:** Make them sound as if you were speaking.
- **Friendly:** Use positive words and expression — not forgetting 'please' and 'thank you'.

Your aim is to be understood correctly by using language which works effectively on two levels at once:

- **Practical:** The message must make sense, so your style needs to be efficient.
- **Psychological:** The message must have the desired effect, so your tone must be appropriate. You do not want the reader to take your letter the wrong way or to 'read between the lines'.

Your style will of course affect your tone. Bursts of very short sentences sound jerky and abrupt. Long rambling sentences, often the result of poor dictation technique, sound indecisive and wishy-washy. Passive verbs are often clumsy and can sound unfriendly, e.g. 'Your order has been received' rather than 'We have received your order'. Long words often sound remote and snooty. To avoid misunderstanding you should try to adapt your style and tone to suit your *reader(s)* and your *subject(s)*.

(a) The reader(s)

Suppose you had to answer two letters of complaint on the same subject, e.g. a disappointing package holiday; one angry in tone, illiterate in style, and handwritten; the other reasonable in tone, literate, and professionally typed. Would you write the same sort of reply to each? If you did, you would probably fall between two stools. The first reader might find your reply pretentious and pompous, whereas the same reply might strike your second reader as patronising. The first complainant might be less interested in detailed explanations than the second, but both would be equally concerned about what remedy you propose.

The more you know about the reader the closer you should be able to match your style and tone to match the situation. Factors like education, position, age and temperament could all be relevant. So watch out for any clues dropped by the examiners, e.g. 'an awkward customer'; 'a busy executive', etc. If you are supposed to know the reader personally you may use a more relaxed tone — but don't overdo it, e.g. 'See you round the pub some time. Cheers, Pete.'

Circular letters pose a different problem since you have to get the same message through to a number of readers at once. They may be a group with similar backgrounds and a common interest, e.g. the members of a club or professional body; or they might be a mixed group, e.g. all the residents of a given area. The message may be **favourable**, e.g. announcing higher salaries; or **neutral**, e.g. information about a conference; or it may be **unfavourable**, e.g. announcing a rise in subscriptions; or **persuasive**, e.g. stressing the advantages of early retirement to employees over 55. Examiners are keen on circular letters because they test your ability to produce a clear courteous style suitable for a range of readers.

(b) The subject(s)

Sometimes you might have to write two very different circular letters to the same people. For example, if you were the secretary of a club and you had to write first to all members about the arrangements for the annual dinner dance, and then to certain members who still had not paid their subscriptions in spite of a previous mild reminder, there would obviously be a marked difference in tone between the two.

- A letter making arrangements or giving instructions would be **neutral** in tone, e.g. *When you arrive at Palma airport at 1500 hours our Sun Trek representative will be waiting to meet you at Gate Number 8.*
- The answer to a complaint would be **conciliatory** in tone, e.g. *We were sorry to hear of the problems you experienced on your recent Sun Trek holiday in Majorca.*

● A salesletter should sound **enthusiastic**, e.g. *Are you in search of a touch of spice and adventure this year? Sun Trek can make your dream come true on an exclusive safari in exotic Zanzibar.*

You are unlikely to be asked to write letters calling for an extremely **formal** and **frosty** tone, e.g. final debt collection notices, disciplinary/dismissal letters. Most of the letters you are likely to be set will require a **positive** tone. *Remember*: even the simplest message can sound negative and unhelpful.

Negative	Positive
With reference to your order of 20 November, we are unable to supply four bottles of champagne. We cannot despatch goods in lots of less than 12.	*Thank you for your order of 20 November. To keep down packaging and carriage costs, so that we can offer this quality champagne at such a low price, we are unfortunately unable to send fewer than 12 bottles at a time.*

Even when replying to a complaint which you feel is unjustified you should write with courtesy in an effort to restore goodwill:

Negative	Positive
I note that you have written for the second time to complain that the grass verges in your road have not been cut recently. As stated in my letter of 12 July, the heavy rainfall during May has led to a backlog in the Council's normal schedule . . .	*I am concerned that you have again felt it necessary to point out that the grass verges in your road have not been cut recently. Unfortunately our grass-cutting crews have not yet been able to catch up with the backlog caused by the heavy rain in May, but I do assure you . . .*

A positive approach is particularly important when you are trying to persuade the reader to buy something, supporting an idea or back a project:

Negative	Positive
This year we hope to return to Brazil to explore the upper reaches of the Mateo River, but this will not be possible unless we manage to get some sponsorship soon . . .	*Following our successful expedition last year, we are planning to return to Brazil to explore the upper reaches of the Mateo River. We have heard that your company sometimes sponsors projects of this kind . . .*

Even letters of refusal can be courteous and encouraging:

Dear Mr Roberts,

Your expedition to Brazil sounds most interesting and I am sure you will find a firm willing to sponsor it.

Unfortunately, our company has already agreed to sponsor two expeditions this year and I have been told by the Board that there are no further funds available at the moment.

If you plan a further expedition for next year I hope you will apply to us again. Meanwhile may I wish you every success in your enterprise.

A positive approach is particularly important when you are trying to sell yourself in a letter of application for a job (see Ch. 12 p. 210).

Finding the right words

So far we have been concerned with the basic shape of different letters and with your approach to different readers and subjects. This section deals with the nuts and bolts of style, i.e. *vocabulary, syntax and punctuation.* To achieve a clear concise style you need to build up confidence in your sentence construction and choice of words, and to develop the natural rhythm which springs from correct punctuation.

Even if you are already reasonably confident and fluent you will have to work at the particular language skills involved in letter-writing. You may have noticed that communication teachers are stricter about what may seem to you niggling points of grammar than are subject teachers who mark your essays. This is because essays are largely a test of knowledge and argument, whereas letters are largely a test of style. Of course clumsy use of English will show up in an essay, but in a letter it will stick out like a sore thumb. Nowhere is this more obvious than in the opening sentence, which even experienced letter-writers often find particularly tricky.

How to start

Whether or not you use a subject heading, you should use a direct approach.

(a) With a heading

Tropical Fish Tanks

'We are pleased to enclose our latest catalogue which includes several new models especially suited to dentists' waiting-rooms ...' *Not:* 'Enclosed please find ...' *or* 'We are writing to you in connection with our latest catalogue which we enclose ...'

Standard **reply** to enquiry

'Thank you for your letter of 23 March. We would be pleased to supply you with four Finflash models ...' **Not:** 'With regard to be above, we would be pleased to supply ...'

(b) Without a heading

'We enclose our latest catalogue of tropical fish tanks, which includes several new models ideally suited for dentists' waiting-rooms.' *Not:* 'We are writing to draw your attention to the enclosed catalogue of tropical fish tanks, which includes several new models ...'

Standard **reply** to enquiry

'Thank you for your letter of 23 March asking for details of the new range of tropical fish tanks listed in our catalogue.'

This is the simplest way of starting and is always correct. Opening with phrases such as *In reply to* ... or *With reference to* ... is awkward and best avoided. Such phrases are stiff and hackneyed, and often result in unfinished sentences: *With reference to your letter of 23 March in which you state that one of the Finflash tanks you purchased from us is leaking* (no main verb). Or they may plunge you into long and tangled sentences: *With reference to your letter of 23 March concerning the non-delivery of one of the tanks ordered from us, I regret to say that this model is no longer in production owing to the non-availability of materials.* There is also the danger of going off at a tangent: *In reply to your enquiry of 23 March about tropical fish tanks, I have been away on sick leave for the past two weeks.*

Another favourite opening is: *Further to our/following your telephone conversation/call of . . .'* This phrase is useful in reminding the reader of the cue for your letter, but it lays the same grammatical traps.

How to end

It is sometimes difficult to know how to bring a letter to an end. The fear of sounding abrupt leads to useless repetition − *once again may I say . . .* or to tired stock phrases like *Assuring you of our best attention* (no main verb). You should try to point the way forward, e.g. *Please send me your comments by 14 March.* Or you might thank the reader for a service, or wish him well in some venture, or anticipate an event, e.g. *I look forward to seeing you on the 19th.*

How to make yourself understood

Twenty-five per cent of British adults have a reading age of 13 or below, i.e. they would find the *Daily Mirror* heavy going. *The Times* and other 'quality' newspapers demand a reading age of 17. Most business letters should be pitched at an average reading ability of about 15. The Industrial Society urges managers to strive for **accuracy, brevity, clarity** − the ABC of letter-writing. You can improve your style by learning the following rules:

1. Use familiar words

The usual advice given to managers and secretaries is to avoid uncommon words unless you are sure that your reader will understand them. A senior manager of Tube Investments Ltd reports that when the company started issuing biennial confidential reports there were many enquiries as to whether biennial meant six-monthly or two-yearly. One enquirer even asked: 'Who's this bloke Biennial?' (BACIE *Guide to the Writing of Business Letters*).

Communication exams, however, contain questions designed to test and stretch your language skills. You would probably gain marks for choosing precise words like 'biennial' provided you use them appropriately and spell them correctly. So avoid words you do not know how to handle, e.g.

Incorrect	Correct
The accommodation comprises of ten rooms and a rather unique roof garden.	The accommodation/property has/consists of/comprises ten rooms and a unique roof garden.

Accommodation is one of the most commonly misspelt words. *Unique* must always stand on its own; it means 'having no like or equal', so it is an *indispensable* word, i.e. a word you cannot do without. All the words in this illustration are useful ones which need not be replaced by one or more shorter words. However, there is a long list of words which are too often preferred to their simpler equivalents because they are supposed to sound more weighty and official. These words are great favourites with politicians, bureaucrats, businessmen and 'experts'; but they are out of favour with the examiners. Here are just a few of them:

acquire	*gain/get*
ascertain	*find out*
assist/assistance	*help*
commence/commencement	*begin/start/beginning*
endeavour/s	*try/efforts*
locate	*find/put/place*
peruse/perusal	*read/reading*
purchase	*buy*
remittance	*payment*
terminate/termination	*finish/end*

2. Cut out unnecessary words

- Do not use more words than are necessary to make your meaning clear; even a long letter need not be long-winded. Being concise is not the same as being short, nor does it mean being brief to the point of rudeness, e.g. *In reply to your request for our holiday brochure, we enclose same.* But being concise does involve pruning flowery language, e.g. *We have the greatest pleasure in enclosing our very latest brochure which contains an exceptionally wide choice of holidays at amazingly low prices* ... That sort of emotive language should be left for advertising circulars!

  Do not overdo the apologies either; just say you were sorry or concerned, not *very* distressed, *deeply* sorry or *genuinely* concerned.

- Don't tack on redundant stock words, as in:
  Due to the recent drought *conditions*.
  The college lacks workshop *facilities*.
  We must avoid a conflict *situation*.
  This sort of 'officialese' has been the butt of many jokes.

- Replace old-fashioned phrases:

Pursuant to your request	*As you requested*
Please be good enough to advise us	*Please let us know*
We are in a position to	*We are able to*

- Cut out all those pointless little phrases and fiddly extra words:

prior to	*before*
subsequent to	*after*
in connection with	*about*
with regard to	
in the region of £100	*about £100*
at a price of £10	*at £10*
the sum of £10	*£10*

3. Use short sentences and paragraphs

Sentences should average about twenty-five words, otherwise the reader tends to get lost. Try to vary the length of your sentences to give a natural conversational feel. Paragraphs should also vary in length from one sentence to about a quarter of an average page. The first sentence should be a signpost pointing to the topic or theme, so keep it short.

4. Use natural-sounding punctuation

Punctuation marks do the same job in writing as pauses and voice inflections do in speaking; they reflect the natural rhythms of speech and place the emphasis on key words and phrases. You drop your voice slightly as you approach a comma, then drop it more distinctly as you approach a full stop. When you move into the next sentence you rev up again. Managers who dictate letters should speak in the manner of actors, and should also play safe by indicating punctuation:

> *rhubarb ... rhubarb ... comma, rhubarb ... rhubarb ...*
> *rhubarb ... semicolon; ... rhubarb ... rhubarb ... full stop.*

Students tend to worry more about spelling than punctuation, but punctuation mistakes are more confusing to the reader because they can cloud or change the very sense of the message. The eye skips over a misspelt word − maybe a typist's error? − but the brain, the silent voice and inner ear of the reader, stumbles over something like this:

> *The conference centre has an excellent restaurant and two bars,*
> *and a cafeteria, this is very popular at lunch-time.*

You can often avoid punctuation mistakes and improve the fluency of your style by using appropriate linking words (conjunctions):

> *The conference centre has an excellent restaurant, two bars, and a*
> *cafeteria which is very popular at lunch-time.*

Weak writers use too many *ands* and *buts*, while neglecting other useful joining words like *so, although, unless, however, because, despite,* etc. (see also Ch. 6, p. 81). Another handicap is the inability to handle that invaluable punctuation mark, the semicolon (;). You can improve your punctuation by studying one of the guides on style which are listed at the end of this chapter. Finally, Fig. 4.3 provides a useful routine to follow when you are next asked to write a letter.

C. USEFUL APPLIED MATERIALS

Fig. 4.3 Letter-writing routine

T H I N K	AIM?	To inform? To instruct? To persuade? To sell?	**C L A R I F Y**	
	APPROACH?	What action or reaction is expected?		
	STRUCTURE?	What is the best order?		
	LANGUAGE?	What is the appropriate style and tone?		
P L A N	NOTE	What are you going to say?	**J O T**	
	GROUP	How do your points link up?		
			OR	
D R A F T	WRITE	Use simple sentences and clear paragraphs	**D I C T A T E**	
	POLISH	Check for mistakes and omissions		

Fig. 4.4   Letter of enquiry from private individual to travel agency.

12, Brent Road,
Westport WP4 6TM
Tel. 762 523

23 February

Alpha Travel,
21, High Street,
Westport WD3 2TC

Dear Sir,

We have studied your new brochure giving details of summer tours in Austria, and would like to make a booking for two on the Tour No. 43 to Salsburg leaving on the 21st July.

We notice that you give a choice of three hotels, and we should like further details before deciding which would suit us best. We need a double bedroom with bath, if possible with a balcony and a view of the mountains.

Could you please make a provisional reservation. When we are able to choose our hotel we will send confirmation and a deposit.

Yours faithfully,

J K Phillips

Mr. J. K. Phillips

Fig. 4.5 A circular invitation letter

The Sports Council

16 Upper Woburn Place, London WC1H 0QP Tel: 01-388 1277

Chairman **Dick Jeeps** CBE
Vice Chairman **Ian McCallum**
Director General **Emlyn Jones** MBE
Deputy Director General **John F. Coghlan** MBE TD

JMS/ECS

November 1982

Chairman of Committee

Dear Chairman

RECREATION MANAGEMENT SEMINAR AND EXHIBITION 1983

The 14th national Seminar and Exhibition organised by the Sports
Council will be held in the new Conference Centre in Harrogate from
28-30 March 1983. The theme this year will be 'FINANCE AND SPORT -
ACCOUNTING FOR THE FUTURE' and will draw on financial expertise in its
speakers from the public, private and commercial sectors.

The three-day conference will cover a variety of topics all concerned
with the financing of sport and recreation and look at some of the ways
in which partnerships, the use of alternative sources of finance, and
innovative financial arrangements can contribute to the successful
promotion of recreation opportunities. Further sessions will explore
the economics of design and construction methods and the opportunities
for income generation through catering and spectator events. With
papers on sponsorship and participation programmes, the Seminar should
be of interest to all involved in either the promotion or the financing
of recreation in Britain today.

The Seminar is supported by a large exhibition of products and services
available to the recreation field and should be of particular interest
to recreation managers, local authority members and officers, education
authorities, architects in the public and private sectors and commercial operators.

Full programme details and application forms will be available in mid-
December and we will ensure you receive a copy. I do hope you will
reserve these dates in your diary and attend what promises to be an
extremely informative and thought-provoking seminar.

I look forward to seeing you in Harrogate.

Yours sincerely

Bev Stephens

Bev Stephens
Head of
Sports Development Unit

(Source: The Sports Council)

Fig. 4.6 A salesletter illustrating a skilful 'soft-sell' approach to a carefully selected residential area

SOLSAVE LTD
23 Maple Avenue, Southport SC3 8JH
Tel. 0324 587

Dear Householder,

We are a British company looking for suitable properties in the South West as part of our advertising programme for the promotion of solar heating.

Clear and informative introduction of purpose

As thousands of people are finding, even in Britain, solar heating can dramatically reduce fuel bills. Your fuel bill is growing at an alarming rate, and perhaps you are having to turn your heating down to compensate. But there is something positive you can do. Not only to save money, but also to save our natural resources.

Plausible claim

Concern with reader's problem

Points forward

Solar heating can be installed without fuss or mess, requires no structural alterations, and will make a welcome contribution to your energy needs.

Possible practical solution

We are able to make a very attractive offer to households willing to give us a certain amount of help with our advertising programme.

Suggestion of fair swap, rather than hard sell

If you are seriously interested in using solar energy, and would like the opportunity to be considered, then please return the enclosed reply-paid card as soon as possible.

Subtle but businesslike cue to respond

Yours sincerely,

NOW IN YOUR AREA

D.G.Marling,
Marketing Department.

Fig. 4.7 Reply from the travel agency (Fig. 4.4) — blocked

```
                              ALPHA TRAVEL
                    21 West Street, Westport 3WD 2TC
                         Telephone  762 376

Your ref.              Our ref. TR/PL 43            26 February 1986

Mr J. K. Phillips
12 Brent Road
Westport 4WP 6TM

Dear Mr Phillips

                          Tour No. 43

Thank you for your letter of 21 February 1986.  We are pleased to tell
you that we are able to give you a provisional booking for tour No. 43
on 21 July.

We enclose the hotels' leaflets to help you make your choice.  The
Astral is the most modern and comfortable, the Grunewald has the most
spectacular views but few bedrooms with balconies, while the Richthof
is renowned for its cuisine.  Last season's clients gave favourable re-
ports of all three, though our courier usually prefers to stay at the
Astral because of its convenient position and efficient service.

Since our Austrian tours are proving very popular this year we advise
you to confirm your reservation by 4 March, enclosing a deposit of £50.

If you need any further advice please telephone me on extension 24.

Yours sincerely,

      Sue Tomlinson
Miss S R Tomlinson

Enc.
```

D. RECENT EXAMINATION QUESTIONS

Question 1 Writing a letter of enquiry

Eight of your friends who help run a youth centre at Bradfield Road want to organise their first-ever dance. It is already agreed that it is to be on Saturday 27 July from 8.00 p.m. to 1.00 a.m. There will be food, a disco and a live band. Prices will be £4.00 with £1 off for the unemployed. A local publican will be asked to provide a bar, and he will apply for the licence.

The local council owns the community centre. Your friends ask you to write a letter to the Leisure Services Officer at your local town hall seeking agreement for your planned use of the community centre.

You may invent names and material you think is essential.

Question 2 Writing a letter of reply

(RSA Communication in Business Stage II)
This question is part of the complete case study paper shown in Ch. 1, p. 2. The assignment involves both a reply to an enquiry and an invitation. You will have to disentangle the jumbled note from Mr Grant and arrange the information in logical order.

Fig. 4.8 Extracts from a typical newsletter

THE NEWSLETTER OF
CAMBRIDGESHIRE
COMMUNITY
COUNCIL

HARVEST

CAMBRIDGESHIRE HOUSE
7 HILLS ROAD
CAMBRIDGE
CB2 1NI

Vol 5 No 4

SUMMER 1985

Large Garden or small farm

The Cambridgeshire Farm College will be running a course for small-scale farmers at Milton on Thursday evenings from 26th September. Topics to be covered include: The Cow, The Vegetable Garden and Beekeeping.

Other short courses for the Amateur Gardener will be run on weekends from October.

Details of these and other courses from Cambridgeshire Farm College, Landbeach Road, Milton, Cambridge CB4 4DB. Tel: Cambridge 860707.

BETTER BRITAIN

The Shell Better Britain Campaign is under way once again. An information and resource pack designed for people running conservation or environmental projects is available. There are also some grants — apply by 30th September.
Details from The Campaign Administrator, Shell Better Britain Campaign, Nature Conservancy Council, Northminster House, Peterborough PE1 1UA.

Youth Development

An interesting experiment in providing youth activities for young people in villages without Village Colleges has been undertaken with help from Impington, Cottenham, Swavesey, Comberton, Melbourn and Bassingbourn Village Colleges.
The first event organised by Jane Kell in the Comberton area attracted an overwhelming response — which caused its own problems!
We wish the project every success.

Running A Voluntary organisation

Do you sometimes consider using an outsider to work with you on a particular problem or area of work to bring a skilled independent fresh approach?
If so, you might be interested in Framework, an organisation of three experienced trainers/consultants — Tim Grant, Sally Hind and Bill Crook. You may have known Sally when she was working in Cambridge City Social Services Department or at Youth Action Cambridge.
Contact the Community Council for brochures which give further details. Anyone interested is welcome to ring Framework, 0533 557453, to find out about the range of charges.

Communications

In the last issue we asked if any groups were interested in our organising a course on communications, marketing and publicity for about £5 to £10. Two organisations were interested — are there any others?

(Source: Cambridgeshire Community Council)

GENERAL INFORMATION APPLICABLE TO ALL QUESTIONS
(Information obtained from one question can be used in answering another)

Assume that you work for John Summerton, owner of 'Tent-Hols' at the firm's office at Mondial House, Station Road, Melchester, Wessex MP2 5WA, telephone Melchester 160356. 'Tent-Hols' specialises in family camping holidays and has tents erected on ten first-class sites in France, Spain and Italy. Families can travel to their chosen resort by car or use the firm's chartered air or coach transport. The tents are fully equipped and laundry, washing and shopping facilities are available on each site. There is an English representative of the firm resident at each site who speaks the local language. During the holiday season, which runs from early June until early September, an average of 400 holidaymakers per week are dealt with by the firm.

1. *Writing a letter*

SITUATION

The following letter arrived in Mr Summerton's post this morning:

> Swift-Fleet Coach Travel,
> 61 London Road,
> Melchester,
> Wessex MP2 5WA
> 9th March, 1982

Dear Mr Summerton,

During discussions with my drivers about our contract made with you for the coming season, I have received several complaints about the procedure to be adopted on arrival at the camp sites with the clients.

It appears that last season my drivers were asked by the campsite representatives to help carry pieces of clients' luggage at the site. The drivers feel, quite rightly in my opinion, that arrangements for carrying luggage should be made by the representatives.

We are looking forward to working with you again this year but should be grateful if this small problem could be solved before the season starts.

> Yours sincerely,
> C. Manson

Mr Summerton adds the following information:

Chris Manson is quite right — I fully appreciate his point that carrying bags isn't his drivers' responsibility. It's up to the representatives to make local arrangements — assure him we'll make it clear to our representatives.

ASSIGNMENT

Draft a letter to Mr Manson for Mr Summerton to sign. Your letter should include an appropriate letterhead and you should use an acceptable layout with which you are familiar. A suitable answer will probably use between 150 and 200 words for the main body of the letter.

2. *Writing a memorandum*

Mr Summerton is concerned about Mr Manson's complaint and wants to ensure the problem does not recur this season. The local representatives are given a budget to finance such arrangements and should have been making their own arrangements such as buying trolleys for use by clients or hiring porters to do the job for them.

(Communication Studies RSA Stage II,1982) (20 marks)

Question 4 Writing a circular letter making arrangements for an event

The factual content of this question is quite straightforward, so the challenge lies in hitting the right 'encouraging and persuasive' tone.

You are employed as a secretary to Comlon International plc, a large company. You work at the Head Office which is about 35 kilometres from London (or, if more appropriate, from the capital of your known country).

You have recently been elected to serve as Honorary Secretary of the Staff Association to which most of the employees belong. It is customary for the Association to organise a staff visit to the capital each New Year for an evening out, including a meal (remember that some people may require special diets) and a seat at a theatre or other place of entertainment. The company defrays 50 per cent of the cost.

You have chosen a suitable programme of events and will shortly need to make the necessary bookings, including transport. A circular letter must now be sent to all Members to set out the details. It needs to mention not only the chief arrangements but also the cost, method of payment and so on. The letter must be encouraging and persuasive in order to overcome inertia and stimulate Members to take part. As far as possible it should anticipate queries, such as whether husbands/wives may take part, whether vegetarian food will be available, the latest probable time of return and so on.

Inventing brief details where necessary, draft a suitable circular letter. It should be presented as if ready for mailing and will probably take a whole page.

(LCCI PSC, 1983) (30 marks)

Question 5 Writing a letter to the press

PA News and Views is a magazine widely read by personal assistants and secretaries. In this month's edition you see the letter reprinted below. Ignore the provocation and **in about 250 words write as an intending PA a dignified reply which answers any or all of the points made by the correspondent.** (Only the body of the letter is needed.)

Where Did All the Secretaries Go?

In the old days we managers depended very much on secretaries whose office skills and personal qualities were second to none. The word 'secretary' really meant something then: a woman of good education and superior attainments who provided a complete office service *par excellence*. She could spell, type immaculately, take shorthand at 120 and be word perfect; she had manners, dress sense, integrity and above all, genuine dedication to her work.

In her place we now have second-rate people providing a third-rate service at a first-rate salary.

Few so-called secretaries nowadays deserve the designation. The better ones have been driven to call themselves 'personal assistants', an inflated title if ever there was one. The rest comprise a motley assortment of under-trained, over-privileged nomads, who flit from job to job, interested only in the money they can get, in leaving the office on the dot at 5 p.m. and in dodging any real responsibility.

Where, oh where did all the real secretaries go?

G.W. Basham
Managing Director Kestingrite Industries

(RSA DPA, 1982) (15 marks)

E. OUTLINE AND TUTOR'S ANSWERS

Question 1

Not quite as straightforward a question as may first appear. Because of the suspicion of residents and officials that youth dances are bound to be rowdy, you need to be diplomatic and reassuring. You may think midnight a reasonable time to end, but the council may insist on 11 or 11.30 unless you can show that you are willing to be co-operative. Since it carries only eight marks you should keep the letter short and to the point.

We demonstrate the tutor's answer in **handwriting:**

Tutor's answer 1

Thorpe Youth and Community Centre,
Bradfield Road, Mareport JB3 9HA,
Telephone 089 554

15 May 1986

Mr. J. T. Kirk,
Leisure Services Offices,
Mareport Borough Council,
Town Hall,
Mareport JH7 8KL

Dear Mr. Kirk,

The committee of the Thorpe Youth Club want to organise a dance at the Bradfield Road Youth Centre on Saturday 27th July, so I am writing to request the Council's permission.

We propose to start at 8.00 and would like to be able to end at 1.00am. There will be a cold buffet, a disco, and live music from the local rock band Brillo and the Padz. The price of tickets will be £4.00 with £1 off for the unwaged. We plan to ask Mrs. Tennant, the landlord of the Queens Head, Bradfield Road, to provide a bar and to apply to the Council for the licence.

Members of the committee will act as stewards to ensure that the event runs smoothly and to minimise noise and disturbance to local residents.

Our next committee meeting will be held on 7 June, when we hope to make final arrangements, so please could you give us a reply within the next two weeks.

Yours sincerely,

Jane Roberts

Jane Roberts.

Margin notes:

- Invent name for centre.
- Give plenty of time for response.
- You should know the name. Invent full address.
- Not Dear Sir,
- Announce your plan and date. State purpose of letter.
- Give details, without taking permission for granted. Invent names.
- Be reassuring about possible problems.
- Politely indicate deadline.
- Not faithfully,

Your ref: EE/JL
Our ref: MG/YT

25 June

Dear Mr Eden,

<u>Eastview Shrub Week</u>

Thank you for your letter of 23 June asking if you could promote your recent book The Complete Shrub Gardener at our garden centre.

We are holding a Shrub Week during the week beginning 21 July which will be launched on the Saturday with a programme of demonstrations and competitions, special offers, free gifts and promotions. The event would provide an ideal opportunity for you to sell autographed copies of your books. You could have a table in the main sales area, or if the weather is fine you may prefer to be outside amongst the shrubs.

The directors would be delighted if you could open the event by saying a few words in praise of shrubs and our display. If you would be willing to perform this short opening ceremony we would be happy for you to sell your books free of charge. If you are unable to help us in this way, we would have to ask you for a charge of 15% on sales.

The event is scheduled to start at 2.00 pm and will close at 9.00 pm. If you are able to accept, could you come to the office entrance at 1.45 in order to avoid the crowds at the main entrance. Please let us know if you would like tea to be provided at 4.00 pm.

We hope that your many admirers in this area will have the chance of meeting you on 21 July.

Yours sincerely,

Mark Grant (Managing Director)

TENT-HOLS
Mondial House, Station Road, Melchester, Wessex MP2 5WA
Telephone: 023 160356   Telex: Holtent

Your ref.   Our ref. JS/pl   10 March 1982

Mr C. Manson
Swift-Fleet Coach Travel
61 London Road
Melchester
Wessex MP2 5WA

Dear Mr Manson,

<u>Luggage Procedure</u>

I was concerned to learn from your letter of 9 March that your drivers have had reason to complain about the arrangements for carrying luggage from arriving coaches to the campsites.

You are correct in pointing out that carrying luggage is not part of your contract, and I regret that your employees were imposed upon in this way. I have advised all our local representatives of your complaint, reminding them that it is their responsibility to arrange for the handling of clients' luggage out of their own budgets. I have warned them that I will not tolerate any such incidents during this coming season.

Please convey my apologies to your drivers, and assure them that if they are ever again asked to carry luggage they are fully entitled to refuse. A number of our clients have written to me saying how much they appreciated the friendly and efficient service given by your company, so I am as anxious as you are to solve this problem before the start of the next holiday season.

I look forward to seeing you at the Travel Trade Exhibition on 23 April.

Yours sincerely,

John Summerson, Managing Director

Tutor's answer 4

COMLON INTERNATIONAL STAFF ASSOCIATION
234 Ongar Road, Epping, Essex EP8 4RT
089 675 ext. 213

25 November 1982

Dear Member,

The association's annual visit to London has been arranged for Friday 3 January. To enable me to finalise bookings I need to know within the next two weeks how many of you want to join in what promises to be a very enjoyable evening. Husbands and wives are welcome.

The coaches will leave from the main entrance at 4.30 p.m. and we plan to return at about 11.00 p.m. At 6.00 p.m. we have booked a large private dining room at the Cumberland Hotel, Marble Arch, who are offering the following menu:

Melon Cocktail	Chocolate Mousse	Muscadet
Chicken in mushroom sauce	Cheese and dessert	Beaujolais
Choice of vegetables	Coffee and liqueurs	

Alternative dishes can be supplied on request for vegetarians and those on special diets.

We have not tried the Cumberland before, but several members of the committee have reported enthusiastically about the quality of the food and the efficient friendly service.

After the meal we will be taken by coach to the Adelphi to see the musical *Me and my Girl* starring Robert Lindsay, described as 'the happiest show in town'. The show starts at 8.00 and lasts about 2½ hours.

The price is only £6.00 per person because the company pays 50 per cent of the cost. If you want to join the trip please fill in the reply slip below and return it to me by 14 December, enclosing your payment.

Mary Younger (Hon. Secretary)

....

I/we shall be coming on the visit on 3 January.
I enclose £6.00/£12.00.
I/we would like alternative dishes (please specify)

Name .... Department ....

It might be useful at this stage to consider the **examiners report** on the actual performance of candidates in answering Question 4.

The examiners' report

Potential private secretaries should have been able to produce a first-class answer to the question which was an exercise in secretarial duties offering tremendous scope to clear-thinking practical candidates. It was surprising, therefore, to find so many poor answers where instructions had been ignored and where there were errors such as the following:

New Year evening out arranged for mid-summer, or for whole day
January outing to include picnic in Hyde Park, trip on the Thames, or tour of London in open-topped bus
Memorandum written instead of circular letter
Incorrect tone
Letter incorrectly addressed or wrongly dated
Letter sent from Comlon International plc and not from Staff Association
Payment to be made to Company instead of to Staff Association
No instructions for booking, for payment of deposit and balance
No final booking date
No indication of cost or of programme
Unrealistic costings varying from £1.50 to £100
No indication of Company's contribution
Unrealistic or incorrect timings, for example, 'will return at 1500 in the morning', 'will be collected from Trafalgar Square at 0100 on New Year's Day'
Offers such as 'bring all your friends', 'fancy dress provided', 'taxis home for all staff', 'baby-sitting service'

The most common error was the lack of a return slip. Some candidates referred to one, but did not include it.
There are special diets other than those for vegetarians, though few candidates mentioned any others.
Mistakes such as 'honary secretry', 'buzy', 'bussiness', and 'sincerly' were inexcusable.
Some amusing inclusions: 'We shall see the sights of London floating down the Thames', 'There will be a cabaret with two singing artists', 'Menu caters for all pallets'.

(LCCI PSC, 1983)

Tutor's answer 5

Mr Basham sounds like a man with old-fashioned and prejudiced views. He was probably 'mothered' for many years by a traditional personal secretary and has been dissatisfied with her recent replacement(s). He certainly appears to know little or nothing about present-day

51

qualifications. You should point out the distinction between shorthand typists and personal secretaries and include some facts about the Diploma for Personal Assistants.

Remember that you are not writing directly to Mr Basham, but to the readers of the magazine.

Dear Sir,

In his letter to the July issue Mr Basham makes some unfavourable comparisons between the 'dedicated' secretaries of 'the old days' and present-day 'second-rate people providing a third-rate service at a first-rate salary'.

Since he chose to make his attack on current secretarial standards in *PA News* I am sure he did not expect his comments to pass unanswered, so I should like to take issue with some of the points he made. His reference to 'nomads' suggests that he has had a succession of unfortunate experiences with 'temps', who might well have been recruited by one of the less reputable agencies. Indeed, one of the reasons why first-rate secretaries now prefer to be called 'personal assistants' is to emphasise the difference between their professional qualifications and the minimal skills of the floating population of glorified shorthand typists.

Part of the problem is that the approach of many managers to recruitment is based on a lack of knowledge of the present range of training and qualifications. All too often they are mainly concerned with shorthand and typing speeds and whether a candidate's appearance happens to suit their personal taste. They overlook the growing importance of administrative and communication skills which demand a high level of intelligence and education.

Many of your readers will know from experience that the Diploma for Personal Assistants is an extremely demanding course for post A level and graduate trainees. It includes communication, law, personnel, economics and finance, as well as secretarial and administrative skills. My 'inflated title' was hard-earned and means that I have more to offer my employer. I am fortunate in working for a company which recognises the value of initiative and flexibility.

Yours faithfully,

F. A STEP FURTHER

The best way of improving your letter-writing is to study as many actual examples as possible. Take note of the layout and pay critical attention to the language. Whenever you have to write a formal letter take particular care to follow the advice in this chapter. Study letters in the press, particularly in your local paper, which argue the case for or against likely exam topics, e.g. recreation facilities, shopping developments, etc.

General textbooks

The following contain useful chapters on letters and points of detail:
Communication at Work, Evans D W. Pitman 1982. One of the best elementary books appropriate to BTEC general, and O level.
People and Communication (2nd edn), Evans D W. Pitman 1984. Chapter 3 is particularly helpful on layout and shows several good examples. It also contains a thorough list of good and bad examples of style and tone. See also Chapter 10 on Use of English.
Mastering Business Communication, Woolcott L A and Unwin W R.

Macmillan 1983. Chapter 1 is a good up-to-date survey with useful examples. See also Chapter 12 on language.

The Business of Communicating, Stanton N. Pan 1982. Chapter 2 is a stimulating approach to a well-worn topic. Chapter 15 gives a useful survey of some of the common problems with English.

English for Business Students (2nd rev. edn 1982), Pincott M. Longman 1985, pp. 31–46, 57–61, 95–107. Mainly aimed at secretarial students.

Modern Business Correspondence (3rd edn 1984), Gartside L. Macdonald & Evans 1976, pp. 156–269. A comprehensive book on all aspects of the topic.

Communication in Business, Little P. Pitman 1983, Chapter 8. Chapters 3, 4, 5 and 6 provide an excellent and detailed guide to style. Essential reading for more advanced candidates.

Get it Right, Temple M. John Murray 1978. Will help you to polish up your style.

The Plain English Story M. Cutts and C. Maher. The Plain English Campaign, 1986, shows many examples of ghastly 'officialese'.

Books for managers

Effective Writing, Turk C and Kirkman J. Spon 1982, Chapter 12. Although aimed particularly at engineers and scientists, the author's advice should be heeded by all potential managers.

Janner's Letters, Janner G. QC MP. Hutchinson 1983.

Useful booklets

A Guide to the Writing of Business Letters. BACIE, 16 Park Crescent, London W1N 4AP.

Letter Writing. The Industrial Society, 3 Carlton Terrace, London SW1Y 5DG.

Films

Letter Writing at Work. Rank Educational Films. An excellent and unexpectedly amusing film available to colleges.

The Business Letter Business. Video Arts (with booklet).

Chapter 5   Internal written communication

A. GETTING STARTED

In small organisations day-to-day internal communication is usually so informal that very little has to be put on paper. Messages and instructions are exchanged face-to-face or over the telephone. But success and expansion breed distance. Managers become more specialised; their offices more partitioned; their diaries fuller with outside engagements. They are no longer in daily contact with all employees, and see less and less of their immediate colleagues. This results in more and more routine messages having to be written, reproduced and distributed.

As the organisation grows the written tasks multiply, with more and more people needing to be informed and instructed, warned and reprimanded, thanked and congratulated.

Lengthy and complex forms of internal communication, such as reports, are dealt with in separate chapters. Here we deal with several other writing tasks which do not merit a chapter each. **Memoranda** and **notices** are covered in some detail because they are often set as complete questions or as parts of composite questions. Other topics are dealt with in a way designed to help you answer general and quiz-type questions, e.g. those which ask you to choose an appropriate form of communication for a given situation, or to compare the advantages and disadvantages of different forms. Of course some questions of this type will also demand an awareness of the general principles and theory of communication.

You are advised to pay particular attention to cross-references in this chapter, since there is an unavoidable degree of overlap with related topics covered elsewhere in the book.

B. ESSENTIAL PRINCIPLES

All forms of communication can be roughly divided into categories according to their purpose. The original B/TEC National Syllabus used four main headings:

Informing: e.g. a memo confirming the delivery of a new photocopier and for what purposes; the photocopier manufacturer's manual; the rules of a competition; the procedure for internal telephone calls.
Persuading: e.g. a leaflet, brochure or letter about the qualities of a particular photocopier; a piece in the newsletter urging staff to enter a competition; a circular memo asking staff to save telephone bills by making non-urgent calls at the cheaper afternoon rate.
Operating: i.e. the choice of appropriate means of communication, based on an understanding of communication systems and relationships.
Co-operating: e.g. in teamwork, meetings and group discussions.

Of course most writing tasks have more than one of these purposes. For example, the installation of a new photocopier might involve writing a circular memo informing staff of new arrangements, placing the manual near the machine, and pinning up a notice in the photocopying room urging the economical use of paper.

MEMORANDA

The word **Memorandum** (memo for short) originally meant a reminder or confirmation. It has since come to include a wide variety of written messages exchanged between people working within the same organisation. Memos range from handwritten one-liners to two or more pages of typescript. They might be hand delivered by the writer, put in the internal post by secretaries, carried through the streets by despatch riders or sent electronically. Their contents are usually neutral and routine, but can sometimes be sensitive and confidential. They are the internal correspondence of an organisation, and are not supposed to be read by outsiders.

Most memos end up in filing cabinets or waste-paper baskets. Indeed, a common complaint of office life is that there are far too many of them; and the larger the organisation the more they multiply. In an average school, college or university your course will probably generate several memos per week, concerning anything from changes in the syllabus to the attendance record of an individual student.

Why send a memorandum?

It is easier to ring an extension or scribble a note than to go to the trouble of writing a memo. So why bother with the formalities? Why should these two messages be turned into memos?

(a) *Please put your department reference number, which is now 404, on all letters sent out to customers.*

(b) *Jim. Let me have a breakdown of last year's sales to overseas customers on a monthly basis by the end of next week. And I'll need a similar analysis for this country by the 31st.*

The answer is that memos provide a written record, can be written and read without interruption whenever convenient, and they are certain to reach the intended person. And Jim will see that particular memo in his in-tray every day he puts off the task. It will jog his memory and his conscience until he writes his memo in response.

Types of memorandum

Most memos are messages from on high. They are the usual means of communication from *senior to junior* level in order to:

1. **Convey information**, e.g. to tell employees how many parking spaces are available and who is entitled to use them.
2. **Request information**, e.g. ask for lists of names, cars and registration numbers of employees in need of parking spaces.
3. **Give instructions**, e.g. tell employees which spaces they are allowed to use, where to get display discs, etc.
4. **Deliver reprimands**, e.g. point out that certain employees have been parking in the wrong places and how this will be stopped.

Many such memos are like internal circular letters in that they are mass produced and delivered to a number of people at once, sometimes with an additional copy for the notice-board. (Note that important information of a confidential nature, e.g. pension schemes, early retirement, impending redundancies, are often distributed as circular letters, individually addressed in envelopes.)

Memos sent from *junior to senior* level are usually responses to requests, e.g. providing lists of names, cars and registration numbers. But the memorandum is also the usual means whereby a junior formally conveys information and ideas to his seniors without having been asked to do so. For instance, he may think the car-park is badly laid out, or that arrangements for the disabled are inadequate, and wish to suggest improvements. In this case he might write a memorandum/report (see Ch. 7, p. 96).

Of course many memos are exchanged each day between *equals*; arranging meetings, asking for information, placing orders for equipment, etc.

Format

A memorandum is like a letter which has been topped and tailed. It has no letterhead, no 'Dear X', no 'Yours Y', etc. and is often delivered without an envelope. It may have the name of the organisation and/or department across the top, or simply be headed 'Memorandum', e.g.

MEMORANDUM

From:	Ref:
To:	Date:

Subject:_____

This is all you are likely to have to remember for your examination, whether you are asked to write a brief A5 memo or an extended memo/report. Most organisations have their own memo pads for short routine messages. Some have additional columns, tear-off reply portions, multicoloured undersheets, etc.

It is a good idea to draw a frame round a short memo, particularly if it needs marking off from another part of the question, e.g. when attached to a report. If you have used your full name at the top you need only put your initials at the bottom. End with your full name (not a signature) if you have not used it at the top, e.g. From: The Marketing Director ... B.W. Smith.

Structure

Memos fall into most of the same basic shapes as letters, depending on their content and on the relationship between the writer and the reader(s). All but the briefest and most informal would normally follow the sort of pattern shown in Fig. 5.1.

Fig. 5.1 The structure of a memo message

```
Subject:        Heading


Reason...............purpose...............context...............
............


Information.........instructions.........explanations............
questions...........comments........etc.....................


Indication of response required.........deadline................
............


Maybe a parting word or two......Well done........................
Thank you for your co-operation.........etc.
```

Tone and style

Few employees see the letters sent out from an organisation, but many will receive and act upon memos. So the impression of an individual or department will depend to a large degree on the tone and style conveyed through memos.

If messages from *senior* staff are too brisk and bossy, or too 'official' and impersonal, they will invite sour comment and get grudging compliance. If they are too clumsy and long-winded they will be shrugged off. They are more likely to gain respect and co-operation if they are clear, concise and friendly.

Even if the purpose is to reprimand or keep people 'up to the mark' it pays to sound firm but reasonable, rather than threatening or self-important. So avoid openings like 'It has been drawn to my attention that ...' In a memo you should be frank and straightforward: 'I have had several complaints recently about ...' This advice particularly applies to exam questions which ask you to follow up an outside complaint with a memo to an employee or colleague.

If you are supposed to be a *junior* employee writing to a senior, your style and tone should be neutral and impersonal, not grovelling or smarmy. For example, *not*: 'I fully realise that you must be dreadfully busy, but I would be so grateful if you could possibly manage to give your consideration to this matter ...'; *but*: 'I hope you will be able to consider ...'

If the role or situation outlined in the question involves communication between *equals*, your message is aimed at a smaller, more knowledgeable and probably more sympathetic audience. You should be able to drop the routine formalities and courtesies appropriate to letters, e.g. 'Thank you for your extremely informative memo dated ...' and launch straight into the subject: 'Thanks for the information ... it will be very helpful etc. ...'

Memos tend to be written or dictated in a hurry between appointments and telephone calls, so less trouble is taken than with letters to polish the language. Some rough edges are acceptable provided the message is clear and the tone is appropriate to the reader(s). The rules to remember are:

1. Always use a heading to identify the subject to the reader and to make sure it is correctly filed.
2. Be brief and direct, but pleasant in tone. Do not include anything the reader does not need to know. People expect memos to be crisper than letters, but not too brisk and bossy.
3. Use short paragraphs, and in longer memos covering several different topics use numbers and subheadings.
4. Make sure that technical or statistical information is clearly presented.
5. Add a final pay-off comment if appropriate, e.g. thanks, congratulations, warning, etc.

NOTICES

Notices are used, particularly in large organisations, for communicating messages to the whole workforce in circumstances where it would not be practicable to send memos to everyone, including shop-floor workers. They are the usual means of conveying information which needs to be continually on display, e.g. fire drill and safety precautions, also for announcements on matters such as canteen arrangements, staff car-parking, etc.

Most notices are a *downward* form of communication from those at executive level to those in middle and junior positions. There is therefore little scope for immediate feedback, so it is important to ensure that the tone does not provoke resentment or cynicism. Whatever the message, it must be straightforward and briefly worded.

It is advisable to keep separate notice-boards for different interests, e.g. for the sports and social club, the trade unions, one for internal vacancies and promotions, etc. If this is not possible then a single notice-board should be divided into sections with a clear permanent heading for each. People will then get used to knowing where to look for information they are interested in.

Someone should be responsible for checking the boards and making sure that no unauthorised notices are pinned up. Notices should be attractively displayed, following the principle that people are used to reading from left to right, so the ones they read first will be those at eye-level on the left-hand side. Flapping, overlapping and tattered notices should be regularly tidied up, and 'dead' out-of-date notices removed.

Heavy borders, underlinings, capitals and an additional colour are eye-catching additions to simple typed notices (see Fig. 5.2).

Fig. 5.2 A management notice about safety precautions

```
                        CALCO CHEMICALS

    TO:  ALL STAFF

                   PROCEDURE FOR VISITING THE WAREHOUSE

    1. ALL VISITORS MUST FIRST REPORT TO THE WAREHOUSE OFFICE AT THE MAIN
       ENTRANCE.  DO NOT USE THE SIDE DOOR.

    2. ANYONE NEEDING TO ENTER THE WAREHOUSE WILL BE ISSUED WITH PROTECTIVE
       CLOTHING AND WILL BE ACCOMPANIED BY A MEMBER OF THE WAREHOUSE STAFF.

    3. ANY ITEMS REQUIRED SHOULD FIRST BE REQUISITIONED FROM THE STOCK
       ORDER OFFICE.

    THESE INSTRUCTIONS ARE DESIGNED FOR YOUR SAFETY AND THE SECURITY OF OUR
    PRODUCTS.

    12 March 1986                              J. K. Evans
                                            Distribution Manager
```

WRITING INSTRUCTIONS

An instruction is worthless unless it is 100% clear. Nothing is more infuriating than finding yourself in the middle of assembling a piece of equipment, and having to undo the job and start again because of a poorly worded instruction. The Plain English Campaign's 1984 booby prize went to the instructions for the assembly of a child's car, which began:

> 'Attach front wheels to steering column, firstly place on large domed fastener on axle pass through wheel (recess outermost) and long spacer. Through column, long spacer and wheel, secure with fastener ...'

Instructions tell us *what* to do, and usually, *how* to do it. Sometimes they also tell you *why* it has to be done, *what* the results will be, and the dire consequences of not doing it, or of doing it incorrectly. For example, photocopier manuals always tell you to fan the paper before loading; some will then tell you how to turn the pack and flick the edges, while others will point out *why* this routine is necessary — it eliminates electrostatic, which is the usual cause of misfeeds.

Clear instructions should be:

(a) **Simply expressed**, e.g. 'Always display your parking disc.' *Not:* 'Your parking disc should be affixed to your windscreen in such a way as to be always visible.'

(b) **Unambiguous**, e.g. 'Only one disc per member of staff will be issued. Owners of more than one vehicle are asked to transfer the disc from one car to another when necessary.' *Not:* 'Do not display your disc on more than one car at a time.'

(c) **In the correct sequence**, e.g. 'Switch power OFF. Open fuse box and remove blown fuse.' *Not:* 'Open fuse box and remove blown fuse, having first switched power OFF.'

(d) **Complete**, e.g. 'Turn the red knob at the back of the machine anticlockwise.' *Not:* 'Turn the knob at the back.'

The simplest and shortest way of writing instructions is to use *imperative* verbs, either in the positive or the negative, e.g. '*Load* the paper into the cassette. *Do not overload* the cassette with paper.' The imperative is best for operating instructions in handbooks and manuals where clarity is the main priority, and the reader expects to be told what to do. Extra clarity is achieved by illustrations and diagrams (see Fig. 5.5).

However, notices and circular memoranda phrased entirely in the imperative would sound brisk to the point of rudeness. If a manager were concerned about wasted paper in the print-room he would be ill-advised to start like this: 'Do not waste paper. Load paper correctly. Use both sides of the sheet.' And so on throughout the message. He should introduce the matter with an explanation, e.g. 'Consumption of paper has increased by 15% over the last quarter, which has cost the company over £500. Some of this increase is due to an increased workload, but a great deal is being wasted unnecessarily through incorrect operation of the photocopiers.' He would then proceed to urge members of staff to avoid misfeeds by studying the manual, to save paper by using both sides of the sheet and by making reductions. The style should use a mixture of persuasive and imperative verbs, e.g. 'Wherever possible, you should use both sides of the sheet.' 'In case of breakdown, call the technician.' 'Please try to cut the queues by leaving long runs to off-peak periods.'

Algorithms

The clearest way of reducing a set of instructions to a simple foolproof form is to turn it into the sort of flow-diagram known as an **algorithm**. Algorithms are particularly useful in taking you through a series of steps which includes variables, e.g. *If indicator light shows GREEN do X; if it shows RED do Y*. This enables you to miss out steps which do not apply. (See Fig. 5.6, also Chapter 10, Visual Communication).

BRIEFING NOTES

Briefing is one of those awkward examination topics which touches on a variety of contexts and takes several different forms. You should first be clear what is meant by the term itself.

The noun 'brief' is best known as the name given to the summary of facts and relevant points of law prepared by a solicitor for the barrister who is to represent his client in court. The term can also apply to someone's 'terms of reference' for a job or commission, e.g when an outside consultant is called in to sort out a particular technical or financial problem, he will need to know the exact scope of his brief.

For instance, a structural engineer might be given the brief of studying the cause of cracks in a building. Before starting on his study he would need to be 'briefed', i.e. given all the relevant information. He in turn might call in his assistants to a briefing meeting to give an outline of the job. Then he will assign them each a detailed brief for a particular aspect. The assistants will then keep him briefed as the job develops. So when we speak of someone being 'well briefed' we mean well informed.

Junior managers are often asked by senior colleagues to provide them with notes on a topic that is likely to come up at a meeting or conference to enable them to make an accurate and up-to-date contribution to the discussion. For example, an accountant would be expected to provide his finance director with the latest costs of a building project; a senior secretary/PA may be asked to provide guidance notes on new office equipment for a manager who has to argue the case to the board for purchasing particular items; a local government officer may be asked to provide notes for a councillor who has to make a speech or answer questions in a debate.

Briefing notes have the same purpose as short informal information reports, and are written in an impersonal businesslike style. You dispense with report section headings such as Introduction, Recommendations, and simply list the facts under a main subject heading, e.g. <u>Purchase of Office Equipment</u>, with appropriate subheadings, e.g. Typewriters, Photocopiers.

If the notes are to be used as a guide for a talk or presentation, they should include some indication of illustrations and visual aids, e.g.

PHOTOCOPIERS	VISUALS
The two models best suited to our needs are:	
The *f*X 1000B @ £580	
The PM 20BK @ £720	Show brochures
The definition of PM copies is slightly sharper but the difference is probably too marginal to justify the much higher price.	Show some examples of
. . . etc.	copies

If the notes are going to be referred to in the course of a speech, it is especially important to arrange the facts in a logical order, and to make the key points stand out by use of bold headings (see Ch. 10).

HOUSE JOURNALS AND NEWSLETTERS

There are three distinct types of 'in-house' publication:

(a) A *glossy prestigious magazine* aimed at clients and shareholders as well as staff, containing feature articles about the organisation and subjects of general interest such as travel and wine. These are produced either by the company's own public relations staff or by outside professionals.

(b) A *monthly newspaper or magazine* for staff only, containing news of the organisation, work-related articles on personnel matters such as pension schemes, sports and social reports, profiles of individuals or departments, competitions, etc. It may also carry official notices and lists of vacancies.

(c) *Local weekly bulletins or newsletters* which are pinned up on noticeboards and circulated among staff. These are usually simple duplicated sheets produced by the personnel department, listing appointments, retirements, announcements from clubs and committees, etc.

The main purpose of house journals and magazines is to keep staff informed about the organisation at all levels by giving an overview of objectives, activities, and news about products, services and personnel. For large companies, which may have factories and offices scattered over a wide area, magazines provide a link between people working far apart, and foster a sense of belonging.

To overcome the common suspicion that house magazines are the 'mouthpiece of management', staff are encouraged to contribute by suggesting possible topics, sending letters to the editor, writing reports on events, submitting photographs and entering competitions. If the magazine is too heavy in content few employees will read it, so about a third of the space is filled with snippets of gossip, sports reports, gardening and cookery tips, crosswords and competitions. There is often a regular slot about the winners of suggestion schemes.

The language of staff journals is pitched at a level suitable for a wide readership. The style and tone should be chatty and positive, without being too jolly or patronising. Items of a controversial nature such as industrial disputes are usually avoided. The nearest parallel is with a local newspaper minus the 'shock horror' stories.

A typical issue would contain all or some of the following:

- A report on recent company results (perhaps illustrated by a graph), adapted by the editor from a report or speech and signed as if by the managing director.
- The announcement of a new appointment or promotion, with a profile and photograph.
- A report on new technology in an office or factory, featuring the members of staff involved.
- A report on the launch of a new product or service, and/or an account of an advertising campaign.
- An article about an aspect of personnel management, e.g. training, pensions, early retirement, job appraisal.

- Picture features of events, e.g. retirement parties, sponsored runs, award presentations, etc.
- A sports page featuring the organisation's teams, and individual achievements, e.g. an employee winning an angling contest.
- Practical tips on gardening, cooking, DIY, etc.
- Puzzles, competitions, cartoons.

The examiners will expect you to have a background knowledge of the use of house journals and bulletins as both downward and upward channels of communication, and to be able to write a variety of items — usually an article, a letter or an announcement (see also Ch. 13).

Feedback

To ensure that house journals are read and appreciated by staff, surveys are sometimes conducted to assess responses and preferences. Such surveys usually show that the majority of employees are mainly interested in reading about company activities, while the lighter gossipy sections are skimmed for items of particular interest. Feedback can also be measured by the number and range of letters and contributions received. A journal that has to be assembled and written entirely by the editor is a sure sign of staff indifference.

C. USEFUL APPLIED MATERIALS

This memorandum could also be pinned up on a notice-board.

Fig. 5.3 A routine circular memo about car-parking

```
                          MEMORANDUM

From: Buildings Officer              Date: 7 November 19..

To:   All Staff

Subject:  Staff Car Park

The extension to the car park will be completed in three weeks time.
This will involve the reallocation of spaces.  Arrangements are being
made for the issue of  new parking discs which will be numbered and
have your initials on them.

All members of staff requiring a disc should return the reply slip
below to my office by 14 November to enable me to prepare a revised
register and issue the new discs before the extension is opened.

One disc only per member of staff will be issued, and owners of more
than one car are asked to transfer the disc when necessary.  The car
park attendant has instructions not to allow cars to enter unless
they are displaying a currently valid disc.

The new discs will be issued through Departments during the week
beginning 21 November, and should be displayed as from Monday
28 November.

P. L. King

...............................................................

Name

Department

Registration number
```

Fig. 5.4 Request from junior to senior level

```
                              MEMORANDUM

From:      John Paynter, General Office        Ref:   JP/GO

To:        T. W. Kent, Training Officer        Date:  6 May 1986
      cc Janet Wright

Subject:   Leave of Absence 12 June

As you know, I am attending a day-release course at Weston College on
Thursdays.  Our Law Lecturer has arranged a tour of the Inns of Court on
Tuesday 12 June and has asked if any students in this Thursday group would
be able to make up the numbers on the coach to London.

I am keen to go because it will help towards my end of term project.  I
realise that this will mean taking a day off work at a particularly busy
time of year, but I would be prepared to make up the time lost out of my
annual leave or by working unpaid overtime.

The College needs to finalise arrangements by 27 May, so I hope you can
give me your answer in time for my class on the 20th.

                                          JGP
```

In reply :

```
                              MEMORANDUM

From:      T. W. Kent, Training Officer        Ref:   TWK/SG

To:        John Paynter, General Office        Date:  11 May 1986

Subject:   Leave of Absence, 12 June

I have discussed your request for leave of absence with Mrs Wright.  She
says that although the General Office will be under pressure that day,
you could make up the time during the following fortnight.  She will
arrange the details with you.  I note that your reports from the college
have been favourable, and hope you do well in your project.

Enjoy the trip.

                                          TWK
```

Notes

- The reply might have turned down the request, or been stricter about the overtime, but the tone should be reasonable and friendly.
- The subject heading mentions a date; otherwise it might at first glance seem to have been about leave of absence in general.
- 'I hope you can' sounds less brisk than 'please'.
- 'cc'. It is courteous procedure to send a copy to your immediate boss, even if she does not have the final say. In this case, you would probably have already raised it with her.

Fig. 5.5 An extract from a photocopier manual

LOADING PAPER
How to Load the Cassettes with Paper

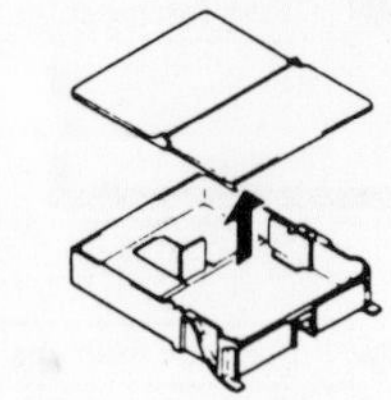	1. Remove the Cassette Lid.
	2. Remove the Paper from its package. 3. Fan the paper thoroughly. NOTE The paper should be loaded into the Cassette so that the surface facing the sealed side of the package faces upward.
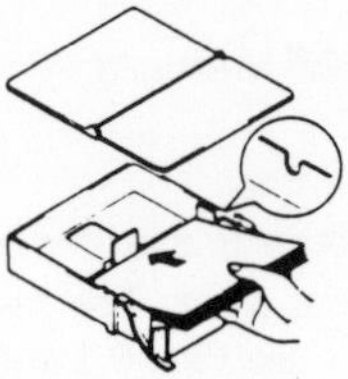	4. Align the front edge of the sheets of paper. 5. Place the Paper into the Cassette so that the Tailing Edge presses against the Paper Stop. Then lower the Leading Edge to load the Paper completely. At most, the Upper and Middle Cassettes can hold 250 sheets each and the Lower Cassette 500 sheets of 75 g/m^2 paper. Never load the paper to a level higher than that of the notch in the Paper Edge Guides.
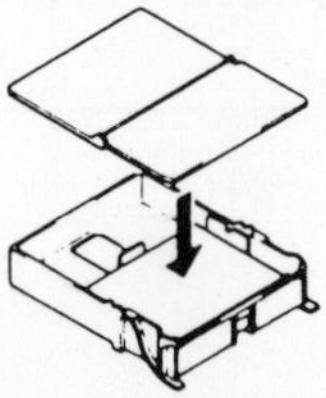	6. Replace the Cassette Lid. The Protective Cover should be closed when the Cassette is not inserted into its Port and when it is in storage.

Note the variations from the imperative, e.g. 'Remove', 'Replace', to the persuasive, e.g. 'The Protective Cover should be closed . . .'

(Source: Minolta EP 650Z Manual)

Fig. 5.6 Algorithm from the photocopier manual

TROUBLE SHOOTING
The machine does not turn ON after the ON switch is pressed.

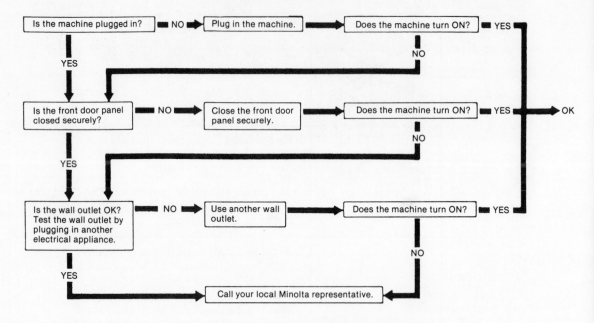

(Source: Minolta EP 650Z Manual)

The design of **algorithms** is a skilled job, but once mastered, it is simpler than presentation as a list. The instructions are certainly easier for the reader to follow — see Figs 5.5 and 5.6.

Note how direct questions replace the repetition of sentences beginning with '*if*', e.g. *Does the machine turn on?* followed by alternatives, rather than *If the machine does not turn on, either X, or Y, and therefore you should do this or that.* (The use of algorithmic techniques in form design is discussed in Chapter 11.)

Fig. 5.7 A selection of typical items from a house journal

Kellogg's NEWS

DECEMBER 1984

New Board appointments

AT A board meeting on the 26th November, Chairman Ross Buckland and the Board of Directors announced a number of new appointments.

Two Deputy Managing Directors were appointed: David Brenner, formerly Marketing Development Manager — Europe; and Geoff Lord, formerly Director — Manufacturing and Engineering.

Four other Directors were also appointed: Wilf Hamilton — Scientific Affairs; Russell King — Logistics; Neil Makin — Human Resources; Brian Moore — Sales.

It was announced that Chris McNaughton has been appointed President of the US Food Products Division and will be relocating to the United States in the first quarter of 1985.

Present Chairman Ross Buckland re-assumes the combined role of Chairman and Managing Director.

Christmas Message

1984 will mark Kellogg Company of Great Britain's fifth year in a row of record sales. This success has only been made possible by the individual and combined efforts of all Kellogg people.

We wish to use this occasion of the holiday season to extend to each of you our thanks for your help, dedication and a job well done! With strong performances from our existing products, and the successful introduction of our new products, START and FRUIT 'n FIBRE, we, with you, look confidently forward to an even more successful 1985.

Best wishes for a very enjoyable Christmas and a Happy New Year.

Ross Buckland

Christopher J. McNaughton

NEW LOOK FOR 'RICE KRISPIES'

1985 will see a brand new look for RICE KRISPIES packets on the supermarket shelves, and a brand new television commercial too.

The past year has been a tough one for RICE KRISPIES, with mounting competition from private label crisp rice brands. The new carton and advertising will help to ensure, however, that consumers are right in keeping RICE KRISPIES in its long-held position of one of the best selling cereals of all.

The carton strongly features the 'Snap, Crackle Pop' characters, and they are the stars of the exciting animated TV commercial which will appeal to children of all ages.

The TV campaign will highlight the good food value of RICE KRISPIES, as well as being among the most action-packed commercials appearing on Britain's screens during the year.

Packets of RICE KRISPIES will feature back panels which children can design themselves, using rub down transfers (free in all packets) to re-crete SNAP, CRACKLE and POP's TV adventures.

Initial screening of the commercial will start in January, and run throughout the year.

RICE KRISPIES, famous for 'Snap, Crackle and Pop' was first launched in 1928. The new year's developments will see to it that it remains a family favourite for all ages.

(Source: © 1984 Kellogg Company)

Fig. 5.8 Extracts from Kellogg's weekly bulletin which is circulated and posted on notice boards. The communications co-ordinator is also the editor of the company house journal Kelloggs News.

 *GRAPEVINE*

AUGUST 1986

NUTRI-GRAIN

August sees the first transmission of T.V. commercials for the newest Kellogg product – NUTRI-GRAIN.

There are four different commercials; one of 40 seconds, covering the whole range, and three twenty second commercials – one for each NUTRI-GRAIN variety.

Early indications show a good level of distribution has been achieved in the market place, and the television campaign planned for the next few months should result in 92% of housewives seeing the commercial on average over 13 times.

NUTRI-GRAIN will be advertised on both ITV and Channel 4, with the first 'spot' in 'News at Ten' on Tuesday, 5th August, at 10.15 p.m..

Service Anniversaries

Congratulations to Ben Baker (Manufacturing Engineer) who completes 30 years service during August.

Maureen Farrell and Ian Miles, of Finance Department, complete 25 years service this month, whilst Pietro Dicello and Walter Brown of Maintenance Department complete 20 years with the Company.

Thank You ...

The National Blood Transfusion Services passes on thanks to everyone who donated blood during the recent visit to Kellogg's.

202 donations were received, bringing the total donations from Kellogg employees to 8,715 since the first visit in 1950.

Thank you again to all donors.

PHOTOGRAPHIC COMPETITION

Details of this year's KELLOGG'S NEWS PHOTOGRAPHIC COMPETITION will be announced in the near future, with a closing date in mid-November.

The contest is open to all Kellogg people, at all locations, and both slides and prints are accepted.

Last year saw a record entry, so, sort out your best photos now and win some prize money for Christmas.

(Posters with full details will appear at all locations).

(Source: © 1986 Kellogg Company)

D. RECENT EXAMINATION QUESTIONS

Question 1 (a) Briefly describe two methods which the management of a large organisation can use to communicate important messages to their workforce.

(10 marks)

(b) Discuss the relative advantages and disadvantages of these two methods as ways of ensuring effective communication and developing good relationships between management and workforce.

(ICSA, 1984) (15 marks)

Question 2 Give four points to consider in displaying an important notice.

Question 3 You work at Philips and Jones plc as private secretary to Mr G Anderson, the Chief Office Administrator, among whose responsibilities is ensuring that adequate administration services are provided for the 150 staff, including mail, typing services, filing and photocopying. Yesterday Mr Anderson had this to say to you:

'Something will obviously have to be done about the photocopier in the print room – it's broken down again. That's five times in the last fortnight! Staff are always ready to complain when this happens but I'm convinced the breakdowns are caused by people not using it properly. I knew we would have this problem when it was agreed to allow staff free access to the wretched machine – people putting the paper in wrongly or being very clumsy using the controls. They don't seem to realise an expensive machine needs careful handling. Apart from this, they don't know how to get the best results out of the machine – not printing on both sides of the paper or reducing A4 sheets on to one. And it's alarming to see how many copies have been thrown away in the waste bin! I've discussed the matter with senior staff and they agree that something has to be done – the present problems will take the whole of tomorrow to sort out – and this situation is affecting the general efficiency of the company. It's very inconvenient and frustrating for those who do use the machine properly. I want to send something out to each member of staff today, explaining the situation and getting some information from them – how often they use it, how many copies they make in an average week, whether they would like some basic training, etc – in fact, any information that may help us to sort the matter out. They may, in fact, want all copying done by a trained operator who can be in absolute control of the machine. If I can have their replies by 15 July, I'll be able to work something out to put to the next senior staff meeting.'

(a) Prepare a suitable communication (using about 200 words) for Mr Anderson.

(20 marks)

(b) Prepare a reply form to accompany (a) for staff to complete. This should provide Mr Anderson with the kind of information he requires.

(15 marks)

(LCCI PSC, 1984) (Total: 35 marks)

**Question 4
Briefing
notes**

Assume that you work as personal assistant to Mr Derek Thomas, Personnel Manager of Fabrica Products Limited, a company which manufactures a range of wallpapers and home decoration products.

The company's head office comprises the following departments:

Sales, Marketing, Accounts, Office Administration, Personnel, Transport.

Each Department is administered by a departmental head and is made up of some 3−5 middle management staff, some 5−10 clerical staff, and some 5−7 secretarial staff, ranging from the junior to the more experienced in terms of age and length of service.

At a recent meeting, the Managing Director said he thought that the company had not been paying sufficient attention to staff development.

At present staff turnover − especially among junior staff − is unacceptably high, and senior management has recently complained about a general 'lack-lustre' performance overall at head office.

Mr Thomas has felt for some time that an initiative ought to be taken to improve matters and had this to say to you earlier today on the subject:

'I've just been reading this article by Professor Anderson of the London School of Management in last month's *Management in Action*. It's called 'Staff appraisal − what's in it for *your* company?' You know, it's high time we looked carefully at the whole question of employee appraisal for our head office staff.

I'd like you to prepare a briefing on the benefits of employee appraisal and whether it could be introduced here. You need only concentrate on the junior staff in your briefing as I imagine the scheme would be introduced progressively. Oh, and reference should be made to any visual aids you feel relevant.'

Compose a suitable briefing to meet Mr Thomas's needs in a format you think appropriate, of between 300 and 400 words.

Note: You should indicate the nature of any visual aids, but should NOT attempt to reproduce them.

(20 marks)

(RSA DPA, 1980)

Question 5

In this question from a case study exam you are asked to write two memos and a notice. (See also Question 2, Ch. 3, p. 21).

You are employed as Senior Accounts Clerk in the Accounts Department of the Brunswick Trading Company Plc, Wolverhampton, West Midlands.

There are 12 people working in the office altogether:

The Accounts Office Manager, Mr Blunt
His secretary
2 clerk/typists
2 filing clerks
1 Senior Accounts Clerk (yourself)

Your company operates as suppliers of office equipment and supplies.

Your superior, Mr Blunt, the Accounts Office Manager, is a very busy man, known to be short-tempered but fair in his treatment of staff. He prides himself on his discipline/efficiency and expects the same from everyone else. He seems to be however, unsure of himself in some ways and does not seem to relate easily to people. He is surprisingly poor at making conversation and making decisions. Over the 18 months in which you have been in your present position, he has come to depend on you in some respects and values your views on some matters. He respects your honesty and integrity.

He is inclined to be somewhat abrupt and even rude with junior staff, and in the past young office trainees tend to leave on this account.

It has been established practice in the past for all staff within the company to be granted use of the company switchboard to make personal phone calls, provided they identify their name and extension number, and the number they wish to call, stating the personal nature of the call.

This information is then relayed by the switchboard operator to the Accounts section, and it is your responsibility to make out Personal Telephone Accounts for Staff each month, which are forwarded to them by internal mail.

Recently the following facts have come to your attention:

1. The switchboard operator maintains that some stores staff do not state the personal nature of their calls, although the same numbers are called by the same people regularly.
2. Despite repeated bills being presented, an increasing number of staff are not paying them.
3. The overall volume of personal calls is increasing.

You approach Mr Blunt about the matter and tell him of your observations. He tells you to:

● circulate staff immediately with an appropriate Memorandum to try to resolve the problem;
● suggest, in Memorandum form, what action could be taken (with reasons) if the situation does not improve by the end of the month;
● take any other immediate action you consider necessary.

TASK 1: Write the circular to all staff   (20 marks)

TASK 2: Write the Memorandum to Mr Blunt   (15 marks)

TASK 3: Draft a notice to be placed on all notice-boards which may help to resolve the situation
(10 marks)
(AAT specimen paper, 1985)

E. OUTLINE AND TUTOR'S ANSWERS

Tutor's answer 1

(a) (i) Circular memoranda or letters
Methods of distribution will vary from department to department. Office staff usually have desks or pigeon-holes. Supervisors are responsible for distribution to manual staff. Very important or personal messages, e.g. of redundancies, might be sent to employees' homes. The circular should end by indicating if a response is needed.

(ii) House magazines
An excellent medium for presenting non-confidential facts about company results, products, advertising campaigns, etc. Also suitable for conveying information about personnel policy, e.g. pension schemes, job appraisal, training, etc. Professionally produced magazines or newspapers usually issued monthly to all employees, often supplemented by brief weekly newsletters.

(b) Circular memoranda or letters
Suitable for conveying bad news or instructions because it is more courteous to approach people individually. Sure to reach everyone, more likely to be read. Cheap and quick to produce, but sometimes difficult to distribute, e.g. to manual staff.

House magazines more suitable for conveying good news and raising morale. Excellent for eye-catching presentations, e.g. the managing director's summary of the annual report. Expensive and slow to produce. May be skimmed or ignored.

Other methods you might have discussed include: notices, consultative meetings, amplified paging and tannoy for brief announcements.

Outline answer 2
1. Prominent eye-level position.
2. Bold design and lettering.
3. Positioned away from less important notices.
4. Regular updating.

These notes could be easily amplified into full sentences for an exam.

Outline answer 3
The use and misuse of photocopying facilities is an all too familiar topic in most organisations, prompting numerous memos, instructions and notices. The speed and convenience of having machines instantly accessible to all staff have to be balanced against the risks of machine breakdown and paper wastage due to inexpert and hasty operation. In this case it appears that Mr Anderson is at the end of his tether, and determined to sort the problem out once and for all. The tone of his message is impatient and irritable, but it would be a mistake to make him sound like a headmaster addressing a group of stupid and irresponsible schoolchildren. You need to explain the problem, stress the need to find an acceptable solution and invite a constructive response.

MEMORANDUM

From: Chief Office Administrator
To: All Staff   Date:

Subject: PHOTOCOPYING ARRANGEMENTS

Decision to allow free access of all staff to print-room. Result has been frequent breakdown of photocopier. On most recent occasion problem took whole day to sort out. Effect on efficiency of company.

Problems include:

Faulty paper loading.
Clumsy use of controls.
Failure to get best out of machine by using both sides of paper and making reductions.
Consequent paper wastage.

Situation cannot continue. Need for alternative arrangements. Two main options are:

Continue as at present but give basic training on correct use.
Have all copying done by trained operator.

Information needed on usage and preferences in order to find acceptable solution. Please return reply form by 15 July.

Note: part (b) is answered on p. 190.

Outline answer 4

This is an example of a particularly challenging type of question in which the subject-matter is drawn from another area of the syllabus – in this case administration/personnel. A successful answer needs four ingredients:

(a) an adequate knowledge of staff appraisal – the meaning of the term, its advantages and disadvantages, the techniques involved;

(b) the ability to present the information as a briefing rather than as a fully fledged report or as a memorandum;

(c) the imagination to relate the topic to the personnel problems of Fabrica Products;

(d) the ingenuity to suggest at least three visual aids to illustrate a topic which, at first sight, seems to have little or no visual content.

APPRAISAL OF CLERICAL AND JUNIOR STAFF	A/V AIDS
(a) <u>Definition</u> = Assessment of extent to which employee's performance fulfils job specification.	Sample specification of clerical job. Hand-out or O/H projection
(b) <u>Purpose</u> = To gain maximum potential from employees by matching people to posts and thus reduce turnover – particularly among junior office staff – by improving: ● Motivation: promotion, transfer, training. ● Communication: encouraging more discussion between senior and junior staff staff about context and details of jobs.	
(c) <u>Methods</u> = Annual reports by immediate superiors, usually by giving ratings on knowledge, accuracy, speed, co-operation, initative. Overall grade from A to E, plus comments on training needs and promotion potential. Reports lead up to one-to-one appraisal interviews.	Sample form/report Hand-out or O/H projection
NB Important for all involved to be clear about purpose and procedure, otherwise employees get apprehensive and reluctant to speak frankly, i.e. appraisal interviews distinct from disciplinary interviews. Best to start gradually, concentrating on problem areas, e.g. our office juniors.	Interview video *How am I doing?* (Video Arts)
(d) <u>Application to Fabrica</u> = Present low morale of office junior staff. Need for better motivation, reduction in turnover. *Conclude*	

that appraisal is now needed for about fifty clerical and secretarial employees, leading to more mobility, variety, training opportunities. Audio-typists need particular attention because isolated. Fabrica's personnel dept could tackle appraisal programme.

Suggest further reading for managers likely to be involved (Mr Thomas and office admin. supervisor). The article mentioned in the question, a personnel textbook, e.g. *Human Resources Management* by H T Graham (Macdonald and Evans).

Questions?

Sample employee questionnaire

Reading list hand-out

Name
Date

These notes are about two-thirds of the allowed length, and could be expanded into a full briefing by using complete sentences, though some abbreviations, e.g. Admin. would be acceptable.

Outline answer 5

This question concerns a matter which crops up regularly in many large organisations. The main concern of the company is to cut its telephone bills, relying on your department to keep a close check that the rules are complied with. Your immediate boss, Mr Blunt, is in the firing line on this matter and will be most anxious to resolve the problem as quickly as possible. The background information about him suggests that he is the type who might get people's backs up over a disciplinary matter like this, so you must steer him into reacting firmly but tactfully. You want to warn the culprits in a manner which will not offend employees who follow the rules.

Task 1

The circular memo

MEMORANDUM

From: Accounts Office Manager   Date:
To: All Staff

Subject: PERSONAL TELEPHONE CALLS

● Outline of present policy. Until recently this has worked well, but evidence that now being abused.

● Reminder that staff must ALWAYS tell switchboard if call is personal. Too many unauthorised calls now being made.

● Reminder that bills must be paid promptly. Growing delays in payment.

● Inform staff that volume of personal calls in increasing.

● Worrying situation that cannot be allowed to continue. Further restrictions necessary unless there is immediate response. Appeal to fairness and co-operation.

Your memo to Mr Blunt
- Enclose circular, and ask for immediate approval.
- Point out that you have not singled out culprits at this stage.
- If situation does not improve suggest that no personal calls be accepted from non-payers. Inform stores supervisor that you know who culprits are and warn that if abuse continues a payphone will be installed and all outside calls will be checked.

A tutor's answer to question 5

Task 1
The circular memo

BRUNSWICK TRADING COMPANY plc

MEMORANDUM

From: Accounts Office Manager   Date: 20 April 1986
To: All Staff

Subject: PERSONAL TELEPHONE CALLS

It has long been policy to allow staff to make personal calls through the switchboard provided they follow the correct procedure, and pay their private telephone accounts promptly. Until recently the system has worked well, but there is evidence that it is now being abused.

The volume of personal calls has greatly increased recently, causing inconvenience to the switchboard and to the accounts office.

1. You must ALWAYS identify yourself and your extension number, and tell the switchboard operator if you are making a personal call. Too many unauthorised calls are now being made.

2. Bills must be paid within one month. There is now a growing number of bills dating back several months which are still unpaid in spite of repeated reminders.

These abuses cost the company money and create an atmosphere of mistrust. Further restrictions will have to be imposed within two weeks unless all overdue bills are paid and no more unauthorised personal calls are made.

I am sure that you would not wish the majority to suffer from the selfish behaviour of a minority, so I hope I can count on your co-operation.

H P Blunt

Task 2
Your memo to Mr Blunt

MEMO

From: J Smith   Date 20 April
To: Mr Blunt   Ref: JS/tr

Subject: PERSONAL TELEPHONE CALLS

Here is a draft of the circular memo you asked for yesterday. Could you check it and make any amendments or additions you think necessary, so that I can send it out tomorrow?

I think it would be a mistake to be too heavy at this stage. I've tried to suggest that we know who the culprits are and what they've been doing, but we're giving them a chance to fall into line.

If things don't improve within two weeks I suggest the following:

1. No more personal calls this year for those who haven't paid their bills.

2. Inform the stores supervisor, Mr Thompson, that we know most of the trouble comes from his section, and ask him to convey this to his staff.

3. Tell him that if the abuse doesn't stop we'll install a payphone outside his office, and keep an extra close check on all outside calls from stores staff.

I have also posted the enclosed notice on all notice-boards. Please let me know if there's anything else you want me to do.

JS

enc.

Task 3
The notice

> ### PERSONAL TELEPHONE CALLS
>
> Staff are reminded that only essential private calls should be made in working hours.
>
> — Always tell the switchboard operator that it is a personal call
> — Pay your bills promptly each month
>
> Unless these rules are followed, use of the switchboard will be restricted.
>
> H. P. Blunt
10 April 1986

F. A STEP FURTHER

Memoranda
Notices

People and Communication (2nd edn), Evans D. Pitman 1984. Chapter 4 contains some excellent examples.
Communication in Business (3rd edn), Little P. Pitman 1983. Chapter 11.
Secretarial Skills, Freeman A, Martindale R and Mancktelow J. Longman 1986 (Longman Exam Guides).

You should make a habit of looking at noticeboards wherever you go, and studying the sort of notices which you might be asked to write for an exam. This is hardly a textbook subject, but there are useful pages in:

Communication at Work, Evans D W. Pitman 1984.
Communication in Business (3rd edn), Little P. Pitman 1983. Ch. 11.

Instructions, handbooks and manuals

Again, this topic needs plenty of raw material e.g. Health and Safety Handbooks, instructions for domestic appliances, car and cycle maintenance, etc, manuals for photocopiers or other equipment.

Communication in Business (3rd edn), Little P. Pitman 1983.
Effective Writing, Turk C and Kirkman J. Spon 1982. Chapter 10 has useful guidance on writing technical instructions.

Company publications

For this topic there is no substitute for the real thing. If you work for an organisation which has a house journal, bring a selection of back numbers into college for the benefit of fellow students. They will not only help you answer questions on this particular topic, but provide a gold-mine of useful background information for a range of questions which demand an element of plausible role-playing.

Specialist books

Public Relations, Jefkins, Frank. Macdonald & Evans 1980. Chapter XII discusses the specialist's approach to internal and external house journals. *Editing and Design*, Evans H. Heinemann 1984 (5 vols). A comprehensive guide for trainee journalists.

Chapter 6   Comprehension and summaries

A. GETTING STARTED

As managers become more senior in business or public administration, the more information they are expected to absorb and respond to. It is therefore essential that they are saved the time-consuming, temper-fraying chore of ploughing through pages of indigestible closely printed text. They need to be able to see quickly what a document is about, whether it is relevant to them, and what the main ideas are. Often, they will demand that lengthy documents are filleted and boiled down by someone else in the organisation. Comprehension and summary questions in exams cast you in the role of that someone else.

In order to convey information effectively to others you first have to assess why they need it, what they already know and how they might want it presented. Your job is to select only the relevant facts or ideas, guided by your own understanding (comprehension) of what the writer intended to communicate, your skill with language, and your familiarity with various business formats. You must always be aware of the need for information to be communicated and absorbed quickly and accurately so that the right decisions are made and the appropriate action taken. For example, a concise, clearly presented summary of a 400-page report about a subject to be discussed at a meeting, circulated beforehand, will ensure that those who have not read the full report will nevertheless grasp the main issues.

By including comprehension and summary questions the examiners are testing whether you have been trained in the essential skills of summing up and re-expressing someone else's writing without changing the meaning. Indeed, all exams are in themselves tests of comprehension and summary. More marks are lost through misunderstanding the question and answering irrelevantly and long-windedly than because of the more obvious and simple errors of spelling and layout.

You will find detailed tips on concise style within different formats in the appropriate topic chapters, particularly in Chapter 4 – Letters, and Chapter 7 – Reports; but the basic skills involved in comprehension and summary should be applied to the whole range of writing tasks you are likely to encounter. There is no room in communication exercises for lapses into the sort of waffle and padding which fills out so many essays on academic subjects. Communication candidates will benefit greatly if they apply the same rigorous standards of style and presentation to their written assignments in allied subjects such as law and economics.

B. ESSENTIAL PRINCIPLES

COMPREHENSION

Most standard comprehension questions present you with a passage on a business topic, and ask you to:

(a) express particular points in your own words;

(b) give the meaning of specific words or phrases as they are used in the passage;

(c) give alternative words or phrases which are exact substitutes for those used in the original.

Comprehension needs to be tackled methodically in the following stages.

| Stage 1 | Reading the text | • Study the title; this sums up the theme of the passage.
• Skim through the passage to grasp the main gist.
• Read it again carefully. Imagine that you have to understand it well enough to tell someone else what it is about. |

| Stage 2 | Reading the question | • Scan all the questions to get an overview of what is expected.
• Read each question carefully, underlining that part of the text which contains the word or phrase to be 'translated' or explained. |

| Stage 3 | Planning | • Jot down the answers to longer questions in rough.
• Check your answer against the question to ensure it is complete. |

| Stage 4 | Writing | • Follow the same order as on the question paper, and use the same numbering, e.g. (a), (b), etc.
• Answer in complete sentences unless instructed otherwise.
• Use your own words as far as possible, but avoid adding your own views.
• When asked for the equivalents of several words or phrases, list the originals on one side and your alternatives opposite, e.g. |

$$erudite \;=\; learned$$

(Remember to give only one answer)

• If you are asked for a substitute word or phrase make sure you use the same part of speech, i.e. a noun for a noun, e.g.

$$householder = property\text{-}owner, \quad not \; owning \; property.$$

• Look at the mark-scheme for an indication of length.

- If you use a dictionary, choose the meaning which best fits the context, but avoid copying definitions word for word.

Stage 5 Checking

- Eliminate punctuation and spelling mistakes. Both are penalised. Some candidates lose marks through miscopying from the text, particularly the names of people.

SUMMARY

1. Précis

Some exams, e.g. LCCI (PSC) 1982, require a summary of a passage on a business topic in continuous prose within a strict word limit. You may not have done a traditional précis since O level English language, and so be feeling rather rusty. The step-by-step routine in Fig. 6.1 will help you to develop a methodical approach to this sort of exercise. We show the draft stage of the routine (Fig. 6.1) being applied to the opening paragraph of exam question 2 answered on p. 90.

Of course in the exam you will have to speed up this process because you may be faced by up to 1,000 words to reduce to 300 or fewer in 40–45 minutes flat. It is therefore essential to get as much practice as possible at timed exercises.

Fig. 6.1 Summarising routine

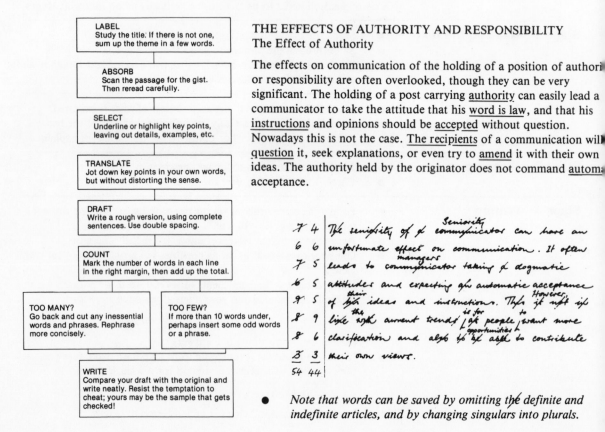

THE EFFECTS OF AUTHORITY AND RESPONSIBILITY
The Effect of Authority

The effects on communication of the holding of a position of authority or responsibility are often overlooked, though they can be very significant. The holding of a post carrying <u>authority</u> can easily lead a communicator to take the attitude that his <u>word is law</u>, and that his <u>instructions</u> and opinions should be <u>accepted</u> without question. Nowadays this is not the case. <u>The recipients</u> of a communication will <u>question</u> it, seek explanations, or even try to <u>amend</u> it with their own ideas. The authority held by the originator does not command automatic acceptance.

- *Note that words can be saved by omitting the definite and indefinite articles, and by changing singulars into plurals.*

2. Summaries in business format

Most examining bodies now expect summaries to be presented in formats which reflect real office needs. You are usually presented with an article or an extract to digest and reassemble for a particular person with a specific requirement. You may be told which format to use, e.g. a memorandum, report, briefing notes, etc. or it may be left to you to choose the appropriate format for the situation. More specialised candidates may have to turn unedited notes of a meeting into minutes. You are usually given a rough word limit, but if in doubt reduce to about a third of the original.

The passage will usually contain inessential background material and illustrations, and it may be written in an order inappropriate to your brief, so you will have to shorten and adapt it by selecting the relevant points and rearranging them to suit the person and the purpose. You will need to think carefully about how to use schematic layout with headings, subheadings, underlinings and indentations to make the points clearer. Sometimes, e.g. when asked by a superior to prepare a summary for presentation at a meeting, you may need to attach a short separate memo explaining that you have completed the summary requested, and asking for comment or further instructions.

Guidelines for presenting in note-form

The question might say that you may use *note-form*. This often worries candidates because they are not quite sure what is and what is not permissible, so here are some guidelines:

- **Do not** use personal note-taking type abbreviations of words, such as *gvt, info, admin*; or symbols for *therefore* ($\therefore$) and *because* ($\because$). You can use the standard abbreviations of Latin terms, such as NB, etc., cf.; but do beware of the common confusion between i.e. (that is to say/in other words), and e.g. (for example).
- **Do not** use too many colloquial abbreviations. Common shortenings of 'not', as in *don't, hasn't, aren't*, are acceptable, but do not risk other common contractions like *you'll, they'd, should've*, in a formal piece of writing.
- **Do** write full grammatical sentences, however short; e.g. *The government plans to change the law. Not: Gvt to change law.*
- **Do** be careful when using brackets and dashes that the overall grammatical structure is correct (see Ch. 7, p. 99).

The routine for answering non-précis questions can be adapted from Fig. 6.1. When highlighting selected points, decide if and how the order of the original needs changing (see the outline answer on p. 89). Then map out your headings and subheadings before doing your draft. Your final count need not be as exact as for a précis; provided the summary is clear, concise and complete, ten words either way are unlikely to be penalised.

Word-saving tips

1. Find the most appropriate and economical joining words (conjunctions). Strings of 'ands' and 'buts' sound long-winded and amateur. Add variety and fluency by using *which, while, because, so, since, with, although*, etc:

The Conference Centre is set in beautiful parkland and it is modern and comfortable. It has a large lecture theatre and seminar rooms, and also a licensed bar. (28 wds)	The Conference Centre, which is set in beautiful parkland, is modern and comfortable, with a large lecture theatre, seminar rooms and a licensed bar. (24 wds)

2.   Use other useful summarising words which can replace phrases, e.g. *despite, otherwise, nevertheless, however, therefore, whereas.*

3.   Use dashes or semicolons to avoid starting a new sentence:

The park has its own swimming pool. This makes it ideal for delegates who like to cool off between sessions.	*The park has its own swimming pool — ideal for delegates . . .*

4.   Avoid repeating words:

We enclose a list of useful books. If any of these bo̸oks are unobtainable . . .

The final programme has now been confirmed. We hope you will find it ~~the programme~~ *both interesting and enjoyable.*

5.   Replace fiddly phrases with single words, e.g. *prior to* = before, *in the event of* = if, *in the region of* = about.

6.   Use hyphenated double adjectives, e.g. *time-saving, well-chosen, counter-productive, eye-catching, long-winded.*

3. Notes for a talk or speech

You may be asked to make notes to guide you or an associate — usually a superior — through a speech or informal talk. What the examiner is looking for in this type of question is a logical arrangement of relevant information and sensible content with realistic detail. This topic is dealt with in detail in Chapter 9, but remember that such notes should include:

- the title of the talk or speech;
- the opening sentences;
- the key points you would make in the body of the talk or speech, set out in sections;
- the closing remarks.

4. Notes for a telephone call

Notes following a telephone call or notes before making a telephone call should include:

- A heading making the subject of the call quite clear, e.g. *Call to J. Smith & Sons re late delivery of cold steel bars.*
- The telephone number, extension, name and/or position of the person you are calling, or who has called.
- Any reference numbers relating to orders, delivery notes, invoices, files, letters, etc.
- What you want to say, or what was said, logically arranged, and including a brief outline of the background to the call and what action needs taking, e.g. Order no. 124 delayed two weeks: promised for 11 May by Mr Smith in his letter of 12 April — steel urgently needed.

Remember: The test for notes made for another person following a telephone call is whether they make sense, and whether they include all the essential details.
(See also Ch. 9, p. 147).

5. Telex

A telex message, if this is set as a question, must be set out in the accepted format as shown in Fig. 6.2, unless just the text is asked for. A telex must be concise but unambiguous, so questions which involve drafting a telex are tests of your ability to be clear and brief. Telex messages are charged according to distance and transmission time.

Fig. 6.2 Telex message

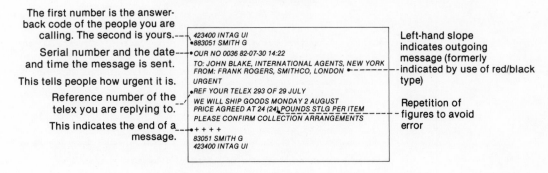

The first number is the answer-back code of the people you are calling. The second is yours.

Serial number and the date and time the message is sent.

This tells people how urgent it is.

Reference number of the telex you are replying to.

This indicates the end of a message.

```
423400 INTAG UI
883051 SMITH G
OUR NO 0036 82-07-30 14:22
TO: JOHN BLAKE, INTERNATIONAL AGENTS, NEW YORK
FROM: FRANK ROGERS, SMITHCO, LONDON
URGENT
REF YOUR TELEX 293 OF 29 JULY
WE WILL SHIP GOODS MONDAY 2 AUGUST
PRICE AGREED AT 24 (24) POUNDS STLG PER ITEM
PLEASE CONFIRM COLLECTION ARRANGEMENTS
+ + + +
83051 SMITH G
423400 INTAG UI
```

Left-hand slope indicates outgoing message (formerly indicated by use of red/black type)

Repetition of figures to avoid error

(See also *Exam Guide to Office Practice and Secretarial Administration*.)

C. USEFUL APPLIED MATERIALS

Fig. 6.3   A monstrous memo cut down to size

(a)

```
                              MEMORANDUM

To:        Mr B.N. Nash, Production Controller        Date:
From:      Mr R.Y. Turner, Manchester Contracts Manager    Ref:

Subject:  Syndicated Engineering Limited.

       In the recent past I have checked on the likely availability of Piston Rings, and
it seems that there should be some spare by February/March next year.  It would now
appear that these could be profitably used to convert Type 12 pistons to Type 14 pistons,
since the rings available next March will include some suitable for Type 14 pistons.  I
have spoken to Mr Murray, and he will convert as necessary, provided the piston rings
arrive at a pre-agreed date, and provided he can obtain from you one or two other spare
parts.  Will Mr Murray please inform Mr Nash by means of a list of parts exactly what is
required,. 25 pistons will have to be converted as we have received an order for this
number from Syndicated Engineering Limited, as you will know from your copy of
T6/749/tdr.  I have put in hand the necessary arrangements for releasing 25 pistons on
programme for next year from the allocation to Hydraulic Engines Ltd., who will not
require the pistons until the summer.  Mr. Clewer has organised the transfer of these
pistons, which are Type 12 pistons, from the Fluit Pumps under construction for
Hydraulic Engines, but as you realise in this form they will not be suitable for
Syndicated Engineering, which is why the above-mentioned conversion has been proposed.
Will Mr Murray please let Mr Nash know at what date he will require the spare parts
and inform Mr Clewer when he would like the 25 pistons sent up for conversion.  It may
be that Mr Murray would like to take this opportunity to convert Shaft Assemblies at
the same time.

       I would be grateful if you could make the spare parts available to Mr Murray as he
requires them.  I see that we have just received a request for a Type 14 piston from
Ring Mechanics Limited, and therefore the number of conversions will need to be increased
to 26.  These pistons can, as I have said, be released from the Hydraulics contract,
for conversion to Type 14 pistons, and replaced next February/March by these in next
years programme.

                              R.Y. Turner
                      Manchester Contracts Manager.
```

(b)

```
                              MEMORANDUM

From:      R.Y. Turner, Manchester Contracts Manager    Date:
To:        B.N. Nash, Production Controller             Ref:
           A.B. Murray

Subject:  Piston Conversions

Orders Received.

1.    25 pistons (Type 14) for Syndicated Engineering Ltd (Ref. T6/749/tdr)

2.    One piston (Type 14) for Ring Mechanics Limited.

Conversion Required.

      To meet the above orders, Mr Clewer will release 26 pistons (Type 12) from the
allocation for Hydraulic Engines as Hydraulic Engines will not need them till next
summer.

Action.

1.    Mr Murray   I understand you will be sending a list of the spare parts you need
                  for this conversion, to Mr Nash: with the dates by which you would like
                  delivery.  Please inform Mr Clewer when to send the pistons for
                  conversion.

2.    Mr Nash     I would be grateful if you could make the necessary spare parts
                  available to Mr Murray as he requires them.

cc.  A. Clewer
```

The following very long question has been chosen, not only as a demanding exercise in **summary**, but also because the content of the passage provides an interesting account of company communications. Since the article was written, all the procedures described in the article have been successfully implemented. Examples of Kellogg's company publications are shown in Chapters 3 and 5.

(Note that the numbers in the margin and textual emphases have been added for your guidance by the authors.)

Question 1 John Enright, the newly appointed Personnel Director of a large manufacturing concern with a poor record of labour relations, is trying to devise a more effective employee communications policy for the firm. As his personal assistant you see the following article.

In 300−350 words prepare for Mr Enright a summary which evaluates Kellogg's approach to their communications with employees.

Use this margin for your notes

Giving Employees Something to Chew On

(1)
A 10-week strike at Kellogg all but removed the morning plate of cereal from millions of British breakfast tables last year.

The dispute was essentially over pay, but a confidential <u>poll</u> of workers' attitudes conducted by the company revealed that a contributing factor could have been the poor standard of communications with its 3,000-strong workforce.

According to the workers, management hardly ever kept them <u>informed</u> about the company's performance or plans; neither were they told the reasons for major decisions.

The opinions of staff were also generally ignored and there was seldom any <u>consultation</u> when changes were made in conditions of employment.

In general, the local and trade Press and radio were quicker to publish information than the company was to inform staff.

To make no bones about it, the company − as it now admits − had no employee communications policy to speak of and, as the poll demonstrated, morale was at a very low ebb.

(2)
In an attempt to reverse this situation Kellogg has recently established a procedure to keep all employees informed about the company's activities, performance and personnel policies.

(5)
Within a remarkably short space of time, Kellogg claims, its new communications policy has created 'a much better spirit' in its six factories scattered around the country and has brought it several benefits.

In the first place, Kellogg says the improved level of communications helped smooth the latest pay negotiations, which resulted in an 18 per cent award for most workers. 'We got through the settlement without any trouble at all', a spokesman said.

Secondly, the company believes that the new policy has been instrumental in staving off the approaches of an <u>additional</u> trades union. The Association of Scientific Technical and Management Staffs (ASTMS) had been recruiting among the 600 non-unionised administrative staff and subsequently appealed to the Arbitration and Conciliation Service (ACAS) after the company refused to recognise it. Three months ago, however, ASTMS suddenly withdrew its application because it had attracted insufficient membership.

'We think we are now satisfying the communications needs of our staff, which means that they have one less reason to join a trades union', the company says.

(2) Kellogg's new policy represents a departure from the common British practice of using trades unions as one of the vehicles for disseminating certain company information among their members. In effect, the new policy establishes a procedure that bypasses them in this. But it is not intended to affect the company's traditional relationship with existing unions over such issues as pay and conditions.

(5) The new policy has been generally welcomed by Kellogg's unions, the largest of which is the Union of Shop, Distributive and Allied Workers.

George Cheetam, USDAW's branch chairman at the company, described communications as 'an awful lot better' since the dispute last year. 'All that the company is doing is informing the workforce <u>direct</u>. It saves us a job actually'.

(3) The man brought in to implement the new policy under the title of manager, public affairs, is Nicholas Cole, a former public relations executive.

(2) For a man more used to calming controversy he is surprisingly forthright about the role of unions. 'Unions have taken away from management the duty to communicate and that was wrong', he says 'in the past the company's hourly-paid workers usually got their information either on the grapevine or through their union. This method sometimes led to <u>misunderstandings</u>. We are now asserting our duty and right to communicate. Unions still have a distinct function in representing their members but that does not include communicating company information'.

Cole says that shop stewards will get information on the basis of their function as employees, rather than as officials of a trades union.

(3) The implementation of the policy revolves round a monthly departmental meeting chaired by a director and attended by all 24 departmental managers. Company information such as trading performance and sales projections is systematically released for communication to employees. Each manager provides the meeting with departmental information, either verbally or in briefing notes. The managers then communicate this information at one or more meetings with the members of their departments. Department heads subsequently pass the information to the foremen who, in turn, inform the company's 2,600 part-time workers.

So, information which basically used to be communicated through the unions will now be passed through the foremen after a chain of meetings. The procedure can also operate in the reverse direction, as an upwards channel of communication.

Under the new communications policy Kellogg is also providing a two-way forum for the company's <u>administrative staff</u>, none of whom belongs to a trades union. Through a staff committee, which meets regularly, they are able to contribute ideas and opinions about their work and conditions of employment and to have prior discussions about major changes affecting their jobs.

(5) Kellogg describes the meetings as 'tending to be a bit of a bitching session, so they are not proving to be particularly useful yet'. But the company is confident that 'they will settle down in time and become a constructive forum'.

(3) While the staff committee is able to discuss many aspects of staff employment, it does not have any negotiating rights; Kellogg makes an annual pay award to its administrative staff.

In addition the company is considering involving the total workforce in its annual management conference. One way of doing this would be to extend the gathering into an all-employee conference, but apart from the wider policy negotiations, Cole says this is still being appraised because of the logistical problems.

An alternative would be to videotape the proceedings and make the tape available to all workers – an experiment tried out with some success at the latest annual meeting in February this year. A decision will be made later in the year, says Cole.

(4) The company also intends to disseminate information in other ways. An employees' annual report will be published and the coverage of *Kellogg's News*, the company's monthly newspaper, will be enlarged. The company feels that there should also be a weekly bulletin of general news to be posted on all notice-boards. Thus, the recent visit of Trades Union Congress general secretary Len Murray to the cereal packaging plant outside Manchester was announced before it was revealed in the local press.

The employees' annual report will be an uncomplicated review by the management and will contain reports from all departments such as human resources (personnel, etc.), logistics (distribution, purchasing), marketing, finance and production. It will be the only report produced by the company in the UK. Usually any account of UK activities is referred to briefly in the US parent company's statutory annual report. The first UK document is expected to be circulated in February next year.

Having implemented its policy Kellogg is clearly experiencing the first flush of success after a period of low morale. The policy is less than a year old and its effectiveness will naturally depend on whether it can stand the test of time.

(5) It hinged on two uncertainties. Can the staff committees evolve from being 'a bitching session' into a more constructive forum? Secondly, will the series of meetings down the line lead to fewer misunderstandings than in the past?
(Kransdorff, Arnold, 'Giving employees something to chew on', *Financial Times*, 24 Sept. 1980)

(RSA DPA, 1981) (25 marks)

Question 2 Your employer, concerned about the need for better communication within the firm, is arranging a seminar for senior staff. He has asked you to produce a simplified version of the passage printed below for circulation at the seminar. He wishes you to re-express the ideas in a condensed form.

Write the shortened version, using not more than 120 words.

THE EFFECTS OF AUTHORITY AND RESPONSIBILITY
The Effect of Authority

The effects on communication of the holding of a position of authority or responsibility are often overlooked, though they can be very significant. The holding of a post carrying authority can easily lead a communicator to take the attitude that his word is law, and that his instructions and opinions should be accepted without question. Nowadays this is not necessarily the case. The recipients of a communication will question it, seek explanations, or even try to amend it with their own ideas. The authority held by the originator does not command automatic acceptance.

Nevertheless, authority does add weight to a communication, and the wise communicator in this position uses this to add force to his message whilst at the same time he takes into account the likely reaction that may result. He will probably find it necessary, therefore, to temper his authority with explanations in order that he may gain the response he requires.

<u>The Effect of Responsibility</u>

Whilst the holding of authority gives rise to considerations of acceptance, the holding of responsibility gives rise to considerations of consequence. The fact that the communicator will be held responsible for the outcome of his communication should make him use more caution than he would if he were not to be held accountable for the consequences of his communication. Perhaps the most public example of the way responsibility affects attitude can be seen in Parliament. The party in power talks and acts with much more caution than it did when in opposition: in the latter case it knew quite well it could not be held accountable for its ideas or its utterances. Responsibility usually, therefore, causes more care and consideration to be given to the possible consequences of words and actions than if there were no responsibility, and this in turn results in more restrained and carefully worded communications. The use and abuse of authority and of responsibility in communication have a considerable effect on staff receptiveness and hence on the effectiveness of communication within an organisation, particularly vertically downwards.

(334 words)

(from: *Effective Communication Made Simple*, Eyre, E C,
Reprinted by permission of William Heinemann Limited)
(LCCI PSC, 1982) (30 marks)

Comprehension

Question 3   Reread the passage used in Question 2 and answer the following questions:

(a)   Give the meaning of the following 3 words as they are used in the passage.
amend   (line 5)
accountable   (line 16)
restrained   (line 23)   (6 marks)

(b)   Give the meaning of the following phrase as it is used in the passage.
temper his authority   (line 10)   (4 marks)

(c)   What recent change in attitude towards authority is outlined in the passage?

(5 marks)

(d)   Summarise the political analogy used in the passage.

(5 marks)

**Question 4
Writing a
telex
message**   You are to assume that you work as personal assistant to Patrick Forster who is Managing Director of Comfycover Ltd, Elm Lodge Industrial Estate, Bradwell, Lemeshire LM3 9XH. The company produces a wide range of bedding accessories and in recent years it has expanded its range of products to include non-bedding items such as table-cloths.

It is decided to package the table-cloths in the same transparent plastic bags that are used to pack continental quilt covers and the appropriate insert placed inside the bag. These bags, measuring 30 cm × 40 cm are supplied by Jameson's Printers Ltd of Hertford Road, Derby DE6 7ST (telex No. 86-39274) and are plain transparent plastic with the firm's logo or trade mark on the bottom right-hand corner. There will be one change, however, The logo will be printed on the top right-hand corner of the bags used for table-cloths. Jameson's are quite happy to accept minor printing amendments such as this and it is normal practice to inform them by means of telex. The packaging department will also need to be informed of any changes made.

(RSA Communication Skills in Business, 1982 Stage II)

E. OUTLINE AND TUTOR'S ANSWERS

Outline answer 1

The article is about 1,200 words long and it jumps about between topics, e.g. there are several references to unions, so the first step is to identify groups of related points. Then arrange these groups in logical order: (1) introduction; (2) the new policy; (3) implementation; (4) future plans; (5) results. You will also need a concluding line or so of 'evaluation'. Your summary should be introduced by a brief accompanying memo.

Select only those points likely to interest Mr Enright and omit unnecessary details such as names of shop stewards. You can assume that he would know the unions by their initials. Your evaluation should not go so far as to make recommendations, though you might draw some parallels, e.g. your firm also has several factories on different sites, or has recently been approached by ASTMS. Some background knowledge, particularly about unions, will help you to sound plausible and practical, e.g. you should not infer the collapse of the entire ASTMS!

MEMORANDUM

From: Your name
To: Mr Enright   Date:

Subject: <u>Improving Communication with Employees</u>

I recently read an article (author, title, publications and date) relevant to your current concern with labour relations. I thought you would be interested in its account of how Kellogg's dealt with similar problems, so I have written a summary with a brief evaluation.

KELLOGG'S COMMUNICATION POLICY

1. <u>Background</u>
   Recent Kellogg's strike partly caused by bad communications. Poll revealed two problems:
   (a) Lack of information about performance, plans, decisions.
   (b) Inadequate consultation – staff's opinions ignored.

2. <u>New Communication Policy</u>
   (a) New downwards channels for informing 3,000 employees in 6 factories about company activities and personnel policies.
   (b) Regular briefings for employees. Trade unions used to pass company information to members which led to misunderstandings. Unions' role now confined to negotiating pay and conditions.

3. <u>Putting the Policy into Practice</u>
   (a) Appointment of manager with public relations background.

(b) Monthly meetings of director and department managers, leading to chain of meetings between:
  (i) department managers and their staff;
  (ii) department managers and foremen;
  (iii) foremen and part-time workers.

   Chain also works from bottom upwards.
(c) Staff committee provides two-way forum for administrative staff − no negotiating rights.

4. Future Plans
  (a) Involvement of whole workforce in annual management conference, possibly through video.
  (b) Simplified annual report for employees.
  (c) Enlarged company newspaper; also monthly bulletins.

5. Results
  (a) Better morale.
  (b) Smoother pay negotiations.
  (c) Policy welcomed by existing union (USDAW). Withdrawal of ASTMS.
  But − too soon to judge whether misunderstandings will be avoided. Staff committees not very effective so far.

6. Conclusions
  (a) Similarities between our situation and Kellogg's suggest these methods worth exploring.
  (b) Key to success is appointment of specialist manager.

Your final version could be expanded into semi-note form rather than continuous prose, e.g.

2. The New Communication Policy
  (a) New downwards channels of communication have been established to keep the 3000 employees in 6 factories better informed on company activities and personnel policies.
  (b) Regular briefings for employees have been introduced, thus bypassing the trade unions. Company information used to be passed by the unions to their members, which led to frequent misunderstandings. Now the unions are confined to their traditional role of negotiating pay and conditions of employment.

Worked answer 2

7 4		The seniority of a communicator can have an
6 6		unfortunate effect on communication. It often
7 5		leads to communicator managers taking a dogmatic
6 5		attitudes and expecting an automatic acceptance
9 5		of their ideas and instructions. This is not if However,
8 9		like the current trends is for people want more to
8 6		clarification and also to be able to contribute opportunities
3 3		their own views.

6	6	To achieve the desired response, ~~competent~~ *perceptive*
6	5	~~communicators~~ *managers* are firm but sensitive; they
8	6	are ~~aware that they~~ *acknowledging the* need to explain the
4	4	reasons behind their instructions.
6	4	The responsibility of managers ~~has~~ *which comes* because
7	5	~~with seniority~~ of his senior position should increase his *managers'*
6	7	awareness of the effects *of* their communications.
7	8	~~have.~~ They should therefore be careful ~~in~~ *need to how*
4	5	~~phrasing~~ *they express their* communications / messages, because
8	8	this will have an effect on staff reaction.
7	6	~~They should use their position carefully to~~ *Authority and responsibility should be handled*
4	6	*tactfully to* ensure effective internal communication,
6	6	especially from senior to junior level.
143	120	

Final version

The Effects of Authority and Responsibility

Seniority can have an unfortunate effect on communication. It often leads to managers taking dogmatic attitudes and expecting automatic acceptance of their ideas and instructions. This goes against the current trend of people wanting more clarification and opportunities to contribute their own views. To achieve the desired response, perceptive managers are firm but sensitive; acknowledging the need to explain the reasons behind their instructions.

The responsibility which comes with seniority should increase mangers' awareness of the effects of their communications. They therefore need to be careful how they express their messages, because this will have an effect on staff reaction. Authority and responsibility should be handled tactfully to ensure effective internal communication, especially from senior to junior level.

Outline answer 3

Here we give suggested answers to a selection of each type of question. For (a) and (b) you should find a word or brief phrase in the same part of speech as the original. Questions (c) and (d) need succinct paraphrases in your own words.

(a) amend = alter
    accountable = responsible
    restrained = circumspect
(b) temper his authority = exercise his power with moderation.
(c) Staff are less willing to accept authority without question.
(d) When in power political parties have to take more responsibility for their words and deeds than in opposition.

Tutor's answer 4

The marks for this question would probably be allocated between layout and content equally. Layout should include the given recipient's number and your invented one for Comfycover, both repeated at the end in reverse order. The date and the time the message was sent should be indicated; also **to** and **from** with the appropriate names.

```
86 39274

54 32097 COMFY

OUR NO. 1080 85 – 05 – 21        15.03

TO:      JAMESONS PRINTERS LTD. DERBY

FROM: PATRICK FORSTER, COMFYCOVER, BRADWELL

REF: TABLE-CLOTH BAGS

PLEASE SUPPLY 50,000 (50,000) BAGS 30 × 40 CM IDENTICAL TO CONTINENTAL
QUILT BAGS BUT WITH OUR LOGO ON TOP (REPEAT TOP) RIGHT-HAND
CORNER NOT BOTTOM RHC.

DELIVERY ASAP.      PLEASE CONFIRM

54 32097   COMFY

86 39274
```

Notes on answer

ASAP (as soon as possible) is accepted in business and vital details –
e.g. the number of bags and the changed position of the logo – are
repeated as a safeguard. RHC (right-hand corner) is acceptable as the
phrase has already been spelt out. A request to confirm has been included
as a feedback to assure Mr Forster that there are no problems about
delivery.

The marks for content would be awarded for including a description
of the bags, the number required, clear details of the change, the required
delivery time and the correct names and telex number of the receiver.
Marks would be deducted for miscopying details, e.g. writing 'Foster'
instead of 'Forster'.

F. A STEP FURTHER

The most useful way of improving your performance in comprehension
tests is to read widely, regularly and actively. Start keeping a note of new
words you come across and checking the meaning in a dictionary.

Never just read a textbook passively; summarise the important points
of each chapter in examination-style note-form with schematic layout.
Practise summarising documents of different lengths on to just one side
of A4.

All the standard textbooks contain sections on summarising. See
particularly:
Communication in Business, Little P. Pitman 1983. Chapters 6 and 7
are exceptionally clear and helpful.
People and Communication (2nd edn), Evans D W. Pitman 1984.
Chapter 4.
English Survival Kit, Bailey R F. Longman Cheshire.
Effective Writing, Turk C and Kirkman J. Spon 1982. Chapter 8 is
excellent for more advanced candidates.

Chapter 7   Reports

A. GETTING STARTED

The term **report** is familar in everyday life as in:

- reports on radio and TV news bulletins: 'our reporter was at the scene'.
- medical reports: 'temperature 38 °C, pulse 80'.
- school reports: 'could do better'.

In business and public life a report can be defined as the communication of information and advice from someone who has collected and studied the facts to someone who needs to be informed in order to make decisions and take action.

Of course some reports have more than one author, and they usually have a number of readers. The weightiest reports of all are commissioned by the government and produced by committees.

At the other end of the scale, most organisations will expect quite junior members of staff to make routine reports, usually by inserting words and figures on to pre-printed forms, e.g. accident reports, monthly sales returns, etc. They may also have to give oral reports to groups of senior managers or colleagues on matters too urgent or too specific to require the usual formal treatment; or to deliver an oral introduction, summary or update to a report they have written and distributed to a committee or board of directors.

This chapter is mainly concerned with writing one-off reports, of the type you are likely to have to write for examinations, and with writing investigation reports and analytical reports which describe and evaluate a past event. You will also need to know a certain amount about other types of report in order to answer general and quiz-type questions. It should also be useful to those taking other subjects which frame questions in report form, e.g. **law**, and **office practice and secretarial administration**.

Most students approach the subject of reports as if it were something new and alien to their experience. Yet they probably have more experience and knowledge of reports than they realise. Some will have seen routine reports at work, or have filled in pre-printed report forms. Some may be members of clubs, trade unions or voluntary organisations which report on matters such as finance and membership; or they may have money invested in a company or building society which issues an annual report. Local authorities are now required by law to send potted versions of their annual reports to every household.

Even this sort of sketchy experience will help towards an awareness of the context in which reports are written. Although most exam questions give you a certain amount of background material (thereby also testing your ability to summarise), you will usually have to invent some details. If you rely solely on your imagination you will sound implausible and amateur, so it is worth while collecting useful background information from your own direct experience and from lectures on related subjects in your course.

B. ESSENTIAL PRINCIPLES

Fig. 7.1 Circulation of reports

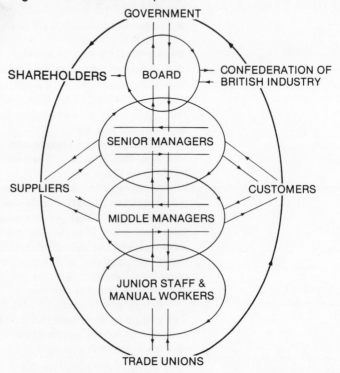

In any large organisation reports are circulated internally in an endlessly repeated pattern:

- **vertically** − from senior managers to juniors and vice versa;
- **horizontally** − between colleagues of equal status;
- **radially** − around the various departments.

This same pattern is reproduced in the relationship of the organisation to the outside environment in which it operates; reports are received, sent out, circulated, acted upon, or stored away and quietly ignored. Indeed, reports are all too often requested in order to keep people safely occupied, or to postpone decisions by a call for further information.

TYPES OF REPORT

Reports can be classified according to **purpose and content, length** and **format**.

Purpose and content

All reports have one function in common − **to provide information**. In the case of many regular routine reports this is their only function, so they consist simply of facts and figures relating to the day-to-day running of the organisation, e.g. monthly sales returns, safety inspections, etc. This type of report is reproduced as a matter of course by whoever is responsible for supplying the information and is usually presented in standardised form.

Occasional investigation reports which are written as one-off exercises are usually commissioned by a superior, a colleague, a client, or a committee. Their purpose is to investigate a particular process, product or problem. Some investigation reports consist entirely of detailed presentation and analysis of factual material, and are for information only, e.g. an accident report giving an account of a case of electric shock and an investigation of its causes. Others also include comment, opinion and advice, and it is this type of report which you are usually asked to write in exams. For example, the accident report might prompt a further report containing a thorough survey of the wiring, plugs and cables in a particular building, and recommendations for their replacement. Some of the material for such a report might be drawn from the regular safety inspection reports.

Length

The length can range from the equivalent of several thick telephone directories, right down to a single side of A4. The average length required in exams is between 200 and 400 words. Usually the maximum will be specified, though sometimes the question will simply ask for a 'brief' report or a 'summary' report. (Some candidates may have to submit a project or case study in the form of a longer report of about 3,000 words; e.g. B/TEC Higher Level, AEB, A Level.)

Format

All reports, whether long or short, 'formal' or 'informal', follow one of the following systems for organising and presenting the material in a clear and digestible form.

(a) Pre-printed forms for regular and routine reports

These cut the amount of writing to a minimum. Often all the employee has to do is tick boxes, enter figures into columns, and supply names, dates, etc.

(b) Letters and memoranda

Some simple reports may be submitted within conventional letters and memos, with the information divided into numbered sections under headings. Profile reports of candidates for interview often use this format, with headings such as: **Qualifications; Experience; Personal characteristics**, etc.

Reports which have not been asked for, but are written by someone who comes across interesting information or who has a suggestion to make, are usually presented as formal memoranda. For example, a middle manager or senior secretary might become frustrated by the inadequacies of the photocopying arrangements in the organisation which have attracted an increasing number of complaints from colleagues. He or she starts to write a brief memo to the head of department, but finds that the subject needs more detailed treatment, i.e. a report within a formal memorandum (see Fig. 7.2).

Fig. 7.2   The structure of a memorandum report

MEMORANDUM

From: Ref:

To: Date:

Subject: Report on Photocopying Provision

I have become increasingly concerned about complaints by several key members of staff over the difficulties and delays they experience in processing important documents in the Reprographic Room, and thought I ought to bring the matter to your attention. I have made a preliminary investigation of the problem, and would like to suggest some modest improvements.

Present Arrangements.
....
....

Problems and Complaints.
a) ....
b) ....

Possible Improvements.
....
....

(c) Conventional report format

Whatever the format, reports should always be presented **schematically**; i.e. divided into sections and subsections which are systematically numbered under headings and subheadings. The longer the report the more formal and detailed the scheme and layout needed to guide the reader through the weight and complexity of material. However, even single-sided A4 reports follow a basic schematic layout. A clear system of signposting the sections is particularly important if a report is to be discussed at a meeting, when everyone present will need to be able to refer quickly and easily to a particular point.

For example, suppose the result of the memo report on photocopying is to prompt the management to review and expand reprographic facilities throughout the organisation, a further more detailed report would be called for. The author would probably attend a high-level meeting to present his report and answer questions on the 'nuts and bolts', e.g. the average daily consumption of paper. So readers would need to be able to refer to a specific point in the report, e.g. a table on page 3, section 2.b.

In some advanced-level examinations you might be asked to write a **briefing** in note or report form (see p. 73), or a report of a meeting as opposed to conventional minutes (see p. 125).

It is essential to remember that the content, length, format and to some extent the style and tone of a report should be adapted to suit:

(a)   the *context*, e.g. a fact-finding visit, the launch of a new product, purchase of equipment, etc.;

(b)   the *reader(s)*, e.g. a superior, a colleague, a committee.

You might also have to bear in mind the characteristics and position of your reader(s), e.g. whether or not your boss is technically minded, or whether a committee is united and decisive, or divided and dithery.

PRESENTATION OF REPORTS

Be generous with space and signposts when setting out a report:

- Leave a margin each side of the page.
- Leave a clear line between sections.
- Use a consistent scheme of headings, numbers and indentations.
- Clarify statistics with diagrams where appropriate.

In formal reports of over about 1,000 words there are two accepted conventions, as detailed below.

Decimal system

7.   Topic Section Heading Underlined and Numbered

8.   Topic Section

8.1   Paragraph.

8.2   Paragraph.
8.2.1 Sub-paragraph
8.2.2 Sub-paragraph
     (a) Sub-point or a) or a.
     (b) Sub-point   b) or b.

Alternative system

I MAIN SECTION HEADING IN CAPITALS MARKED BY ROMAN NUMERALS (I, V, X etc)

A   Topic Section Heading Underlined and Marked by Capital Letters.

B   Topic Section.

1.   Paragraph

2.   Paragraph
      (a) Sub-paragraph
      (b) Sub-paragraph
        (i) sub-point
        (ii) sub-point

Unfortunately, once students are shown these conventions, particularly the clumsier second version, they tend to stick to them slavishly, using the same sledgehammer to crack all shapes and sizes of nuts. The results are usually ridiculously self-important, and invite sour comment to this effect in the examiners' reports. So for reports of between about 400 and 1,000 words you should practise using either the decimal system, or the following simplified version of the alternative system.

Simplified alternative system

A MAIN SECTION HEADING IN CAPITALS (e.g. CONCLUSIONS)

1. Topic Heading in Capitals and Lower Case Underlined.
    (a) Sub-Heading Indented and Underlined.
      (i) Sub-point

This scheme can be further simplified for reports of about 300 words:

1. Main Section Heading in Capitals and Lower Case Underlined.
    (a) Sub-paragraph.
      (i) Sub-point

An even simpler scheme, which is becoming more and more widely used, is not to number the main or subsection headings, but to number each paragraph in decimal sequence right through the report. Subpoints are still indicated by (a) and (i), etc. For example:

8. Paper Consumption

8.1 The company uses a total of 2.54 million sheets per annum . . .
(a) A4 . . .
(b) Foolscap . . .

8.2 It is estimated that approximately 10% of the total is wasted. . .

You should not need more than three indicators for the average exam question. If you do suddenly feel in need of a hidden punch, use bullet points ●, as used at the beginning of this section, asterisks * or dashes – to mark a short list of brisk points. They are specially useful when you are in a hurry but want to impose some sort of visual order. If you are not confident about when and where to bring them into play, it is safer to stick to lower case lettering and numerals for minor indented points.

The main thing is to choose a simple scheme which gives you confidence and then to use it consistently. It is a waste of time and marks to dither over whether to put IV, D, 4 or d. Note that the conventional order of weight is: I, A, 3., (a), (i).

Figure 7.3 sums up the essentials of correct presentation of a formal and an informal version of a report.

Figure 7.4 sums up the classification of types of reports.

NB Remember that when you are presenting statistical information one diagram can often replace a whole page of words and figures (see Ch. 9 and Figure 7.6.).

Style

Reports should be written in plain functional language. Avoid jargon and cliché, and keep a within a rough maximum of thirty words a sentence; otherwise you will lose your readers in the fog.

There are two important skills you must develop for report writing:

1. Matching the grammar of introductory phrases in subheadings with that of subsequent points, e.g.

The reprographic facilities in Room 30 could be improved by:

(a) providing one additional machine for short runs (*or* the provision of . . .);

(b) widening the gangway between the large photocopier and the paper stack (*or* the widening of . . .);

(c) removing the store cupboard (*or* the removal of . . .).

Not:

The reprographic facilities in Room 30 could be improved:

a. by providing one additional machine for short runs.

b) The gangway between the large photocopier and the paper stack is not wide enough.

c also the store cupboard should be moved out.

The second version contains only a sample of the most common and irritating mistakes in grammar and punctuation that make examiners twitch.

Recommendations are usually introduced by the word 'that':

It is therefore recommended that:

(a) one additional machine for short runs be purchased at a cost of £. . .;

(b) the width of the paper stack be reduced by 1.5 m;

(c) the store cupboard be moved into the corridor.

Note that readers often prefer to be offered alternative courses of action (options), so (a) could be: 'either one additional machine for short runs be purchased at a cost of £. . .; *or* 'two more desk-top machines be provided in the sales department'.

2. Using impersonal neutral constructions: e.g.

42 members of staff returned completed questionnaires.

or: *42 questionnaires were completed and returned.*
not:
We got 42 completed questionnaires back from members of staff.
or: *members of staff gave us back 42 questionnaires filled in.*

It was evident that ... **not:** *I could easily see that* ...

The figures show ... **not:** *You can see from the figures* ...

This convention can be carried too far. Many textbooks advise you never to use 'I' or 'we', as if this were some kind of rigid taboo. But in some cases it would be ludicrous to twist everything round to avoid it, especially by turning active verbs into passive. For instance, if you were asked to write a report of a visit or of work experience, it would be silly to say *the personnel manager was met by us* rather than *we met the personnel manager*. But there are other ways round these wording tangles, e.g. *the group had a useful meeting with the personnel manager*. The use of 'I', 'we', 'me' 'us', etc. is more acceptable in the introductory and concluding sections than in the main body of the report; e.g. *we visited the site, it is my view that* ... or: *In our opinion* ... Another convention is to refer to the author(s) in the third person: *the working party formed the impression that* ...

Note that the instruction to write an 'informal' report is not an invitation to dash off a few cryptic notes, e.g. *Store cupboard needs moving*. Nor does it mean that you can drop into a chatty casual style, e.g. *I looked into the reprographics room one day last week at the height of the mid-morning rush, and it was packed with frantic secretaries clutching urgent papers*. The language of reports should be fluent but correct and concise.

Remember: the examiners are looking for a structure that looks clear, and a style that sounds decisive. No matter how well you have memorised the main sections of formal reports, the content will fall apart unless you have absorbed the background material, fed in your own knowledge and imagination about the context, and formed your own views about the facts/problems; i.e. your **conclusions**.

You will get more marks for a clear, fluent and plausible account and analysis of the situation than a series of correct formal headings above irrelevant or clumsily worded paragraphs.

| The process of writing reports | If you were a manager, an expert, or a civil servant or local government officer who had been asked to write a report, you would go through the following stages: |

1. Settling the terms of reference.
2. Collecting the information.
3. Sifting and sorting the information.
4. Organising the material into sections.
5. Drafting the factual body of the report.
6. Preparing tables, charts, maps, etc. to be inserted into the text or added as appendices.
7. Drafting the introductory and concluding sections.

(cont'd p. 103)

Fig. 7.3 Schematic presentation of reports

INFORMAL
VERSION

FORMAL VERSION

Covering Memo – 'I enclose the report your requested . . . etc.'
(Optional – depends on wording of question.)

Drop actual
word 'title'

TITLE. REPORT ON . . .

Combine
into an
INTRODUCTION 1.

A. TERMS OF REFERENCE. Why and for whom report has been written.
Definition of subject. Scope of report. (Indicate if recommendations
have been requested.)

B. PROCEDURE. How the writer collected the information.

Drop actual
word 'findings'
Use topic headings
2, 3, etc.

Briefer,
with fewer
sections
and subsections
and simpler
numbering
scheme.

C. FINDINGS. The facts, methodically grouped and numbered.

This section should be split into paragraphs and sub-paragraphs clearly marked
1., 2., 3., etc. and a., b., c., etc. Sometimes 3 subdivisions may be necessary, e.g. 2.,
b.,(ii). In lengthy and complex reports the usual convention is 1.,1.1,1.2; 2., 2.1,
2.1.1, etc. *ad infinitum*, with indentations within paragraphs marked a., b., c., etc.
and/or (i), (ii), (iii), etc.

Alternatively, use I, A, 1., a., (i), etc.

Major subject divisions should be indicated by general headings, e.g. THE
PRESENT SITUATION, FUTURE DEVELOPMENTS, Advantages, Disadvantages,
Costs, etc. Minor section subheadings are more specifically related to the subject-
matter of the report, e.g. Paper Supplies, Maintenance Photocopiers, User
Manuals, etc.

Avoid mere
repetition.

Comment and
evaluate.

D. CONCLUSIONS. Summary and analysis of findings. Length and emphasis vary
according to purpose and nature of report, i.e. whether it is designed just to
provide background information or to prompt decisions; also whether the factual
section was short and simple or long and complex.

Your opinion/evaluation should emerge at this stage, and various
alternatives/options presented.

If requested.

Usually
between two
and five in
short reports.

Clearly
numbered.

E. RECOMMENDATIONS. Proposed solution(s) and course(s) of action (or
inaction). Usually presented prescriptively, e.g. 'that an order be placed with X & Y
Ltd for 2 desk-top copiers at a cost of £ . . .' Sometimes presented flexibly to allow
choice of options depending on balance of conclusions, e.g. 'alternatively, 2
similar machines could be leased from FG and Co. at an annual cost of £ . . .

Recommendations should always be specific, and individually numbered:
1,2,3, etc. or a,b,c, etc. or 7.1, 7.2, 7.3, etc.

Date.

Name.

Position.

Margin for readers' notes.

Leave one line clear at the bottom of the page.

Fig. 7.4 Classification of reports

Report	Type	Readers	Format	Possible results
Report on 2 alternative sites for new offices/factory/club.	Investigation report, assessing advantages and disadvantages of sites and advising on choice	Board of directors, executive committee.	Medium length in four sections: Introduction, 'body' of report, Conclusions, Recommendations. Appendices with plans, photographs, detailed costings.	Decision on choice of site.
Report on visit to an outside organisation.	Information report with Conclusions.	Senior managers, specialist colleagues.	Short, 'informal'; 3 main sections: Introduction, Findings, Conclusions.	Management update on latest needs and/or developments in relevant areas of operation.
Report on accident in workshop.	Factual account by witness of incident; its causes and results.	Safety officer, health and safety committee.	Pre-printed form.	Replacement of dangerous equipment, warning against carelessness.
Government report on what children eat for breakfast.	Investigation report to assess nutrition policies and publicity.	Politicians and officials, parents, teachers, journalists.	Long, formal, covered and bound. Detailed appendices.	Political debate. Health campaign. Survey of school dinners.
Report by Marketing Department of food manufacturing firm on what children eat for breakfast.	Market research report to on potential demand for new breakfast cereal, perhaps including advice on publicity and packaging.	Directors of company and its advertising agency.	Flexible, 'informal'. Detailed appendices.	Launch of new product
Consumer report on dishwashers.	Investigation report, testing and comparing different brands.	Subscribers to *Which* magazine. Journalists, newspaper readers.	Factual article/report with tables and illustrations. Recommendations on best buys.	Better informed customers. Good and bad publicity for products. Improved standards.
Company's annual report.	Information report for Annual General Meeting.	Shareholders, readers of financial press.	Glossy, illustrated with photographs, diagrams, detailed tables of figures.	Rise or fall in price of shares.
Profile of candidate for interview.	Information report to brief interviewers.	Interviewer(s), personnel officer.	Memorandum, outlining qualities, aptitudes and experience.	More effective interviews.
Emergency report on fire	Account of disaster, and measures taken to remedy situation.	Responsible committee or group of managers.	Oral report, perhaps with visual presentation.	Decisions on immediate action.

8. Editing, polishing and shaping.
9. Adding the appendices.
10. Writing and inserting a summary of the report.
11. Getting the great work bound, covered and circulated.

All this would then be followed by: discussing, debating and defending: monitoring decisions or non-decisions and implementation or non-implementation; experiencing triumph, frustration, oblivion; and all too often, coming back 10 years later with 'I told you so . . . it was all in my report.'

Exam exercises try to put you through some of these hoops in a reasonably realistic fashion, though the time limit obviously means that you have little hope of doing justice to the subject. If you are given lengthy background material, just concentrate on pulling that into shape with one or two timely additions from your own background knowledge and practical imagination, e.g. plausible references to other members of staff or departments of the supposed organisation. Some candidates panic when they are given a lot of material to summarise and points to include; others panic when they are expected to invent most of the detail. So you should spend up to 10 minutes sizing up the question, and about half an hour answering it. Try to organise your time as follows:

1. Decide exactly what **type of report** is being asked for. Too many candidates churn out the full formal version regardless of the context and instructions supplied. Your approach should be confident and flexible enough to adapt your content and presentation to the particular question. Examiners are out to test you by varying the ingredients, but they always expect you to remember the basic recipe. Usually this will take the SUMMARY/ INFORMAL shape, sometimes contained within a formal memorandum.

2. Define the **terms of reference**. These may be spelt out in detail, including a full account of your role, and whether or not recommendations are required, or they may be left rather vague. One common mistake is to exaggerate your position and powers. Junior accountants do not decide the advertising budget, nor do secretaries tell the managing director where to move the head office, but they may recommend efficiency measures or the purchase of items of office equipment.

3. Read the question again and make **notes** about the main factual points to be dealt with, adding your own informed common-sense detail to the given material, e.g. results of possible questionnaire, consultation with other departments, etc.

4. Sort out the factual body of the report into **headings** and **subheadings,** and decide − quickly − what you have concluded and might recommend.

5. Write a suitable **title** at the top of the page, or after the word 'Subject:' on a memorandum format.

6. Write the **introductory paragraph** or paragraphs, and begin your numbering scheme at this stage. (If you write a covering memo to

the person who asked for the report it will not count against the word limit.)

7.   Write the **body** of the report, following a clear sequence of **numbered** headings and subheadings using a consistent scheme of capitals, underlinings and indentations.

8.   Finally, **sum up** and emphasise − without mere repetition − and, if required, make your recommendations. (Reports of 300−500 words usually have between two and five.)

9.   Carefully reread and **check** for errors of spelling and punctuation, and remember to put your name and the date at the bottom.

NB Do not endlessly repeat the name of your organisation in full; your readers know it already.

C. USEFUL APPLIED MATERIALS

Fig. 7.5 A typical local authority report (abridged and adapted)

SOUTHWICH CITY COUNCIL   AGENDA ITEM: 6

LEISURE AND RECREATION COMMITTEE   SUBJECT: SAFETY SURFACES ON CHILDREN'S PLAY AREAS

Date: 13 December 1986   AUTHOR: CITY LEISURE AND RECREATION OFFICER

1.   INTRODUCTION

1.1 On 12 October the Committee received a petition from the Southwich Playground Action Group urging the Council to improve the safety of surfaces under play equipment. The officers were then instructed to investigate the problem, assess types of safety surfacing available and their costs, and to recommend a programme of improvement for consideration at the December meeting.

1.2 Many new products have recently been developed and several expert reports have been published. The most comprehensive was a study commissioned by the Greater London Council, which provides some of the information used in this report.

2.   THE NEED FOR SAFETY SURFACES

2.1 Play equipment is provided to entertain, and to develop children's physical abilities and stimulate their imagination. An element of risk is part of the fun. However, the likelihood of injury can be reduced by including safety features such as tyre or composition seats on swings.

2.2 Children fall off all equipment - whether it is just a few inches from a toddler 'rocker' or several feet from a climbing frame. The surface below will to a large extent determine the degree and type of injury.

2.3 Statistics of playground accidents which result in medical treat- are not formally recorded, and few are reported to the Council - on average 3 or 4 a year. However, several recent studies suggest that the total number of accidents on UK playgrounds could exceed 15,000 a year, with injuries caused by falls on to tarmac, con- crete or hard earth accounting for about 85%.

3.   TYPES OF SAFETY SURFACE

3.1 Safety surfacing falls into three basic types - rubber carpet, safety tiles, and loose fill.

(a) Rubber carpet

This is a resin-bound rubber granule or shred surface which
can either be laid on site in the same way as tarmac, or
bought in carpet form, with thickness depending on the heights
of possible falls. Both require a hard and even base to which
they are bonded with adhesives, but are easy to lay around
existing equipment

(b) Safety tiles

These are concrete slabs with a safety layer bonded to the
surface, which are laid on a base of sand or mortar. They
are difficult to lay around existing equipment and are
easily lifted by vandals.

(c) Wood bark, sand, or pea gravel.

These materials can be laid to a depth of 300 mm in pits
excavated around the equipment. They provide the safest
surfacing, but are difficult to lay around existing struc-
tures, and are unsuitable under moving equipment. Also,
they need constant maintenance to ensure that the surface
is evenly spread and free of dangerous objects. Sand has
the added disadvantage of being attractive to dogs. All
need regular topping up, and bark needs completely changing
every 3-5 years because it gradually decays. (Specifications are given in Appendix C.)

3.2 A comparison between the different surfaces can be made by
defining from what height a child has to fall before suffering
injury. The system used below is based on research into car
accidents. If a head fall results in a 'severity index' of
1,000 or more there will almost certainly be concussion or
serious injury. (See diagram in Appendix B)

4.   SOUTHWICH PLAY AREAS

4.1 There are 64 play areas in the city with 290 pieces of equipment.
Most have an average of 5-6 widely spaced pieces, each needing a
separate safety surround.

4.2 The newly landscaped area in the Linden Estate has been designed
to conform to modern safety standards and is surfaced in bark.
This has proved very popular, but needs more frequent maintenance
than traditional playgrounds.

4.3 The 5-year-old play area in Winston Park has swings and slides on
a rubber carpet surface; this is wearing well, apart from some
lifting at the base of the slide.

4.4 All other equipment is sited either on tarmac or grass. Climbing
units are inserted into the grass, whereas with swings, see-saws
and roundabouts a tarmac surface is usually laid to avoid bare
patches.

5.   COSTS

5.1 Safety surfacing is not cheap. Tiles cost between £42 and £80 per
square metre and rubber carpet £30-£100 per square metre, depending
on depth. The deeper and safer the surface, the higher the price.
Installation costs will vary according to the state of present
surfaces.

5.2 Day-to-day maintenance costs for rubber tiles or carpet are
similar to tarmac, but the life expectancy will be lower. Manufacturers predict an average of 10 years.

5.3 Bark or sand is cheaper to install - about £25 per square metre, but needs almost daily attention and regular topping-up and renewal.

Examples of costs: £

(a) Double Swing. Rubber carpet on to existing base.
    Supply and install area of 5 m x 6 m   1,300

(b) Junior Slide. Bark pit 5 m x 4 m
    Creation of pit   130
    Lowering of slide   150
    Bark   120
                                                             ─────
                                                              400

    Replacement after 5 years   120
    Maintenance   50

5.4 The estimated cost of surfacing under all appropriate equipment in line with the recommendations of this report would be:

(a) Bark pits   56,000
(b) Rubber carpet and tiles   118,000
                                                         ────────
                                                         174,000

(A detailed programme is attached as Appendix A)

6. CONCLUSIONS

6.1 There is increasing pressure from parents for safer surfaces on the city's playgrounds, and the Playground Action Group has wide support.

6.2 Safety surfacing is most effective when installed in new or completely redesigned areas, where a combination of bark pits under climbing frames and rubber carpet under swings and roundabouts provides safety without appearing too tame, but there is also scope for improving existing areas.

6.3 There are sufficient funds in the budget for this year to finance the resurfacing of about 20 of those play areas in the worst condition. Any further work in 1987/88 will need additional finance.

7. RECOMMENDATIONS

7.1 That safety surfaces continue to be installed on all new play area areas.

7.2 That a detailed programme be prepared of replacing present surfaces, starting with the playgrounds in the worst condition.

7.3 That the Committee make a bid for £15,000 for 19../.. to finance the next phase of the programme.

7.4 That a group of members and officers visit the Exhibition of Playground Equipment in Birmingham on February 18. (Details enclosed.)

P. D. Hanson
City Leisure and Recreation Officer.

JWD/jg

Enc. Manufacturers' brochures.

After discussion in committee the recommendations might be amended to include further participation from the Action Group; e.g. that a representative be included in the group to visit the exhibition, and/or that they be circulated with the report and invited to comment (see Ch. 8 – Meetings).

Fig. 7.6 An extract from a Police Report, showing the use of diagrams.

VEHICLE CRIMES

Overall, offences associated with motor vehicles, which include theft of vehicles, taking motor vehicles without the owner's consent and theft of property from vehicles has remained constant, with 6,261 offences recorded - an increase of 10 offences (+ 0.15%).

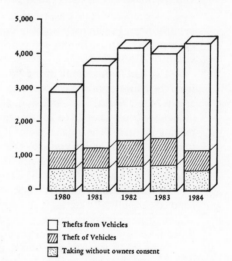

Diagram showing Five Year Comparison of Vehicle Crimes

☐ Thefts from Vehicles
▨ Theft of Vehicles
▨ Taking without owners consent

Offences involving motor vehicles continue to account for one fifth of the annual recorded crime (20.75%). The actual number of vehicles either stolen or taken without the owner's consent has in fact decreased by 359 cases (- 11.70%). Of the 1956 vehicles taken during the year, 342 have not been traced (17.48%).

(Source: Chief Constable's Annual Report 1984/85. Cambridgeshire Constabulary)

D. RECENT EXAMINATION QUESTIONS

Question 1 Give four reasons for writing a report.

RSA Communication in Business Stage II. This question is part of the case study paper shown in Ch. 1, p. 2.

Question 3 You work as personal assistant to Mr Michael Chalmers, Managing Director of Enamellon Utensils Limited, a small company manufacturing a range of cooking utensils which it sells to wholesalers and chain stores in the UK and in a growing export market. The company's factory is situated at 196–198 Surrey Road, Exwell, London EW3 6SR. The factory emplloys 50 skilled, 100 semi-skilled and 200 unskilled employees, while its adjacent offices employ 38 administrative personnel.

The company's products are being sold in increasingly competitive markets, so any cost-savings would be welcome. At present, some 60 per cent of UK sales are made to customers located south of the line from Bristol to the Wash.

This morning Mr Chalmers called you into his office and had this to say:

'As you know, our lease on the Surrey Road premises comes up for renewal in six months' time. Preliminary negotiations have confirmed that we shall find it difficult to meet the expected increase in rent without shedding factory and administrative staff, which could seriously affect sales.

'I've had another look at the Winsfield Estate prospectus. Winsfield's about 20 miles from the major port of Mereport and some five miles from the M58 motorway spur. The area is in the North West, and so qualifies for government development aid, and it looks as though we could save up to 25 per cent of our manufacturing and administrative costs by moving up there. The area is one of higher than national average unemployment, and is traditionally trade-union conscious – something we've not much experience of.

'At present there's not enough office accommodation on the site, but there's plenty of land included with the factory. The trouble is, we couldn't wait for buildings to be put up.

'If we *did* decide to move, lock, stock and barrel, the whole thing would need to be handled carefully. I'd certainly like to take our skilled people with us at the very least, but you can't just uproot people at the drop of a hat. In any case, the office staff could probably find something similar round here if they had to.

'Now this is what I'd like you to do. Get up to Winsfield and have a look round. See what you think of the possibilities. Weigh up our present situation as it obtains here. Then I want you to write a report for me outlining the pros and cons and supplying your own recommendations. I've a Board Meeting in a fortnight and I'd like another view of the subject, reached independently, before any initial discussions. I'll need to have your report on my desk in a week's time.'

Compose a report, based on the above information, but including any additional material you consider appropriate, to meet Mr Chalmer's requirements.

Your report should not exceed 500 words.

(25 marks)
(RSA DPA, 1980)

E. OUTLINE AND TUTOR'S ANSWERS

Tutor's answer 1   A simple 'quickie' quiz-type question. Obviously there are more than four reasons, so choose a selection of the most important ones. Think about the various contexts which call for reports.

1. To investigate a problem or opportunity.
2. To research the market for a new product or service.
3. To review the progress of a new product or service.
4. To assess candidates for interview.

Outline answer 2

The background material is given in about 460 words, so you have to reduce it by more than half. You need a suitable informal summary structure, perhaps with a covering memo.

Ideally, the list of shrubs would look best displayed in columns under headings as Size; Advantages; Disadvantages, etc., but you are stuck with A4 width. So you will need some system of conventional headings and numberings.

There is a danger of repeating the notes in slightly different words; this can be avoided by regrouping the shrubs according to types as mentioned in the additional note. Your report will be more useful if it relates the various shrubs to the site, so invent some relevant features, e.g. sunny or shady and emphasise the characteristics most likely to please the elderly residents.

The examiners have been very vague about cost − perhaps deliberately − so you will have to decide whether to invent some plausible figures. You should also decide whether to mention the partner's wife alluded to at the beginning of the question. The names of the partners are given in a later question. This shows the importance of reading right through 'case study' papers.

Outline answer

> Covering memo to Mr Grant saying you have prepared report requested, and asking for comments. (Informal way of reminding him of your terms of reference.)

REPORT ON SHRUBS FOR ST JUDE'S HILLSIDE HOME

1. INTRODUCTION
Agreed at partners' meeting of 20 Feb. to donate 20 shrubs. Mr Holder suggested 8 species. Total cost between £100 and £150.

2. THE SITE
Main entrance path X metres long, narrow beds each side. Faces west, so gets afternoon/evening sun, morning shade. Rather windy and exposed. Alkaline soil, so 3 on original list excluded.

3. SUGGESTED SPECIES
(a) Deciduous:
    (i) Fuchsia. Very popular, etc … … … …
    (iii) Forsythia. Might grow too large and hide plaque.
(b) Flowering evergreens:
    (i) Skimmia. Scent would be appreciated by partially sighted.
    (ii) Viburnum … … … …
(c) Deciduous evergreens:
    Chamaecyparis … … … …

4. CONCLUSIONS
Any one of above would be suitable for site. Suggest matron asks residents for preferences, e.g. on evergreen v. deciduous, flowers, scent, etc. Also ask Mrs Newman for her opinion.

An interesting and challenging question, which gives you about 350 words of usable material and 150 to invent.

Mr Chalmers obviously does not confine the talents of his PA to the usual range of office duties. Not only does he want you to give a first-hand account of the industrial estate, but he also seems to expect you to write a report on the 'pros and cons' of moving – in one week flat. Many candidates might therefore feel that this is a rather implausible question, but many PAs do quickly find themselves catapulted into this degree of initiative and responsibility, particularly in small organisations.

The examiners seem to be inviting you to go 'whole hog', and tell the MD whether or not to move his company, but it would be more realistic to form conclusions one way or the other and suggest further investigation, without banging in just one overriding recommendation – to move or not to move.

The usual mistake in questions of this kind is to treat it as a summary and simply rearrange and regurgitate the given facts. Mr Chalmers presumably knows the address of his company and how many people it employs, so obviously the bulk of 'additional material' will come from your visit – which breaks new ground; you would hardly be expected to come up with financial wizardry enabling you to stay at Surrey Road at no extra cost.

One quick reading of the question is enough to give the feeling that the cards have been heavily stacked in favour of moving, though you could perhaps decide to find the Winsfield Estate nothing like what it is cracked up to be and invent all sorts of snags. Then you would have to say something about redundancies, and land up in even deeper water.

Remember that the examiners try to be topical, so background material goes quickly out of date, and last year's question is no longer such good practice material in purely factual terms but still valid as an exercise in organisation and presentation. You will be more impressive if you slot in the odd fact or comment which indicates an awareness of relevant current events, e.g. changes in government's regional and relocation policies.

Outline answer

REPORT ON POSSIBLE MOVE TO WINSFIELD

1. <u>Intro</u>.

   Problem/reason for report/background.
   Instructions/brief/terms of reference.
   Information collected by:
   - visit – what seen, who met, etc.
   - consulting key staff.

2. <u>Present premises</u>

   - The site.
   - Implications of rent increase.

3. <u>Winsfield</u>

   - The location, regional and export trade potential.
   - Description of estate.
   - The factory.
   - Adjoining land – offices.
   - Labour and trade unions.

4. <u>Advantages of move</u>

- Financial — government incentives, lower running costs.
- Geographical — near to port and motorway — trade potential.
- Labour available.

5. <u>Disadvantages of move</u>

- Financial — capital cost of building offices, inducements to staff, redundancy payments.
- Geographical — 60 % of present sales in South.
- Labour — militant TUs. Retraining for local recruits.

6. <u>Conclusions</u>

Advantages outweigh disadvantages. Problems can be overcome; more detailed research needed.

7. <u>Recommendations</u>

- Detailed financial appraisal.
- Market research on North-West and Mereport export outlet.
- Personnel manager to investigate TU situation.
- Short-term offices — Portakabin? Long-term — tenders from local builders.
- Survey of staff attitudes. Arrange visit.

Remember that you can save words by writing a covering memo to Mr Chalmers on a separate sheet or in a box at the top of the report to indicate that it is separate. This would take care of part of your introduction, but since it is not clear whether he is going to show it to the board or just use it to help him write his own report, you will have to make the format suitable for either eventuality. So you would be equally correct to put the whole report into a formal memorandum format.

ENAMELLON UTENSILS LTD

MEMORANDUM

From: Your Name.   Ref:

To: Mr M. Chalmers   Date:

Subject: Possible Move to Winsfield.

1. Introduction.
   . . . . . . etc.

ENAMELLON UTENSILS LTD

REPORT ON PROPOSED MOVE TO WINSFIELD

1. INTRODUCTION

The renewal of the Surrey Road lease has prompted the Board of Enamellon to consider moving to the North-West. The managing director asked me to visit and report on the Winsfield Estate, to assess the present situation and the advantages and disadvantages of moving, and to make recommendations for the board meeting on 19 November.

During a two-day visit I made a thorough survey of the estate and a brief tour of the surrounding area, including Mereport. I met representatives of other firms on the estate, and of the local CBI and Amalgamated Engineering Workers Union.

The finance director, the production manager, the personnel manager and the office supervisor of Enamellon have also been consulted.

2. PRESENT PREMISES

Enamellon has been on its present site for 53 years, and there is little room for further expansion. The finance director estimates that the proposed rent increase of 12% will mean redundancies in both factory and office staff and a consequent cut in production leading to a serious loss of sales.

3. THE WINSFIELD ESTATE

(a) Winsfield is 19 miles from Mereport, which handles an increasing export trade. The M58 provides an easy route to motorways linking the North-West to London and the South-West. The estate is on the main road to Mereport.

(b) The estate is well landscaped, and has ample parking space.

(c) The factory is well insulated and spacious. An office building could easily be fitted on to the site (see attached ground-plans). Temporary Portakabins can be hired at £50 per month.

(d) Comparable companies on the estate are prospering.

(e) Housing for sale or rent is plentiful and cheap.

4. ADVANTAGES OF MOVE

(a) Winsfield qualifies for up to 25% government development aid. Rent and rates would be 20% lower.

(b) The premises allow for expansion.

(c) There are potential export and regional markets.

(d) High unemployment in the area will ensure rapid recruitment of labour.

5. DISADVANTAGES OF MOVE

(a) Building new offices will need a high initial capital outlay.

(b) It would be inconvenient for some of our present retail outlets in the South-East.

(c) Manual workers would be unionised.

(d) Present office staff would be reluctant to leave London.

6. CONCLUSIONS

The Winsfield Estate is purpose-built and conveniently situated. However, there would be problems in persuading present staff to move to the North-West, and in recruiting key skilled staff. Administration would be hampered during the construction of new offices.

If these short-term problems can be overcome, it would be in the long-term interests of the company to move.

7. RECOMMENDATIONS

This report is based on brief preliminary research, so it is therefore recommended that:

(a) a detailed financial analysis be undertaken of comparative costs;
(b) further market research be carried out in the North-West;
(c) a series of meetings be held with staff, and a visit to Winsfield be arranged for key personnel;
(d) estimates be invited from local builders for the construction of an office block.

N.C. Grant   11 November 19. .

Notes on tutor's answer

There are two alternative forms of presentation:

(a) *Decimally*:

4. ADVANTAGES OF MOVE

4.1 Winsfield qualifies for up to 25% government development aid. Rent and rates would be 20% lower.
4.2 The premises allow for expansion.
4.3 There are potential export and regional markets.
4.4 High unemployment in the area will ensure rapid recruitment of labour.

(b) *More formally:*

I.   TERMS OF REFERENCE

On the instructions of the managing director, to report on the suitability of the proposed Mereport factory site; to assess the company's present situation and the advantages and disadvantages of moving to the North-West; and to make recommendations for the board meeting on 19 November.

II. PROCEDURE

This report was compiled after a visit to the Winsfield Estate, Mereport, during which representatives of other firms on the estate, and of the local CBI and Amalgamated Engineering Union were interviewed. Consultations were also held with the finance director, personnel manager, production manager and office supervisor of Enamellon.

III. FINDINGS

A. Present Premises.

B. The Winsfield Estate.
    1. Location
    2. Premises

       (a)

       (b)

3. .... etc.

F. A STEP FURTHER

General textbooks

The most useful general textbooks are:

The Business of Communicating, Stanton N. Pan 1982. Chapter 11 contains a typical short report with a letter format version on the facing page. Sensible advice on headings and numbering.

People and Communication, Evans D W. Pitman 1984. Chapter 4 contains a definitive section on layout and the example is clearly structured, though being a demonstration piece has led to top-heavy headings and numberings.

Communication in Business, Little P. Pitman 1983. Chapter 9: The example is a demonstration of full formal layout.

Mastering Business Communication, Woolcott L A and Unwin W R. Macmillan 1983. Chapter 2 contains a good modern-style example.

Specialised books

How to Write a Successful Report, Mort S. Business Books 1985. A comprehensive and up-to-date guide for professionals.

Report Writing. BACIE Booklet 1981 (obtainable from 16 Park Crescent, London W1N 4 AP).

Report Writing. Industrial Society Booklet 1984.

How to Write a Report, Fletcher J A. Institute of Personnel Management 1983. A brief guide for managers, with excellent advice on style.

Effective Writing, Turk C and Kirkman J. Spon 1982. Especially helpful on technical reports.

Research

You should look through as wide a cross-section of actual examples as possible. Most libraries stock a wide variety of reports of public interest, from companies, central and local government, registered charities, etc. They are usually more interesting than the necessarily neutral examples in the textbooks.

Chapter 8   Meetings

A. GETTING STARTED

Most important management decisions are taken at meetings. The more senior the manager, the more time he will spend in meetings; meetings within the organisation, between organisations, and between the organisation and outside individuals or groups. Because meetings are such an essential and frequent form of communication, involving both oral and written contributions, they are included in all communication syllabuses and provide a wide variety of exam questions.

Whatever course you have been following you will probably have learnt a certain amount about meetings, but there will have been wide differences in emphasis and pursuit of detail. The main difference lies in the degree of practical work demanded. GCE communication courses are angled towards the social and psychological aspects of how people behave in groups (see also Ch. 9 – Oral Communication). Most general business studies and management courses expect a broad knowledge of the purpose, procedure, personnel and paperwork involved, whereas secretarial courses demand a more detailed study and practice of the terminology and documentation of meetings.

So you first need to decide precisely what and how much you need to know by studying your syllabus carefully and looking up as many past questions as you can find. Are they short **quiz** type questions which test your factual knowledge, e.g. 'What is a *quorum*?' or 'What is the difference between a *subcommittee* and a *working party*?' Or are they **social/psychological** type questions, e.g. 'What are the most important qualities required of a chairman?' or 'What are the advantages and disadvantages of calling a meeting rather than consulting people on the telephone?' or are they **applied skill** type questions which give you a situation from which to write an agenda or minutes? Of course you may get examples of each of these types, or questions which contain elements of more than one type. There is an obvious difference, for example, between 'List the main duties of a committee secretary' and 'As secretary of . . . write an agenda for the next committee meeting.' But a question which asked you what happens when a meeting becomes *inquorate* and then to make an appropriate entry in the minutes would be testing a wider range of knowledge and skills.

Some examinees may have useful experience of meetings as members of clubs, voluntary organisations, trade unions or staff associations. If so, they are at an advantage because they can relate their classwork to actual situations. Some may have been committee officers or members with useful experience to share with the rest of the class. You may have watched a film or video of a fictional meeting, or conducted a simulation in class; or you may have gone along to a meeting of your students' union, if only as part of the audience.

In any building housing a large organisation there are many and various meetings taking place in any one week — some would say far too many. Find out about the meetings which are held at your place of work or the college you attend. Make a list of these meetings and consider how

Fig. 8.1   The power structure within and surrounding a college of higher education

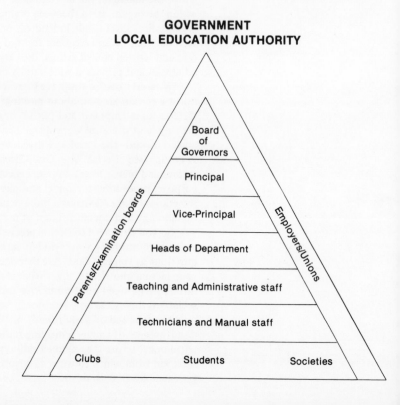

they fit into the power structure. Remember that few organisations are entirely self-contained or immune from decisions taken at meetings held far away and further up the power scale.

Figure 8.1 shows that many of the meetings held within the power pyramid will be part of a wider network. (See also Fig. 7.2 on the circulation of reports.)

Many issues which come up at meetings can be settled on the spot, e.g. the arrangements for the next canoe club outing, whereas others, e.g. a demand by the students' union for an additional common-room, would have to be referred upwards. The overlap and interrelation between committees means that if one meeting fails to convey its decisions to other relevant meetings there can be misunderstanding and delay. That is why important − or self-important − people who attend a lot of meetings are forever consulting their diaries. And that is why examinees are so often asked questions about breakdowns in communication. So it is essential to be aware of the wider context of any meeting you are asked about. As the AEB A level syllabus points out, 'Business does not exist in a vacuum.' Many a candidate has come unstuck through ignorance of the wider implications of seemingly simple tasks such as writing an agenda for a committee meeting.

B. ESSENTIAL PRINCIPLES

The range and variety of meetings are so wide that your first step should be to sort them into categories; otherwise there is a danger of making errors of detail such as minuting a decision of an advisory committee as *resolved* rather than *recommended*, or including *minutes of the last meeting* as an item on the agenda of an *inaugural* or an *ad hoc* meeting. (Some of these specialist terms are explained in this chapter, while others are defined in the glossary on p. 130).

CATEGORIES OF MEETINGS

There are five broad **categories** of meetings:

1. **Annual general meeting** (AGM) − open to all members or shareholders. (There may be occasional need for **extraordinary** general meetings to deal with vital matters such as bankruptcies or mergers.)
2. **Ordinary meeting** − open to all members of an organisation. Held monthly or quarterly.
3. **Standing committees** − formally set up by the parent body on a permanent basis and meeting at regular intervals, e.g. the education committee of a county council.
4. **Occasional advisory committees** − meet several times in order to deal with a specific issue and then disband when the task is completed, e.g. working parties, committees of inquiry.
5. *Ad hoc* **meetings** − called for a specific reason as and when necessary. This category covers the wide variety of one-off meetings which do not form part of any committee structure, e.g. between retailers and suppliers, student representatives and principal of college, etc.

Another obvious distinguishing feature is of **size**, which in turn may dictate another distinction; the **formality** or **informality** of atmosphere and procedure. As a general rule, the larger the gathering the greater the need for formal structure and control. There are other factors which affect the degree of formality, such as the nature of the organisation, the content and context of the meeting, and whether or not the participants know each other. The business of a company AGM is usually conducted very formally, whereas a packed residents' association meeting may be relaxed or even unruly. Three or four strangers may have a rather stiff polite meeting, whereas the committee of a local charity might sit round the kitchen table. Whatever course you are studying, you should at least be aware of this range and variety, even if most exam questions are angled towards meetings within a conventional committee structure.

CHARACTERISTICS OF MEETINGS

You can identify the **characteristics** of a meeting by asking: why it is being held; what authority it carries and what it is expected to achieve; who is attending it and why; and how and when it is conducted and documented.

Why?	PURPOSE
What?	POWER
Who?	PEOPLE
How?	PAPERS
When?	PROCEDURE

The five Ps of meetings

1. PURPOSE

To be effective and worthwhile a meeting needs clear objectives; otherwise it is likely to end in chaos and frustration. The characteristics of a meeting will to a large extent depend on its **purpose**; for example, a meeting called to hammer out a pay dispute might be long and stormy, calling for strong and patient chairmanship, whereas a one-off meeting to plan an advertising campaign would be relaxed and lively, with participants chipping in with off-the-cuff suggestions.

The classification of meetings according to purpose

Purpose	Examples	Characteristics
● To take decisions/ form policy	Boards of directors. College governors. Local authority committees. The Cabinet	Formally chaired, carefully prepared and structured; discussion and debate leading to agreement or vote
● To inform/ instruct	Briefing of trade union branch by regional officer. Update of salesmen by sales manager	Dominated by person who called (convened) the meeting

Purpose	Examples	Characteristics
● To consult/ exchange information/ideas	One-off (*ad hoc*) meetings between managers and outside experts (consultants). Public meetings, e.g. on local planning proposals	Structured but relaxed; no formal decisions
● To persuade/ influence action and policy	Architects/potential clients. Lobby of MPs by pressure group	Presentation of products or proposals; suggestions for action/ policy
● To solve specific problems	Working parties. Advisory panels. 'Brainstorming' sessions/'buzz-groups'. Committees of inquiry into disasters	Informal pooling of ideas and expertise; collaborative, creative and constructive
● To negotiate/ bargain	Union/management meetings. International diplomatic meetings	Tough-talking, sometimes stormy. Often take several sessions to reach agreement/ compromise
● To air grievances	Union/management meetings. Students/ principal. Players/ team manager	Should be informal, conciliatory, with complainants doing most of the talking

2. POWER

The degree of power vested in a meeting depends on its *terms of reference*, i.e. powers and instructions as defined in the **constitution** and **standing orders** or **articles of association** of the organisation and its committees. Usually the ultimate power rests with the parent body, particularly in important matters such as changing the constitution or approving the annual accounts. However, for practical reasons some powers are *delegated* to **standing committees** which meet regularly. These are often called **executive** committees because they have the power to execute, i.e. to act upon their decisions. Delegated powers are used to deal with routine matters requiring prompt action or urgent problems needing swift resolution. Important policy decisions, particularly if they have serious financial implications, usually have to be referred upwards to the parent body, e.g. take-over bids have to be approved by an extraordinary meeting of the shareholders of a company.

Members of organisations sometimes complain that committees take over too much power and that the parent body is reduced to merely 'rubber-stamping' decisions taken by small élite groups. In turn, committees are sometimes jealous of their powers being taken over or overruled by other committees. Hence the suspicion of conspiracies in smoke-filled rooms. The degree of power delegated to committees usually depends on how democratic the organisation is supposed to be. Company boards of directors necessarily have virtually complete power, whereas the executive committee of a trade union is accountable to the members who elect it. Figure 8.2 illustrates a typical democratic power structure.

Fig. 8.2 A typical democratic committee structure

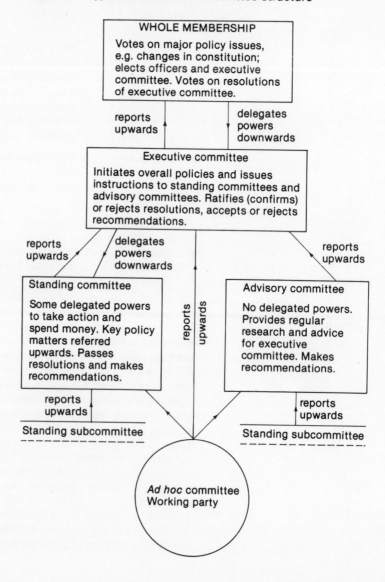

3. PEOPLE

The social character of meetings can range from a collection of individuals who hardly know each other — as when a number of delegations representing different organisations are called together — to small committees which meet regularly and whose members are on first-name terms. But whatever the context and purpose of the meeting or series of meetings, the same assortment of recognisable types tends to emerge:

- Cool and confident members, who stick to the facts, follow the arguments and make constructive contributions.
- Aggressive and impatient members, who often interrupt and are quick to take offence.
- Peacable and relaxed members, who have no axe to grind and whose main concern is to suggest compromises.
- Nit-pickers and know-alls, who constantly raise 'points of order'.
- Sheep-like members, who are anxious to please and confirm, and readily back down if challenged.
- Clowns, who try to turn everything into a joke.
- Dead-beats, who are there because they have nothing else to do.
- Bored and silent members who just want to get away.

The success or failure of a meeting depends as much on how the various personalities present blend and interact as on how efficiently it has been prepared and structured. The main responsibility for ensuring that the participants make relevant contributions and feel reasonably satisfied with the outcome falls on the chairman, particularly in the type of occasional or one-off meeting which is not serviced by all the usual committee officers.

Committee officers

Chairman

The chairman's role extends beyond presiding at meetings. It is the most powerful and prestigious post in any organisation and is often hotly contested. The chairman sometimes has to exercise sole authority on behalf of the organisation, and to be its chief representative to the world outside. So the post involves a wide range of duties and responsibilities both between and during meetings.

Between meetings

- Keeping an overview of the organisation's objectives, monitoring progress and suggesting new initiatives.
- Representing the interests and image of the organisation, e.g. to the media and the public, and at official occasions.
- Supervising the administration in consultation with the secretary and other officers, i.e. checking on arrangements for meetings and functions, and approving agendas, minutes, etc.
- Being well informed by commissioning reports, both oral and written, and by seeking ideas and comments from key people both within and outside the organisation.
- Dealing with complaints and emergencies.

During meetings	• Ensuring that meetings start and finish on time.

During meetings
- Ensuring that meetings start and finish on time.
- Introducing topics clearly and in logical order.
- Summarising each item before moving on to the next.
- Drawing out contributions from other members, and preventing them from being repetitious or acrimonious.
- Obtaining clear decisions, either by general consent or majority vote. Sometimes the chairman will decide an issue on which there has been a tie in the voting by exercising a *casting vote*.

These are just some of the many and various social and administrative skills required of a good chairman. He performs a role rather similar to the conductor of a band; having to assemble the players, keep them in tune, bring them in on time and fade them up and down, and guide them to a harmonious conclusion.

> *NB* Since many organisations are chaired by women, the neutral terms *Chairperson* or *Chair* are increasingly used. During meetings the traditional forms of address, *Mr or Madam Chairman*, can be replaced by *Mr or Madam Chairperson*.

Secretary

The Secretary is the scribe and servant of the organisation. All the administration and paperwork pivots around him – or usually her – so the secretary must be efficient, patient and punctual, and be able to write quickly and correctly. In business and the public services the secretary is highly trained and well paid; whereas in clubs and voluntary organisations he or she is often an overworked 'dogsbody'. (Voluntary unpaid secretaries and treasurers hold 'honorary' posts, and are recorded in the minutes as *Hon. Secretary* and *Hon. Treasurer*.) The main duties and responsibilities of the Secretary are listed below. (Secretarial students should also consult the *Exam Guide to Office Practice and Secretarial Administration*.)

Between meetings
- Receiving instructions and suggestions from the chairman and others on items for the next meeting.
- Drawing up the agenda of the next meeting in consultation with the chairman, and mapping out the content of subsequent meetings.
- Booking and confirming the venue for the next meeting.
- Circulating the notice of meeting and agenda, together with relevant reports and papers.
- Writing the minutes of the last meeting, to be confirmed by the chairman and circulated to members.
- Keeping a correct and up-to-date minute-book.
- Checking that all decisions minuted are followed up and implemented.
- Dealing with routine correspondence and telephone calls.

During meetings	● Preparing the room, and bringing all necessary papers, including spare copies for forgetful members.
	● Listing the names of those present. (In large meetings either taking a count of non-committee members, or circulating an attendance book.)
	● Taking intelligible notes of the proceedings, either in shorthand or longhand, making sure that records of decisions and votes are clear and accurate.
	● Feeding the chairman with information and advice on procedure and speakers.
	● Explaining points of factual detail to the meeting.

Treasurer

The treasurer's main duty is to manage the finances of the organisation. The ideal treasurer should obviously be competent and accurate with figures, and be able to present financial information clearly and intelligibly both to fellow-experts and to innumerate idiots. He should remember that some members will be embarrassed to ask questions which show up their ignorance of financial matters. He should be prudent and therefore cautious of ambitious schemes, but without being automatically negative. As well as explaining why things cannot be done he should try to find ways and means whereby things can be done.

Between meetings	● Keeping careful records of all financial transactions, including invoices, receipts, bank statements, etc.
	● Monitoring the financial implications of the organisation's activities.
	● Preparing a full financial report and balance sheet, getting it independently audited, and presenting it at the AGM.
During meetings	● Explaining the financial aspects of items on the agenda.
	● Pointing out the financial implications of schemes and policies.

Many organisations have **additional officers**, e.g:

● **Vice-chairman**, to deputise when the chairman is unavailable.
● **Minutes secretary**, to take notes and write minutes (Usually a professional.)
● **Membership secretary**, to collect subscriptions and keep records of names and addresses.
● **Social secretary**, to arrange functions and outings.
● **Committee members**, who are either representatives of departments, or (in voluntary organisations) elected by the membership.

4. PAPERS

This section introduces the *principles* of the documentation of meetings; *examples* of documents are shown later in the chapter.

Most large organisations are governed by documents which define their structure and objectives, and guide the procedure and conduct of their meetings:

Constitution	All registered charities, trade unions and political parties, etc. have a formal document defining their objectives, legal status, membership and other characteristics. They are usually written in complex and solemn legal language. Most clubs and voluntary organisations also have formal constitutions.
Articles of association	These are the rules required by company law governing the objectives, activities and procedure of companies.
Standing orders	These include a list of rules governing the calling of meetings, and the procedure and conduct of debate. If a member considers that an item has been conducted contrary to the rules, he can raise a point of order by referring to the relevant entry in the standing orders (See also the *Exam Guide to Business Law*.)
Committee papers	A great deal of time can be wasted at meetings through mismanagement of the paperwork. If members are laden with piles of lengthy reports and wordy minutes, they will often fail to read them thoroughly in advance, and spend half the meeting hastily consulting them. If the papers are too few and sketchy, they will ask unnecessary and ignorant questions. Committee papers should therefore be as concise and informative as possible.

Documents common to most meetings:
(a) Notice of meeting.
(b) Agenda.
(c) Minutes or summary report of last meeting.

Additional documents for more detailed meetings:
(a) Chairman's agenda.
(b) Background papers and reports.

(a) Notice of meeting	Notices should be sent out well in advance (in the case of company general meetings there is a statutory minimum notice) and they should include:

- the name of the organisation and type of meeting, e.g. AGM, committee meeting, etc.;
- the time, date and place of the meeting;
- the name of the secretary.

(In informal organisations the notice is often written at the top of the agenda paper.)

(b) Agenda	The agenda of a meeting is like the synopsis of a play, with each item representing the act and scene number. The order in which items are placed on the agenda is crucial. Urgent matters should be taken early, yet ample time should be allowed for controversial or detailed matters which form the centrepiece of the meeting. Some items cannot be decided until other related matters have been dealt with, and some key people may be unable to stay for the whole meeting, so the chairman will occasionally have to change the order during the meeting itself.

Agendas can be divided into three Acts or sections:

- opening routine items;
- main business;
- closing routine items.

A minimal AGM agenda:

1. Chairman's opening address.
2. Apologies.
3. Minutes of last AGM.
(4. Matters arising. This item is often cut.)
5. Annual reports and accounts.
6. Election of officers/appointment of directors.

The minimal agenda of a sports and social club committee:

1. Apologies.
2. Minutes of last meeting.
3. Matters arising from the minutes.
(4. Correspondence — additional item on some agendas.)
5. Officers' reports.
6. New business, e.g. proposals.
7. Any other business. (AOB)
8. Date of next meeting.

These items can be expanded with appropriate detail, e.g. by specifying the reports and indicating their main subject-matter:

5.1   Treasurer's Report

The deposit account stands at £...... which will
be insufficient to meet the cost of the proposed
bar extension. Discussion of possible fundraising
activities.

The chairman and secretary will often prepare a more detailed **chairman's agenda** with additional notes on who will speak on which items, how long to allocate to each item, and what outcomes or decisions are needed.

Minutes

Format for minutes

There are three accepted formats for recording meetings:

1. **Reports of meetings** do not follow the usual format of minutes, but simply extract and summarise the main conclusions reached and why. Often used to report the results of deliberations in one organisation to other interested organisations; also circulated to participants after conferences, and to the press after newsworthy meetings.
2. **Resolution minutes** in which the decisions only are recorded. Used in a business context where those not at the meeting are told only the results, without any account of the discussion.
3. **Narrative minutes** which record decisions and votes, and summarise the discussion, and occasionally identify participants by name.

Some organisations include an **Action column** down the right-hand margin for the names or initials of the people responsible for implementing the decisions taken. But whatever the style and format adopted, the minutes should always make it clear who is supposed to be doing what.

If you are asked to write minutes in an exam you should adopt narrative style unless instructed otherwise; an Action column is often appropriate, and may gain extra marks. The recent tendency at all levels is to give more and more background material, leaving you with less detail to invent. However, you still have to be careful to make sure that any invented details are plausible and match up with the content of the question. For example, do not pretend that a small club has £100,000 in the bank, or record more votes than there are members present. The agenda provides the synopsis of the plot; the list of those present is the cast; and the minutes are the flat and factual summaries of the ensuing dialogue.

Rules for writing minutes	The rules for efficient minute-writing are fairly straightforward.

1. Follow the order of the agenda, using the same numbers.
2. Give each item an appropriate heading, and leave a clear line between items.
3. Be concise: summarise the gist of the discussion rather than giving a blow-by-blow account of who said what and when.
4. Use reported speech, e.g. *the treasurer proposed opening an account with the Bradifax Building Society to finance the extension to the clubhouse*, **not** *'I propose ...,' said the treasurer*.
5. Make sure that decisions are precisely recorded and accurate on details, e.g. *Unanimously agreed to invest £9,750 in a Bradifax Extra Interest Account to finance the extension to the clubhouse*.
6. Use the appropriate wording for recording decisions. (This is often the trickiest part for examinees and inexperienced secretaries.)
    (a) *Agreed to/that ... wording of decision ...* Appropriate for informal meetings when no vote was needed.
    (b) *Carried by X votes to Y, or Lost by Y votes to X (or Carried: X–Y, Lost: Y–X)* This convention assumes that you have already quoted the proposal/motion under debate.
    (c) *Resolved: that ... wording of the full and precise decision ...* The word used for recording decisions of meetings with executive or delegated powers.
    (d) *Recommended: that ... wording of the full and precise decision ...* The word used for recording decisions of meetings without executive or delegated powers.
7. If several items emerge from matters arising or AOB separate them into items (a), (b), etc.
8. Avoid the repetition of the word *said* by using variants such as *argued, insisted, suggested, urged, queried*, etc. Employ handy phrases to introduce arguments, e.g. *some members argued that ..., whereas others doubted whether ...; Mr X raised the matter of ...*

9.   Sound neutral: do not criticise or ridicule contributions.

So the outline shape of the **minutes** of that minimal agenda of a **sports and social club committee** would unfold as follows:

It is advisable to underline a handwritten heading.

Minutes of Committee Meeting held at 7.0 pm on 12 March 19.. in the clubroom.

List of those present. (Or names of committee and number of members.)

1.   Apologies. Names. (Reasons for absence might also be recorded.)
2.   Minutes of last meeting. After factual amendments (if any) note that they were confirmed as a correct record and signed by the chairman.
3.   Matters arising. A brief mention of the points raised, and any further developments.
4.   Correspondence. The gist of letters read out or reported by the secretary, and how they were dealt with.
5.   Officers' reports. Summaries of reports and subsequent discussions and decisions under headings, and where appropriate, divided into subsections, e.g. Extension to the clubhouse; bar prices.
6.   Visit to Ideal Home Exhibition. Hire of coach, number in party, time of departure, etc.
7.   Annual fête. Summarise preliminary plans. Maybe set up a subcommittee to finalise arrangements.
8.   AOB. Brief mention of minor points made, e.g. announcements.
9.   Date of next meeting. Time, date, place.

5.   PROCEDURE

If you have little or no experience of meetings you may at first find the formal procedure rather pompous and unnecessary, and wonder why a reasonable group of people cannot conduct a civilised and constructive discussion without petty rules and conventions. Yet even small and informal meetings need some kind of structure to stop people straying from the point or all talking at once. At the very least they will usually need a chairman to guide them through the agenda.

The larger the meeting the more need there is for orderly procedure; otherwise people will start arguing or chatting among themselves, the common thread of discussion will be lost, and participants will feel they have wasted their time. Also, the more people there are wanting to contribute, the more pressing the responsibility of the chairman to keep an eye on the clock and get through the business on time.

A skilful chairman will insist that speakers address their comments 'through the chair' so that they can be shared by everyone present, but without being unduly heavy-handed. He should vary his manner to suit the type and purpose of the particular meeting; being brisk or relaxed, severe or jovial, speaking little or at length, as the situation demands. It is important that participants have respect for the 'authority of the chair' and accept the necessity for structured discussion.

The main reasons for formal procedure are:

●   to ensure that everyone gets a fair hearing;

- to keep the discussion to the point at issue;
- to provide a cool and rational atmosphere for decision-making;
- to keep within a reasonable time-limit.

This is how a formal meeting would proceed through a typical agenda.

1. Apologies	The chairman announces the names he has received, and perhaps the reasons for absence, and asks if any other apologies have been sent via members present.
2. Minutes of last meeting	The chairman asks if there are any factual corrections before asking the members if it is their wish that they be signed as a correct record.
3. Matters arising	The chairman invites comments and follow-up questions from members about the minutes of the previous meeting. Those wishing to speak on this or any other item usually indicate by raising a hand. This item provides **continuity** from one meeting to the next. Members pick up loose ends, check on further developments, query whether decisions have been implemented, etc.
4. Correspondence	The secretary is invited to report on or read out any letters received. Members then comment and decide if and how to reply.
5. Reports	Officers are invited to make oral reports, or to introduce written reports. Debate may ensue, after which the chairman has to establish whether members agree formally to *accept/adopt* a report or to ask that it be rewritten. Reports for information only are *noted* (see also Ch. 7).

6. (7, 8, etc.) New business/proposals	The chairman introduces each topic in turn. If a proposal has come from a member he will invite him to introduce the motion. (The seconder might speak immediately afterwards or wait until later.) The chairman will then invite discussion, and if there is controversy, will try to alternate speakers from each side. It is customary for the chairman to remain neutral during debates, unless he has initiated the proposal, in which case he will try to persuade the meeting.
	
	    Amendments to motions under debate should be taken in the order of being proposed and seconded, and must be settled before the original proposal – now the *substantive motion* – is decided. (See the example on p. 135.)
	
	    Finally, he should sum up the discussion and judge whether or not the issue can be decided by consent. If there is no agreement he puts the proposal to the vote and declares it carried or lost. The chairman does not usually vote, but if there is a tie he may settle the issue by using his *casting vote* (see glossary on p. 130).

7. Any other business	The chairman should rule out of order those items which repeat previous business, and suggest that any important new items should be put on the agenda for the next meeting. AOB should be the slot for minor matters which do not merit a specific agenda item. (Many formal bodies do not include this item, e.g. the board of governors of a college.)
8. Date of next meeting	If the particular group does not already have a pre-arranged schedule of meetings, the date is decided after members have consulted their diaries and discussed alternatives.

(For further discussion of informal group discussions and meetings, see Ch. 9, p. 152.)

CONFERENCES

Many of the principles involved in **meetings** can also be applied to **conferences,** albeit on a much larger scale. So you should consider again the five Ps outlined earlier in this chapter, and make the appropriate adaptations.

Why?	**Purpose**	• To inform/learn about recent developments in a particular professional or commercial field. • To pool ideas. • To provide an occasion for useful contacts.
What?	**Power**	• No power to make and implement decisions, but often influence subsequent decisions by those with power.
Who?	**People**	• Delegates representing relevant organisations. • Individuals with an interest or expertise in the broad theme of the conference and/or specific topics in the programme. • Guest speakers.
How? *When?*	**Papers**	• Circular letter of invitation with outline programme and instructions. • Detailed programme and further information about venue, social events, outings. • 'Conference pack' containing background papers, name-badge, full and final details of main and 'fringe' events. • Report of conference circulated later.
How? *When?*	**Procedure**	• Usually open with a full/*plenary* session with speakers and audio-visual aids. • Division into smaller groups to discuss specific topics. • 'Buzz-groups', 'brainstorming sessions', 'fringe' events. • Final *plenary* session with reports back from groups.

ORGANISATION

The arrangements needed for a successful conference are extremely complex, sometimes involving the hire of several hotels or an entire university campus to accommodate a thousand or more delegates from all over the world for up to a week. Even modest gatherings of about a hundred people for one day require very careful planning and detailed administration. Many professional and secretarial candidates will have covered the organisational aspects of this topic in other parts of their course, e.g. RSA Office Skills Applied, and will be expected to apply their factual knowledge in communication questions set in a conference context. (See *Exam Guide to Business Studies* and *Exam Guide to Office Practice and Secretarial Administration*.)

Some large companies organise annual conferences for employees as part of their internal communication policy (see the extract from *Kellogg's News*, Ch. 3, p. 19). Relevant information on other aspects of this topic can be found in the chapters on Oral Communication (Ch. 9), Visual Communication (Ch. 10) and Public Relations (Ch. 10).

GLOSSARY OF TERMS

Ad hoc. 'For the purpose of'. Applied to meetings convened to deal with specific matters and which are then disbanded.

Adjourn. To break off a meeting before completion of business, and resume later.

Amendment. A proposed change to the wording of a motion. Amendments must be voted on before the original motion, and if carried written into the motion.

Casting vote. Additional vote cast by chairman in case of a tie in voting.

Closure. The cutting short of debate by the passing of a motion from the floor 'that the motion now be put'.

Convene. To call people together for a meeting.

Co-opt. To invite a non-member to serve on a committee, often without the right to vote.

Ex officio. Having the right to attend a committee without election because of an official position.

Extraordinary meeting. A special meeting called to consider an urgent or serious issue.

Lie on the table. A matter which is left for the future, and not acted on.

Motion. The correct term for a proposal while it is being debated. The term 'resolution' is sometimes used instead.

Nem con. No one voting against, but some abstentions.

Point of information. The interruption of debate by a member wishing to draw the chairman's attention to a relevant fact.

Point of order. The interruption of debate by a member seeking the chairman's ruling on a breach of correct procedure, e.g. personal insults, overlong speeches.

Proposer. One who proposes a motion and speaks first.

Proxy. A vote cast by a member on behalf of an absent member or shareholder.

Quorum. The minimum number of members required to make the meeting valid.

Resolution. The word used for a motion which has been passed.

Seconder. The member supporting the proposer of a motion.

Sine die. 'Without a date', indefinitely. Applied to adjournments.

Substantive motion. A motion that has been amended.

Ultra vires. Beyond the powers of the meeting.

Unanimous. All voting in favour.

Note: This list excludes some obscure terms and a number of terms which are explained elsewhere.

Fig. 8.3   Notice of Meeting

FLINTWOOD FURNITURE LTD

There will be a meeting of the Management Committee on Monday May 18 1986 at 3 pm in the Conference Room. The Agenda is attached.

J. Wright, Secretary.   Extension 350

Fig. 8.4   Alternatively the notice could be included above the agenda. The example below also shows the right-hand column of a chairman's agenda

---

FLINTWOOD FURNITURE LTD

The next meeting of the Management Committee will be on Monday May 18 at 3 pm in the Conference Room.

AGENDA

1. Apologies for absence.   *T. Lyle away on a course.*

2. Minutes of meeting held on 15 April.   *6. Query on figures.*

3. Matters arising from the minutes.   *8. Check on polishing machine.*

4. Correspondence.   *Letter from Masford College re work experience and day-release. MD on college governors.   (15 mins)*

5. Training Policy.

   To consider the following proposal from Victor   *T. Hinton likely to oppose.*
   Reston, seconded by Sally Garner: 'That the
   Manager Committee request the Board of Directors   *Ask Personnel to do detailed*
   to establish a Training Department to co-ordinate   *report for June.   (20 mins)*
   current and future training needs.'

6. Staff Restaurant.   *Expect complaints. G. Fitch to explain finances.   (15 mins)*

   To receive a report from Mr Fitch on running costs.

7. Retirement of Joan Bateley.   *Might be difficult to fix convenient time for party because clashes with visit of German reps.*

   The Managing Director's secretary is retiring on
   May 26 after 15 years' service.

8. Any other business   *F. Jones on about vending machines again. Cut short because discussed at March meeting.   (5 mins)*

9. Date of next meeting.

FLINTWOOD FURNITURE LIMITED

Minutes of the **Management** Committee Meeting held on Monday May 18 1986 at 3.00 pm in the Conference Room.

PRESENT: Mr John Wilson (Chairman)   Deputy Managing Director
             Mrs Jean Wright (Secretary)   Office Administration Manager
             Mr Paul Thompson   Production Manager
             Mr Victor Reston   Sales Manager
             Mr Robert Hinton   Chief Purchasing Officer
             Mr Gordon Fitch   Assistant Accounts Officer
             Mrs Frances Jones   Senior Secretarial Supervisor
             Miss Sally Garner   Assistant Personnel Manager

In attendance: Miss Juliet Williams

1. Apologies for absence.

   Mr Tom Lyle was away on a course.

2. Minutes of meeting held on 15 April.

   Item 6. The figure for micro-ovens should be £1,940, not £1,540.

3. Matters arising from the minutes.

   Mr Thompson reported that the new polishing machine had been installed.

4. Correspondence.

   A letter had been received from the Head of the Management and Business Studies Department of Marford College asking for help in providing work experience placements. Mr Kent, Personnel Officer, would be in favour if his department were given enough time to prepare a suitable scheme.

   10 copies of the College prospectus were enclosed drawing our attention to opportunities for day-release for craft apprentices.

   Agreed to explore both matters further and to consult the Managing Director, who is a Governor of Marford College.

   S. Garner
   J. Wilson

5. Staff Training.

   Mr Reston outlined current problems with various training schemes. He argued that the present arrangements were too complex, and that there was insufficient consultation between departments. Trainees were not always given adequate super-vision, and were not set precise enough objectives. Department Managers were too busy to attend to day-to-day problems of trainees, let alone think about future needs. He was of the firm opinion that Flintwood needed a Training Department to co-ordinate training and draw up long-term plans. Miss Garner reported that the Personnel Department supported the appoint-ment of a Training Officer since they did not have sufficient time or expertise to devote to detail.

Mr Hinton thought a new department was unnecessary, since current problems were due mainly to recent changes in the Government's Industrial Training policies, and were therefore of a temporary nature.

After thorough debate it was <u>resolved</u> by 5 votes to 2 that the Personnel Department prepare a detailed report with costings in time for the next meeting.

J. Kent
S. Garner

6. <u>Staff Restaurant</u>.

(a) The secretary reported that Mrs Palmer has just resigned as Catering Manageress, but would work out two weeks' notice. Miss Garner reported that morale among catering staff was low.

(b) Miss Garner had received a number of complaints from employees about the size of portions and lack of choice. Mr Fitch insisted that running costs were up on last year, and any improvements would have to be reflected in prices.

After discussion it was <u>agreed</u> to advertise the Catering Manager's post at a higher grade in order to attract applicants qualified to introduce the necessary changes.

S. Garner

7. <u>Miss Bately's retirement</u>.

It was <u>agreed</u> that the Managing Director, would present a cut glass bowl at a sherry reception on Friday 26 May at 5.00 pm in the Conference Room.

J. Wright to organise collection and reception
F. Jones to buy bowl

8. <u>Any other business</u>.

(a) Mrs Jones protested about the prices of drinks from the vending machine. She warned that more and more members of her section were bringing their own vacuum flasks. Mr Fitch pointed out that at 10p per cup, the drinks were already selling at cost, so no reduction was possible. The Chairman ruled that since this matter had been fully debated two months ago the situation be monitored and put on the July agenda.

(b) Miss Garner reported that David Watson (Accounts) had obtained a distinction in his A.A.T. examination, and that she had sent him a letter of congratulation.

9. <u>Date of next meeting</u>.

The next meeting will be on 14 June at 2.00 pm in the Conference Room.

Signed .... (Chairman)

Date:

Notes on Fig. 8.5

Under the list of persons present at the meeting the term 'in attendance' refers to non-members attending the meeting to assist with its business. In this case, Miss Williams is a member of the secretarial staff with the job of taking notes and assisting the committee secretary with the minutes.

In the last paragraph of item 5 'resolved' could be simply recorded as: '*Resolved 5–2*'. If a final decision had been made, the precise words of the resolution would have been reproduced in full. (See Fig. 8.7).

| **Alternative layout** | Typed minutes are often presented with section headings in the *left* margin as shown below. |

```
Apologies for          Tom Lyle was away on a course.
Absence:


Minutes of             Item 6. The figure for micro-ovens
last Meeting:          should be £1940, not £1540.
```

Fig. 8.6 Extracts from a district council's standing orders

```
              RULES OF DEBATE FOR COUNCIL MEETINGS
                     Motions and amendments
14. A motion of amendment shall not be discussed unless it has been proposed and
    seconded, and unless notice has already been given in accordance with Standing
    Order 6 it shall, if required by the Mayor, be put into writing and handed to
    the Mayor or Chief Executive before it is further discussed or put to the meeting.
                       Seconder's Speech
15. A member when seconding a motion or amendment may, if he then declares his
    intention to do so, reserve his speech until a later period of the debate.
                  Only one member to stand at a time
16. A member when speaking shall stand and address the Mayor. If two or more
    members rise, the Mayor shall call on one to speak; the other or others shall
    then sit. While a member is speaking the other members shall remain seated,
    unless rising to a point of order or in personal explanation.
                       Content of speeches
17. A member shall direct his speech to the question under discussion or to a
    personal explanation or to a point of order.
                        Length of speeches
18. No speech shall in the case of the mover of a motion exceed fifteen minutes in
    length or in any other case ten minutes in length without the consent of the
    Council given by reason of the exceptional importance of the subject ...
                       Amendments to motions
20. An amendment shall be relevant to the motion and shall be either:
    (a) to refer or refer back a subject of debate to a committee for consideration
        or re-consideration;
    (b) to leave out words;
    (c) to leave out words and insert or add others;
    (d) to insert or add words;
    but such omission, insertion or addition of words shall not have the effect of
    negativing the motion before the Council.
```

Notes
14.   The notice required is one week.
15.   It is usually advisable for the seconder to 'hold his fire' until he has heard the counter arguments.

16. Points of order and explanation are defined in the glossary on p. 130.
17. Speakers are often challenged for being irrelevant.
20. This rules out simple negatives, e.g. if the motion were 'That hire of the Guildhall . . . be raised by £2.00 per hour', it would be unacceptable to insert the word 'not'; but would be in order to amend £2.00 to £2.50.

Fig. 8.7 Extracts from the minutes of a district council meeting

---

NOTICE OF MOTION

84/24. CUTS IN HOUSING BENEFIT
Councillor Brown moved and Councillor White seconded the following motion, notice of which had been given pursuant to Standing Order 6:

'This Council condemns the cuts in housing benefit due to take effect in April and November 1984 which will seriously affect pensioners and low-income families. This Council is also concerned that further changes to the Housing Benefit Scheme will increase disruption and uncertainty whether correct benefit payments are being made. It therefore resolves that representations be made to the Association of District Councils on the effect of the changes on the City's rent and ratepayers and that the ADC and the City's MPs be pressed to support changes to make more equal the support to tenants and those with mortgages by limiting to the standard rate of tax the tax relief on mortgages to restore the cuts in housing benefit.'

Councillor Black moved and Councillor Grey seconded by way of amendment the substitution of the following for the above motion:

'This Council views with concern further changes to the Housing Benefit Scheme but urges the Government in considering any changes to increase tax thresholds so as to offset reductions in housing benefit.'

On a show of hands 9 members voted in favour of the amendment and 28 against and the amendment was declared lost.
Councillor Green moved and Councillor Rose seconded by way of further amendment the insertion of '(i)' after the words 'pressed to support changes' in the third paragraph of the motion and the addition of the following thereto:

'(ii) to increase tax thresholds so as to offset reductions in housing benefit'.

On the show of hands 36 members voted in favour of the amendment and none against and the amendment was declared carried.
RESOLVED (with 28 members voting in favour and none against)

(1) This Council condemns the cuts in housing benefit due to take effect in April and November 1984 which will seriously affect pensioners and low-income families.
(2) This Council is also concerned that further changes to the Housing Benefit Scheme will increase disruption and uncertainty whether correct benefit payments are being made.
(3) Therefore, representations to be made to the ADC on the effect of the changes on the City's rent and ratepayers and that the ADC and the City's MPs be pressed to support changes—

(i) to make more equal the support to tenants and those with mortgages by limiting to the standard rate of tax the tax relief on mortgages to restore the cuts in housing benefit;
(ii) to increase tax thresholds so as to offset reductions in housing benefit.

Fig. 8.8 Extract from the programme of a 4-day conference organised by the Royal Institute of Chartered Surveyors

DIARY OF EVENTS

Saturday 6 October

0930 **The Creation of a Property Investment**
A graphic demonstration and panel discussion concerning the efficient application of computer techniques to the several phases of property development, from initiation of the scheme to ultimate sale.
A demonstration and discussion will also deal with the relevance of the computer to property management and will illustrate techniques of performance analysis.

Speakers: Ronald Clarke FRICS
Cyril Sweett & Partners, London
Ian Northen FRICS
Capital & Counties plc, London
Jonathan Strong ARICS
Electricity Supply Pension Scheme, London

Computer Exhibition
Chartered Surveyors, whether managing/servicing in local government, property company or private practice can do so with a micro or a mini. Main-frames now are for ministries. A 'live' exhibition by a number of computer suppliers who are experienced in surveying applications will be at the conference hotel. A range of machines and software will be demonstrated to illustrate valuation, agency, investment and development appraisal, cost planning, taking off and bills of quantities as well as general applications such as word-processing and accounts.

1300 LUNCH

1430 **Optional visit to Castle Howard Estate**

To include plant centre; forest tree nursery; arboretum; Shaw Wood (an example of group planting and under planting with original hardwood canopy); Coneysthorpe Village illustrating aspects of property conversion; caravan and camp site; lake amenities and fishing; Park Farm dairy herd of two hundred.

Sunday 7 October

1030 **FINALE**

From Semaphore to Satellite
The changing world of the international fine art auctioneer — experiences and predictions
by Christopher Weston FIA Scot
Chairman, Phillips

1130 **Closing Address**
by The President

1200 **Conclusion of Conference**

Social Programme
running concurrently with technical sessions

(C) North Yorkshire Moors
Nunnington Hall, a large 16th Century manor house, is being specially opened on 6 October for the RICS. Situated on the banks of the River Rye it has been a much loved family home since 1562 and is now run by The National Trust. The Hall is particularly famous for its unique Carlisle Collection of twenty-two miniature rooms, each room one-tenth life size. Coffee will be served in the Dining Room before travelling by coach across the moors via Hutton-le-Hole to Grosmont for lunch on board private Pullman carriages of the North Yorkshire Moors Railway; a rare opportunity to sample a bygone era of luxury rail travel. This fascinating journey passes through the heart of the National Park. The train journey will terminate at Pickering where the coach will be waiting to return to York.

Conference Banquet at Castle Howard
—an evening never to be forgotten
A very special evening awaits at Castle Howard. On arrival guests will be presented with a copy of the Guide Book for a private tour of the house which will culminate with a Champagne Reception in the Great Hall. Guests will then go in to Dinner in the Long Gallery, lit with chandeliers, graced with flowers and laid with fine linen, china and silver.
Dress: Dinner Jacket *Seating:* Round tables of 10
During the evening a male voice quartet from York Minster's choir will sing to the accompaniment of a pianist and violinist.

(See also *Exam Guide to Office Practice and Secretarial Administration*.)

(Source: RICS October 1984. Copyright is held by the Royal Institution of Chartered Surveyors. Conference Administrator: Sue Nickson)

D. RECENT EXAMINATION QUESTIONS

A quick 'quiz-type' question which can be answered briefly in note-form.

Question 1 List the main reasons for having an agenda for a committee meeting.

Question 2 Prepare a list of points to enable a junior secretary to take and transcribe Minutes of a Committee Meeting effectively.

(12 marks)

(LCCI PSC Office Organisation and Secretarial Procedures, 1984)

Question 3 How and why does a meeting become adjourned? Consider the effect of adjourning a meeting.

(18 marks)

(ICSA Law and Procedure of Meetings, 1983)

Question 4
Notice of
Meeting
and
Agenda

This question is Q4 of the case study paper shown in Ch. 1, p. 2.

SITUATION

The last partners' meeting before the shrub event is to take place in Mr Grant's office on 4th July at 10.00 a.m. You have been asked to prepare the agenda; you have asked the partners what they wish to include.

Mr Grant wants the final arrangements for the shrub week to be on the agenda, including Mr Eden's opening. He also wants the donation to the St Jude's Trust to be included and wants to consider the next season's Christmas tree order.

David Lewis (Chief Accountant) wants to discuss the renewal of the Van der Geesingen bulb contract and also the outstanding debts from 1981–82.

Andrew Newman (Personnel Director) wants to discuss temporary staff appointments during shrub week.

Christopher Davidson (Sales and Marketing Director) sends his apologies for absence (he will be at the Norwegian Conifer Convention in Trondheim) but wishes to table his report on the possibility of selling garden barbecue equipment at the centre.

ASSIGNMENT

Write the notice of the meeting and the agenda. The appropriate standard agenda items should be included as well as the above items.

(*notice*: 5 marks)

(*agenda*: 15 marks)

(RSA Communication Stage II, 1984)

Question 5

A longer and more demanding question asking for some invented detail. It would be difficult to give an adequate answer in much under 500 words, but the content is fairly straightforward so you should be able to complete an acceptable answer within 40 minutes.

Prepare minutes for the following meeting, amplifying the information given:

THE WICKBOROUGH COUNTY PLAYERS ASSOCIATION

Notice of Annual General Meeting

The fourteenth Annual General Meeting of the Wickborough County Players Association will be held in Room 224, The Guildhall, Castle Street, Wickborough, on Tuesday 16th June, 1981, at 7.0 p.m.

AGENDA

1. Apologies for absence
2. Minutes of last AGM
3. Matters arising from the minutes
4. Secretary's Report
5. Treasurer's Report

6. Elections: Officers of the Association
    Members of the Committee
    Honorary Auditor
7. Any other business

Synopsis

Five named office holders and committee members attend, along with twenty-five ordinary members. Guy Harding (committee) is in hospital. The Secretary pays tribute to the late James Hennessey, OBE, formerly patron of the Association. The year's main stage productions are reviewed: Alan Bennett's *Habeas Corpus,* Bolt's *A Man for All Seasons* and Alan Ayckbourn's *Absent Friends*; two principal players are praised for their performances. The organised visits to Stratford and one other (named) venue are mentioned. Current membership is reviewed and Jean Johnson's special efforts in forming a Youth section of the Association are noted. The Secretary concludes on a note of optimism.

The Treasurer points to certain items in the Income and Expenditure A/c and Balance Sheet before the members, notably the disturbing rise in costs of props and costumes. Fund-raising efforts are called for. Some stage lighting needs replacing. While *Habeas Corpus* and *Absent Friends* show a profit of £17.26, *A Man for all Seasons* has made a loss of £64.33.

The final financial position is announced. Elections and re-elections take place. Any Other Business includes an enquiry whether money can be had from the local authority; the Secretary will explore possibilities. The Committee and all who have helped them with productions are thanked.

(20 marks)
(RSA DPA, 1981)

E. OUTLINE AND TUTOR'S ANSWERS

This sort of question probably carries half-marks, and since you have only 5 minutes you should think in chronological order, i.e. before, during and after meetings, e.g:

Outline answer 1

(a) To collect and define items for discussion.
(b) To inform members of content of meeting.
(c) To impose order and structure.
(e) To give an idea of likely length of meeting.
(f) To help secretary write minutes.

Outline answer 2

Although this question appears in a secretarial exam, the principles could apply to all candidates expected to have covered this topic. So you should be able to go through a chronological survey of the practical procedures involved in preparing and servicing regular committee meetings, and quickly remember six points worth two marks each, e.g:

(a) The agenda and all other relevant papers.
(b) A list of all present and a seating plan to identify speakers.
(c) A minute-book or other suitable paper for notes.

(d) Fast shorthand and other note-taking skills.

(e) Knowledge of conventions of presentation.

(f) Knowledge of special terminology.

Outline answer 3

An example of a more demanding social/psychological type of question often set in professional exams.

You are being tested here on your understanding of the context of a technical term. A three-paragraph answer is required, corresponding to (a) *how*; (b) *why*; and (c) *the effects*.

(a) The chairman announces that he proposes to call a pause in the proceedings at this point, and to reconvene the meeting later. The pause may last only a few minutes or several days. A meeting may be automatically adjourned if its business is unfinished by the time specified under standing orders, unless the meeting votes to suspend the relevant rule.

(b) A meeting may be adjourned for one of the following reasons:
  (i) Disorder;
  (ii) Deadlock;
  (iii) New and urgent developments relevant to the debate;
  (iv) Time allowed under standing orders is exceeded.

(c) The effects will usually depend upon the reason:
  (i) The cause of disorder will be dealt with and tempers allowed to cool.
  (ii) The parties will go back to consult the appropriate authority, e.g. a trade union delegation will consult its executive.
  (iii) The meeting will resume at a time and in condition to despatch unfinished business.

Tutor's answer 4

An example of the type of practical skill type question often set in O/A English Language Business and Professional Use and in secretarial exams, in which you are asked to interpret instructions and convert them into a conventional format. The Notice is very straightforward and should take you only 5 minutes; the agenda will take more thought and reference back through the paper. Since this is the last of 4 questions in a case study paper, you will need to draw material from previous questions, but by this stage you should be familiar with the developing situation. (See Ch. 4 Q2, Ch. 7 Q2 and Ch. 13 Q1.)

(a) Notice of Meeting.

Eastview Nurseries

MEMORANDUM

To: M. Grant
    D. Lewis
    A. Newman
    C. Davidson

From: Managing Director

The next partners' meeting will be held at 10.00 a.m. on 4 July in the Boardroom.

Your name

AGENDA

1. Apologies for absence. D. Davidson will be at the Norwegian Conifer Exhibition in Trondheim.

2. Minutes of the Meeting of 18 June.

3. Matters Arising.

4. Correspondence.

5. Outstanding debts from 1981–2. (D. Davidson)

6. Van der Geesingen bulb contract. (D. Davidson)

7. D. Davidson's report on possibility of selling garden barbecue equipment. (To be tabled)

8. Donation to St Jude's Trust. (M. Grant)

9. Final arrangements for Shrub Week. Ted Eden has agreed to open the event. (M. Grant)

10. Temporary staff appointments during Shrub Week. (A. Newman)

11. Date of next meeting.

12. Any other business.

Tutor's answer 5

WICKBOROUGH COUNTY PLAYERS ASSOCIATION

Minutes of the Fourteenth Annual General Meeting of the Wickborough County Players Association held on Tuesday 16th June, 1981 at 7.0 p.m. in Room 224, The Guildhall, Castle Street, Wickborough.

Present: James Finch (chairman), Betty Brown (hon. secretary), Sam Carter (hon. treasurer), Liz Roberts (social secretary), Jane Lawson (publicity officer), and 25 members.

1. <u>Apologies for absence</u>.
An apology was received from Guy Harding who was in hospital. Agreed to send get-well card.

2. Minutes of the 1980 Annual General Meeting.
The minutes of the AGM held on 20 June 1980 which had been previously circulated, were approved by the meeting and signed by the chairman as a correct record.

3. <u>Matters arising from the minutes</u>.
In answer to a question from the floor, the chairman confirmed that Sir Peter Willis had accepted the invitation to become patron of the association.

4. <u>Secretary's report</u>.
The secretary paid tribute to the late James Hennessey, OBE, formerly patron of the association, who died in January. Mr Hennessey's constant support and expert advice would be sadly missed.

There had been three main productions: Alan Bennett's *Habeas Corpus*, Robert Bolt's *Man for All Seasons* and Alan Ayckbourn's *Absent Friends*. All had attracted good audiences and had been favourably reviewed in the local press. Special praise was due to Anne Taylor and Bob Stewart for their excellent performances in *Absent Friends*.

The visit to Stratford had been particularly rewarding because of the excellent production of *Twelfth Night*. *Hayfever* at the Nottingham Playhouse was disappointing, owing to a last-minute cast change.

Current membership stood at 50, an increase of 14 over 1980. Jean Johnson had worked hard to build up a youth section which now has 24 enthusiastic members.

Plans were well advanced for the next two productions, and the association can look forward to another successful season. The chairman thanked the secretary for her encouraging report.

5.   Treasurer's report.
A statement of the association's accounts had been circulated which showed a reasonably healthy financial position. The first two productions had made a modest profit of £17.26, but *A Man for All Seasons* had incurred a loss of £64.33. Subscriptions had brought in £248. A book sale in March had raised £75, and bar profits during the three productions were £123. The balance at the bank on 31 May 1981 was £396.

On the debit side, the treasurer emphasised the steep rise in the costs of props and historical costumes. Also, some of the stage lighting was nearing the end of its useful life and would probably need replacing during the current financial year. This indicated a need for additional fund-raising events.

The treasurer's report was approved by the meeting.

6.   Election of officers
Chairman: James Finch was unanimously re-elected.
Secretary: Betty Brown resigned owing to pressure of work. Jo Baker was nominated by Dan Bates, seconded by Bob Stewart; elected *nem con.*
Treasurer: Sam Carter agreed to continue for one more year.
Committee: Guy Harding had resigned because of ill-health. Jean Richards was proposed by Jim Graham, seconded by Jane Powell. Heather Wood was proposed by Liz Roberts, seconded by Bob Stewart. Heather Wood was elected 19–16, with 2 abstentions.
Hon. auditor: Jim Thompson.

7.   Any other business
The secretary will investigate the possibility of a grant from Wickborough City Council.

The chairman thanked the committee for their efforts over the past year, particularly Betty Brown, who had been secretary for 4 years. The producer Jim Graham was congratulated on the excellent standard he had attained.

There being no further business the chairman closed the meeting at 10.15 p.m.

Signed .... (chairman)

Date: B. L. Brown
                                                             Secretary

---

Notes on   Match the style of date used in the question.
the tutor's   3. Less usual at AGMs than at ordinary meetings because of the time-lag and the nature of the
answer   business.
              4. Some minor details could have been omitted. Note that it is customary for officers to be

thanked for annual reports which are then formally 'approved', 'adopted', 'accepted' or 'noted'.

5. When overall figures are not given, make sure your inventions are plausible but not too complicated.

6. You need at least one vote to demonstrate the technicalities. Presentation of this item varies from full lists of nominees, proposers and seconders, with voting figures, to simple entries like 'J. Baker elected'. In formal bodies it may be a legal requirement to record the figures, whereas informal bodies may simply note 'X was elected by a large majority'. If a paper ballot is held, this fact should be noted.

7. 'The local authority' is too vague; translate it into a plausible reality. If no other business is raised omit this heading.

Indicate the space for the chairman to sign and date the minutes at the next AGM.

F. A STEP FURTHER

However much you read about meetings and however diligently you memorise the terminology and procedures, there is no substitute for observing how it all works in practice. The most easily available opportunity is provided by local government. Your nearest public library will have a list of forthcoming meetings open to the public.

Committee meetings give you a good chance to judge chairmanship, to observe the interaction of members, and to study the role of officers. Students on management courses should benefit from hearing the presentation of oral reports, often with displays of visual material, e.g. plans of buildings. Secretarial and administrative students should observe the role of the officer responsible for taking the notes and distributing the written reports and other papers.

Agendas are usually available, and the subsequent minutes are placed in public libraries, so you can compare your memory or your notes of the proceedings with the official version. This will also enable students on more advanced courses to see how complex modes of enumeration are presented and cross-referenced.

For all levels **class simulation** is a valuable exercise. Although role-playing may appear artificial and embarrassing to start with, it is surprising how it can almost turn into a real meeting once the participants enter into the arguments. The group will need a few basic guidelines:

1. Choose a type of meeting close to the experience of as many of the class as possible, e.g. a sports and social club committee.

2. Allocate roles tactfully but firmly. The chairman usually 'emerges' by agreement, but the secretary must be someone who writes quickly and accurately. The treasurer should be someone who can present financial information realistically. There are several other useful roles, e.g. social secretary, membership secretary and departmental representative. Make sure everyone has some pre-arranged role, even if it is just to raise an awkward question under Matters Arising or AOB.

3. Spend about 2 hours fixing the agenda and preparing brief reports to be delivered orally, correspondence, awkward questions, etc.
4. Enact the meeting as realistically as possible, preferably recorded on tape or video. The secretary should take notes.
5. Discuss everyone's 'performance' and perception of others, and how and why items were settled.
6. Duplicate the secretary's notes and circulate.
7. Everyone writes the minutes.

Students following fairly high-level business studies/management courses (e.g. BTEC year 3, DPA, ICSA, IPM, etc.) need to think about the *oral presentation* of information and argument to meetings, with or without visual aids. (See also Chapter 9).

Secretarial students should get plenty of practice in taking notes (shorthand and long-hand) and converting them into minutes. The LCCI produces films for this purpose, though class simulation is perhaps even more useful since it more accurately reflects the meanderings of actual meetings. (See also *Exam Guide to Office Practice and Secretarial Administration*.)

General books

People and Communication (2nd edn), Evans D W. Pitman 1984. Chapter 5 – Excellent diagrams and examples. Complete glossary.
Mastering Business Communications, Woolcott L A and Unwin W R. Macmillan 1983. Chapter 7.

Specialist books

Hours into Minutes, BACIE booklet 1981.
A Guide to Effective Meetings. The Industrial Society 1982.
How to Take Minutes (8th edn), Graham-Helwig H. Pitman 1977.
Meetings, their Law and Procedure, Lawton P and Rigby E C. Macdonald and Evans 1984.

Films

Meetings Bloody Meetings; Video Arts.
More Meetings Bloody Meetings. Entertaining dramatisations starring John Cleese, with an emphasis on the chairman's role.

Chapter 9   Oral communication

A. GETTING STARTED

Most of you will spend much more of your time at work speaking and listening to colleagues and customers than in writing and reading. You will need to discuss tasks and problems, to ask for and to give information, explanations and instructions. So clear and friendly oral communication is essential for achieving co-operation and the positive teamwork needed to solve problems efficiently.

Oral communication is even more of a two-way process than written communication. In a face-to-face encounter the other person's response to what you say is immediate and you can see and hear their reaction. If you are a sensitive *speaker* you will be able to adapt your message according to the response it receives. If you are a sensitive *listener* you should be able to understand exactly what you are being told, and then make an accurate and appropriate response. Sensitivity involves an awareness of the personality and role of the other person.

You can become a more effective oral communicator by:

(a) getting practice in different situations whereby you have to get your message across by talking directly to an individual or audience;

(b) increasing your awareness of the importance of interaction, i.e. the response of the other party or parties, and your adaptation to that response.

All examining bodies expect some awareness of the skills required and problems involved in oral communication. You may be asked general/'quiz-type' questions about the nature of oral communication, questions requiring comment on a situation or dialogue, or questions asking for a set of notes for a talk or an interview. Some exams have an oral test carrying up to 25% of the marks. These cannot be left to common-sense guesswork. You will need rehearsals based on recent exams, often including practice on the telephone.

B. ESSENTIAL PRINCIPLES

The circumstances in which people speak and listen to each other can be roughly divided between:

1. **One-to-one** (face-to-face or on the telephone);
2. **One-to-group** (lectures, seminars, talks, oral reports at meetings);
3. **Group-to-group** (meetings, discussions).

(Interviews are covered in Chapter 12.)

1. ONE-TO-ONE COMMUNICATION

(a) Face-to-face

When only two people are involved rather than several, transmission, reception and feedback follow each other immediately. The speaker is a transmitter and a receiver of information almost simultaneously. Speed and flexibility are essential, because even while you are receiving a message you are analysing it, interpreting it and planning your return message. The advantage is that you can tell by the other person's verbal and non-verbal responses whether your message has got across; the disadvantage is that you do not have time to polish your answers as you would when writing.

Barriers to effective one-to-one conversation

Lack of interaction

One of the participants may be so busy trying to think how to get his views across that he does not listen to what the other is saying. This often happens when people are so convinced of their own view and opposed to the other's that neither party is willing to listen to something they regard as untrue or unwelcome. Or one of the parties may be too distracted or preoccupied with another matter to engage with the topic under discussion. Without interaction and a willingness to listen, effective two-way communication is impossible.

Antagonism — evident or underlying

Differences in age and background, or in position within the organisation, can lead to misunderstandings which may result in open (expressed) antagonism or underlying (unexpressed) antagonism. The way supervisors speak to those underneath them needs to be firm but sensitive, while juniors need to be obliging but not obsequious, i.e. without sucking up.

Harmony between colleagues leads to efficiency of communication and achievement of tasks. Discord and antagonism cause misunderstandings and mistakes, leading to frustration and delay.

Failure to understand

Differences in background, speech, knowledge, education, etc. might lead to misunderstandings. You should be aware of the dangers of using language which goes over people's heads, or, conversely, of 'talking down' to them. There are often difficulties of accent or vocabulary even between people of the same nationality, but English speakers have particular problems when communicating with foreigners. We tend either to assume that they understand English and rattle on as usual, or patronise them by speaking loudly and slowly, rather than adapting and clarifying the message and speaking normally.

(b) Talking on the telephone

Effective and economical use of the telephone is increasingly important as national and international business transactions become faster, and more complex. Quite junior members of staff may find themselves talking on an internal extension to a close colleague one minute, and the next minute be expected to ring a customer 5,000 miles away. Internal calls can be cheap and chatty; but external calls are expensive, so you have to make good use of every second.

Checklist for effective telephone communication

Outgoing calls

1. *Before dialling*
   - Consult the files and note down points you want to make and questions you want to ask. This will help the switchboard operator to put you through to the appropriate person, and ensure that you are ready to state your purpose.
   - Have a notepad ready to write down any points made by the person at the other end. Write the name and number at the top. If you do not get through first time you do not want to look everything up again.

2. *During the call*
   - When the other party answers clearly state your name, organisation and status: e.g. 'This is Janet Brooks of Barnes and Thompson — Mr Green's secretary.'
   - Be careful to speak clearly, taking special care over numbers, e.g. fifty/fifteen. Remember that your listeners cannot lip-read.
   - In the absence of gesture and facial expression use your tone of voice to convey attitude and emphasis.
   - When discussing important and/or complex matters you may need to summarise and check at intervals to make sure your message has been fully understood.
   - End by summing up, referring to future action and written confirmation.

3. *After the call*
   - Note down the name and extension number of the other party in case you have to ring back. Summarise the main points needing further action.
   - Finally, enter dates in the diary, and write any memos or letters arising from the call.

Incoming calls

- If the call comes through direct, start by giving the name of your organisation. If it comes through a switchboard, state your department, then your name and/or position. This procedure helps both parties to decide whether or not the call should be transferred.
- If the person required is unavailable, ask if you can help instead. If your offer is declined, make arrangements for a further call.
- If you need to consult files or find another person, offer to ring back. Do not leave your caller hanging on without an indication of how long you are likely to be.
- If you have to take a message for someone else, make sure it

Fig. 9.1 A telephone message

Wrong   Right

Telephone Message

Taken by: *Susan Smith*
Date: *14 May*
Time: *11.50*
Name of caller: *Mr. Jones - Arko Lighting*
Subject: *Delay in despatch of fluorescent bulbs*
Message: *Please phone Mr. Jones (021-440-3587) before 5pm. today.*

contains all the relevant details: caller's name, company, job title, telephone and extension number, subject of call, time to ring back. Many organisations have specially printed message pads. See also *Exam Guide to Office Practice and Secretarial Administration*.

2. ONE-TO-GROUP

(a) ORAL REPORTS

People who attend a lot of meetings often complain of being buried in written reports. Often, a brief oral report supported by a single sheet of notes or figures is all that is needed, e.g. the presentation of sales figures, an update on progress on a building project, etc. Frequently, events move too fast for the preparation of written reports. For example, a machine may break down and be repaired or replaced in the space of a few days, and the engineer in charge may be called in to give an account. He may then be instructed to write a detailed report, perhaps including recommendations as to how to avoid a repetition.

Structure

Oral reports should follow the same outline and shape as written reports:

(a)   A brief *introduction* explaining why you are giving the report, who asked you to do so and when, and what you are going to cover.
(b)   A succinct *development* of each aspect in turn.
(c)   A *summary* with *conclusions*, stating where necessary what needs to be decided and giving the options.
(d)   Be prepared to answer *questions* when you have finished speaking.

Delivery

Oral reports are usually delivered to small groups of people used to working together, so the approach can be more intimate than when giving a talk to an audience. Unless you need to point to charts, plans, maps, etc. you will not usually be expected to stand up. You should pause between each point and glance round the table to see how people are responding. Take particular note of the chairman's expressions and gestures – he may want to speed you up, slow you down or ask a question.

Use the appropriate language for the particular audience. You should sound informal and relaxed, but not sloppy or slangy. If you know that some of those present will be unfamiliar with technical terms – spell them out, or pause and offer to explain where necessary.

(b) GIVING A TALK

During your time at school and college, and perhaps at work, you will have heard hundreds of, and no doubt have noticed the characteristics of good, bad and indifferent lecturers and speakers. Maybe you have had to give a talk yourself on some occasion, or are reaching a position at work where you will be expected to explain aspects of your job or technical knowledge to trainees.

This is not the place for a comprehensive guide to public speaking; you can find more information in section F at the end of this chapter. But you do need to be ready for exam questions about giving talks, e.g. at conferences, and questions asking for notes for a talk – including the use of audio-visual aids. Some candidates will be asked to give a short talk as part of an oral exam. So you should remind yourself of the key points of preparation and delivery.

Preparation

Even the most experienced speakers feel nervous about an impending talk, particularly if the audience will be large or unfamiliar. The surest way of gaining confidence is to prepare methodically for the ordeal.

1. Clarify the purpose and content of talk. Information? Instruction? Entertainment? Persuasion? Inspiration? A combination of two or more of these?

2. Find out about your audience. How many? Who are they? Well informed or ignorant? Bright or dim? Friendly or cool? A mixture.

3. Find out about the venue. Large or small? Comfortable or uncomfortable? Good or poor acoustics? Blackout and power points for A/Vs?

4. Establish exactly how long the talk should be. Will there be questions?

5. Collect your material and arrange it in logical order.

6. Write notes on postcards or a spiral notepad, using underlining and colour for emphasis. Note cues for quotes or anecdotes. List audio-visual aids and handouts in right margin at appropriate points (see Fig. 9.2).

Fig. 9.2 Notes for a talk

TITLE: *Business Sponsorship of Sport*

DATE *12 April*   TIME *2.0pm.*   VENUE *Harrogate Conference Centre*   AUDIENCE *20-25 Public Relations Officers*

TIMING	STRUCTURE	A/VS Slide projector O/H projector
2 - 2.10	Intro: Famous Examples Joke: Non-smoking snooker players.	Slides
2.10 - 2.20	Total Sponsorship Breakdown per sport	O/H - graph 1980 - 86
2.20 - 30	Need for sponsorship	O/H - costs & attendances
2.30 - 40	What you get out of it. Brand-name Image Prestige	Publicity slides Handouts of adverts.

and so on......

Structure

Remember that the measure of a successful talk is not what you say, or even how you say it, but how much is remembered. Immediately after most talks people remember on average 20% of what was said, 30% of what was shown, and 50% of what was said and shown. Two weeks later their recall has usually faded to about half of that proportion. So your main objective is to be as memorable as possible.

● Start strongly and positively with a challenging statement or question, or appropriate example, illustration or quotation.
● Give an outline of what you are going to cover.
● Develop a few points thoroughly. Do not try to cover too much ground.
● Illustrate your points with examples and stories. Allow your audience to relax from time to time.
● Spend the last 5 minutes summing up and posing one or two challenging questions.

Delivery

Your main aim is to appear confident and relaxed and to sound clear and interesting. If you keep your eyes glued to over-detailed notes you will look stiff and sound monotonous and unnatural. If you rely on the odd glance at a few random jottings, you will look flustered and sound woolly. The well-prepared speaker will be able to pace his talk in a way which arouses and maintains interest.

The most successful speakers have four essential qualities:

Confidence = being well prepared through command of subject-matter, assessment of venue, and expectations of audience.

Charm = looking at the audience in a friendly manner; using humour, gesture and tone of voice to project personality.

Content = having something interesting to say, based on efficient notes, and enhanced by relevant and striking visual illustrations.

Clarity = following a well-planned structure and speaking audibly; pacing delivery to match the concentration span of the audience by using pauses, emphasis of key words, alternations of fast and slow speech. Occasionally repeat or recap main points.

Of course all these qualities are linked. Strong, well-organised content will make you feel more confident, and therefore speak clearly. Confidence will pull you through unforeseen problems, e.g. a larger or smaller audience than expected, technical problems with A/V aids, etc. Charm can sometimes disguise the lack of the other three qualities, but never rely on it — particularly if you are preparing for an oral exam. (See mark-scheme for question on p. 154).

AUDIO-VISUAL AIDS

Virtually every subject can be made more interesting, and therefore memorable, if it is made to appeal to the eye as well as the ear. The main uses of A/V aids are given under the headings below.

1. To convey information

- Giving a breakdown or analysis of complex information, e.g. statistics.
- Showing the stages in a process, e.g. progress of a building.
- Illustrating points about people, places or objects.

(Best for this purpose: overhead projector transparencies, films, videotapes, slide sequences, hand-outs.)

2. To reinforce the spoken word

A/Vs can be used to introduce the subject, to link one part of the talk with another, to summarise, or to pose a question. (Best for this purpose: transparencies, single slides, film clips, flash cards.)

3. To provide background information and atmosphere

A/Vs help to set the tone and mood. The choice will depend on the subject, the venue, and the size and nature of the audience. (Best for this purpose: static visuals such as models, enlarged photographs, posters, charts or chalkboard which can be left throughout the talk.)

Remember: too many different types of A/V in one presentation will be difficult to handle and may distract the audience. Stick to two or three. Keep them simple, and do not dash from one to another.

(A checklist of audio-visual aids is given in Fig. 9.3.)

Fig. 9.3 Checklist of audio-visual aids

Type	Audience size	Advantages	Disadvantages
Chalkboard Marker board	30 – 100	Usually available Keywords can be written up quickly Suitable for instruction and audience involvement No mechanical problems Simple diagrams can be easily drawn Colour can be used for clarity	Association with school Writers often unskilled Speaker has to turn back on audience Erasure often necessary, so permanent record is lost.
Flannel board Magnetic board		Good for simple visual display Items can be moved and superimposed	Fiddly Difficult to transport
Flipchart		Can be prepared beforehand Provides a cumulative record and recap Easy to transport	Speaker has to turn back when writing
Overhead projector	Over 100	Versatile Transparencies can be prepared in advance Can be written on while facing audience Can be rolled back for recap No blackout needed Masks and overlays possible	Special non-glare screen needed Heavy to move Can be noisy
Slides Film Video (large screen)	Over 100	Entertaining and colourful Details can be magnified Movement and sound	Possible technical hitches Needs blackout Breaks flow of talk

3. GROUP DISCUSSION

Working in groups often provides a more effective and stimulating approach to problems than relying on individuals and paperwork, so there has been an increasing trend for organisations to communicate information and reach decisions by talking in groups, either in informal discussions or in meetings.

- More ideas are forthcoming when people collaborate and interact than when they work alone. Discussion stimulates ideas and draws contributions from a wide range of individual talents. This is particularly true of *brainstorming* sessions, when everyone is encouraged to express ideas and make suggestions, e.g. in thinking up new products.
- Ideas can be analysed thoroughly and tested against differing viewpoints before being tried out in practice.
- Decisions are more likely to be carried out when people have been given the chance to participate.

(a) Informal groups

Colleagues in an organisation often meet for informal discussions, either spontaneously or by pre-arrangement. Usually the people involved know each other well and the subject for discussion is familiar. However, even in the most informal circumstances there are certain necessary conditions to make sure that people's time is not wasted:

- Everyone should be aware of what is going to be discussed.
- Everyone should be encouraged to contribute.
- Points should be relevant, and in logical order.
- The atmosphere should be friendly and relaxed, but not so cosy as to prolong discussion by social chat.

Should there be a leader?

In small groups of people who know each other well these conditions can often be achieved without there being an identified 'leader', but in larger gatherings, perhaps including strangers, it is usually wise to entrust someone with leading the disussion. The leader's role is to:

- Set out the topic to be discussed, and make sure the group sticks to the point.
- Encourage quieter members of the group to contribute.
- Curb dominant members by courteously cutting into monologues, and by turning the conversation on to new points.
- Sum up and restate questions at issue, to make sure everyone knows what has been decided and what is the next step.

(b) Formal groups

Discussions need to be formally structured when a lot of people are involved, when the business to be discussed is complex, when representatives of other groups are participating, or when the meeting is part of a regular administrative cycle, e.g. a board meeting, or the AGM of a club.

Meetings are often called by senior management in order to inform or instruct their subordinates. Generally, however, for internal meetings the current trend is towards a greater emphasis on two-way communication. Management seeks to obtain views and share facts so as to avoid conflicts and to prevent cliques developing.

Because formal meetings are often attended by a number of people with different roles and representing different interests, it is important to get through the business thoroughly yet quickly. Set procedures are usually followed to prevent sectional interests from blocking productive discussion and problem-solving, and to ensure that clear decisions are reached. (See Ch. 8 – Meetings.)

Participation in group discussion

Too many groups are dominated by the 'leader' and one or two forceful members. This is often because some people present feel overawed or ignorant, and so make little effort to participate. But even the most junior and inexperienced can take steps to improve their communication skills at meetings; no one need just sit there like a dummy.

- Prepare yourself by thinking about the topics to be discussed. Do some research. Make notes of any facts and figures to support your view.
- Anticipate possible opposition, and have an answer ready.
- Sound reasonable and friendly. Do not direct your points at anyone personally. Express agreement as well as disagreement, and praise the achievements and contributions of others.
- If you are interrupted or disregarded, do not give up or sulk. Try to raise the point again if there is a suitable cue.
- Use humour to get the meeting on your side and relieve tension.

NON-VERBAL COMMUNICATION

Up to 50% of an oral message is conveyed by facial expression, eye-contact, tone of voice, gesture and posture. We convey messages not just by what we say but how we say it, and when we are spoken to we look for clues to the feelings and intentions underlying the words. Often a message can be conveyed without a word being spoken – by a smile, a frown or a nod.

General theories of communication devote a great deal of attention to this 'body language', and to other factors which affect the spoken – and the unspoken – word, such as dress, location and atmosphere. For example, two colleagues discussing a problem in an office on a cold Monday morning dressed in formal suits, might respond stiffly to each other and make little progress; but on the sunny Friday afternoon they may return to the subject while leaning across a cafeteria table in their shirt-sleeves, and solve the problem in a friendly and relaxed manner.

Staff who have to deal directly with the public need to be constantly aware of the importance of non-verbal communication. A frown or a dismissive gesture from a bank clerk might cause offence and lead to a loss of custom; in a DHSS office it could cause an ugly time-wasting scene. British Rail took this problem seriously enough to set up a course for its Sealink ferry stewards showing them how to judge the mood of passengers waiting to be served by reading their 'body language', and how to adapt their approach accordingly.

In the exams under review in this book you are unlikely to find specific questions on non-verbal communication, but since it is sometimes relevant to questions on oral communication, you need to be aware of the basic principles.

A word of warning

Make sure you know the distinction between **oral** communication (the spoken word), **verbal** communication (involving the use of the spoken or written word), and **non-verbal** communication (by means other than words).

C. RECENT EXAMINATION QUESTIONS

It is obviously impossible to provide model answers for an actual oral test since you are never expected to memorise a talk; indeed, you would be penalised if you did. Nor can we entirely predict the course of a face-to-face or telephone discussion between you and the examiner. However, we can give you an idea of what to expect, and how best to prepare for your 'ordeal'.

Question 1

The RSA Diploma for Personal Assistants sets a demanding telephone test which carries 25% of the total communication marks, and which can make all the difference on the borderlines between pass and distinction or pass and fail. Candidates are given the background information 7–10 days beforehand which establishes your role within an organisation and hints at the sort of problems you are likely to have to deal with. Further papers, e.g. diary extracts, timetables, maps, etc. are provided 10 minutes before the test. These give valuable clues as to what to expect. During the test you will be expected to make or respond to 5 calls, usually 2–3 incoming and 1–2 outgoing, and write the relevant notes, within a total time-limit of 30 minutes.

After the last call you have about 5 minutes to write any notes/messages arising from the conversations.

An example

You are PA to the manager of a leisure centre. You receive: (a) a call enquiring about swimming courses in general; (b) an enquiry about a particular course, which involves looking up schedules and booking forms; (c) a caller complaining about a lapse of hygiene; after which you should make (d) an internal call to the person responsible. (e) That person is unavailable, so you have to leave an appropriate message.

The mark-scheme is extremely complicated, with marks allotted for the appropriate practical steps, inclusion of necessary detail, clarity, tone and manner. Candidates on this course will need several discussions and rehearsals for the test.

Question 2

Here we show a test consisting of a case study which you are shown 5 minutes beforehand, and a prepared talk which you have 48 hours to think about.

RSA COMMUNICATION IN BUSINESS II – Oral Test

Part One: Case Study – General information for all Candidates

In this part of the test, you will be asked to imagine that you are giving advice to someone, based on your knowledge and experience. You should read this general information and then your allotted case study. You will have about 5 minutes to prepare your material and you may make notes of up to 20 words. You will then be asked to present a report of up to about 2 minutes to an examiner and you may be asked supplementary questions for a further 1 to 2 minutes.

In each of the case studies someone who is about to change his or her job has come to you for advice about one aspect of his or her new post. Whilst you do not know anything of the details of that particular post, you should be able to offer some general advice and guidance.

(10 marks)

Part One: Case Study A

Imagine you have been approached by a friend who asks the following of you:

'Can you help me please? I'm starting a new job soon. It's quite a senior post but I know I can do the job well. The only problem is that I will be in charge of a number of people who are much older than me and some of them have much more experience of the type of work than I have. I'll be issuing a lot of instructions. What sort of problems could I have, do you think, and how can I get over them?'

Say what advice you would give to your friend.

Structure: 3 marks
Fluency and accuracy: 2 marks
Relevance: 5 marks
Total: 10 marks

Part Two: Talking on a prepared topic

As part of the Oral Test you will be expected to discuss with the examiner which aspects of your Communication Skills course are likely to be most useful to those who are about to take up employment in a business or commercial organisation.

You should consider which communication skills are most important to someone who is to make a career in business or commerce.

You should therefore prepare a statement which sets out your views in a logical manner; this statement should last for 2–3 minutes.

You will be permitted to take *notes* into the examination room and you will have to hand these in at the conclusion of the test. You will *not* be permitted to read a prepared speech. The number of words which may be used for your notes is limited to a maximum of 20.

After you have expressed your own ideas the examiner will discuss the subject with you for a further 1–2 minutes.

You will be assessed on the manner in which you present your material rather than on your knowledge.

Speech: 3 marks
Rapport: 2 marks
Structure: 5 marks
Total: 10 marks

Question 3   A practical question aimed at candidates for professional exams.

(a) Describe ONE recent development in audio-visual equipment

(10 marks)

(b) Discuss how this equipment can be used by the administrator to communicate more effectively in organisations.

(ICSA, 1985) (15 marks)

A question about a breakdown of oral communication, which also touches on problems raised in Chapter 3 and Chapter 8.

Les Howard was Sales Manager of Curtiz Biscuits and he had just had a very bad experience. An hour ago he had been at the monthly Managers' Meeting where he had to take a full ten minutes of criticism about his sales team's failure to do as well as the firm's chief competitor, Greenstreet.

He knew there was some justice in the criticisms but felt that he was being 'got at'. It was always the same at these meetings. Everyone seemed to be just looking for opportunities to run someone else down, everyone examining every statement to see whether they were being blamed for something, being used as a scapegoat for someone else's failures. He was sick of it. Still, he blushed to remember it. Waiting for the wave of comment to subside, and thinking how smug they all looked that it was someone else in the hot seat, he had grabbed at the first defence to come to mind. Picking on the firm's 'Chunky' caramel wafer, which he knew was his team's chief failure, he had answered that it was alright for everyone to blame his men but the truth was that, with this particular product especially, his team were trying to sell something which was of poorer quality than the Greenstreet product.

A hush had descended on the table and Les could still hear the dry voice of the Managing Director.

'If you think back three months Les, I'm sure you'll remember being at the meeting when I announced that Head Office had notified us they had changed suppliers. That we would in future buy our caramel wafers from Ansdale, who would put our label on their products — exactly the arrangement Greenstreet have had with them for over a year. We all know that you knew about that fact at least.'

Les could only admit that he knew about the Ansdale/Greenstreet arrangement. But how could he have attended the relevant meeting and still missed such an important announcement about his own firm?

Accepting that Les Howard had attended the relevant meeting, discuss any communication problems you feel are raised by the above situation, including possible solutions.

(25 marks)

(Scottish Higher National Diploma in Secretarial Studies, 1983)

D. OUTLINE AND TUTOR'S ANSWERS

99% of candidates will have some insight into this problem through arguments with their parents, and many will have had further experience of relationships with older people in weekend and holiday jobs. Remind yourself of all the times you have been proved right — or wrong — in disputes on practical matters. Recall how you felt and how the older person might have felt. Then imagine a typical office and place this imaginary friend into a specific role, e.g. a young secretary with higher qualifications than some of the older clerical staff. Now decide on a structure for your talk. Remember — you will only be able to cover a few aspects of this wide subject, so confine yourself to two or three points.

Outline answer 1 (a) Part one: Case study	**Your notes**	**What you might say**
	PROBLEMS: work methods outdated, resentment of change and of you personally.	Take familiar example, e.g. office might have been run on same lines for years. Old-fashioned methods, e.g. . . . dominant or touchy personalities, e.g. . . . perhaps near retirement? (Give an example from your own or a friend's experience.)
	Overcome by:	
	TACT – consult	Don't rush your changes. Take time to get to know procedures and colleagues.
	FIRMNESS – show confidence	If necessary, stress what needs doing and why. Make you position clear or 'pull rank'.
	FRIENDLINESS – smile!	Get to know your colleagues, and show you are willing to listen and learn.
	(20 words)	

Questions are obviously hard to predict, but expect to be followed up on points you have made, prompted on points you left out, and/or asked to expand on your own experience and observations.

(b) Part two: talking on a prepared topic	**Your notes**	**What you might say**
	Awareness of range of skills needed.	The course has given me an overview of communication methods and problems – written, oral, visual, use of telephone and information technology.
	Writing – letters, memos, documentation of meetings.	I would be able to produce professional memos, agendas and minutes; and other formats involving visual content, e.g. notices and leaflets.
	Oral – dictation, notes at meetings.	I have had regular practice in taking dictation, and an introduction to taking notes at meetings.
	Telephone.	Effective use of the telephone is essential in secretarial posts – perhaps 50% of the job. I have learnt the importance of a good telephone manner, and how to take messages.
	Information technology.	I have had some experience of word processors, photocopiers, etc, but expect to be trained on the job.

Outline answer 3

Apart from the chalkboard and pin-board, most audio-visual aids are comparatively recent, or have recently been improved upon. The most obvious (and most recent) example is **video**, which has developed rapidly over the last 10 years. A possible outline answer would be:

VIDEO
1. Technology available for last 10 years. At first rather cumbersome – heavy and primitive black and white cameras, needing battery recharge or long leads – 20-minute tapes. Complicated playback – poor picture quality. Now – light and flexible colour cameras – 40-minute tapes. Simple playback – good picture quality.

Most important recent developments – projection on to enlarged screen – improved sound – remote control – computer interface for showing graphics.

2. Uses for the administrator:
   (a) Training – showing ready-made videos which can be hired or purchased, e.g. Video Arts material; making 'in house' instructional videotapes – improving performance at interviews, talks, etc.
   (b) Invaluable for public relations presentations to customers and staff; provides excellent material for exhibitions and trade fairs.
   (c) Presentation of data to specialist groups. Video can now be linked directly to a computer. Exciting new development with great potential.

Tutor's answer 4
(a) Problems

Les obviously missed the Managing Director's announcement at the meeting 3 months ago about the change of suppliers because he was not listening. He gets so irritated and depressed by the bad atmosphere at these meetings that he must have 'switched off' at the crucial moment. Everyone seems more concerned to run each other down and 'score points' than to listen to each other and get things clear. He is particularly aggrieved about the Managing Director's insensitive chairmanship; he allows personal jealousies to distort discussion, 'makes announcements' without assessing reactions, and is then sarcastic if they are forgotten or misunderstood.

The documentation of these managers' meetings seems to be inadequate. Les himself obviously failed to take notes of the announcement, but he should have picked it up in the minutes and, if necessary, have raised the point under Matters Arising. Either no minutes were written and circulated, or Les did not receive them, or he failed to read them, or they were inaccurate or incomplete.

(b) Solutions

In the short term Les should apologise and explain to the Managing Director, but point out the frustrations he experiences at the monthly managers' meetings. He should accept the situation, express optimism about the new product, and promise his team's best efforts to improve sales. In the long term, the conduct and atmosphere of the meetings must be improved. The chairman should be less overbearing, and encourage participants to listen and contribute effectively. Minutes should be full and accurate and circulated in good time, and contain an Action column.

E. A STEP FURTHER

The best way to improve your oral skills is to participate in group discussion. College courses in communication should include a high proportion of oral work: informal discussion, role-play exercises, meetings and interviews. Take every opportunity to take plart in meetings of clubs, voluntary organisations and trade unions. You should also give critical attention to radio and TV talks, interviews, discussions and debates. If possible you should go to one or two local government committee meetings open to the public.

General books

Communication in Business, Little P. Longman 1983. Chs 13 and 15.
Mastering Business Communication, Woolcott L A and Unwin W R. Macmillan 1983. Parts of Chs 7, 8 and 9. Ch. 10 on audio- visual aids, and Ch. 13 on non-verbal communication.

Advanced level	*Effective Speaking*, Turk C. Spon 1985. An excellent book by one of the authors of *Effective Writing*. *A Guide to the Use of the Telephone in Business. Tips on Talking.* BACIE booklets. *The Use of the Telephone. Team Briefing.* Industrial Society booklets. *The Floor is Yours.* Mangement Training Ltd/British Institute of Management. Clear and detailed.
Films	*Effective Presentation. Making Your Case. Telephone Techniques.* Video Arts.

Chapter 10   Visual Communication

A. GETTING STARTED

The ability to communicate visually is becoming essential for success in many communications exams, both in specific questions on this topic and as part of questions on reports, leaflets and articles, where you might be asked to reinforce your text with some form of visual illustration. This recent emphasis on skill in graphical presentation is also evident in other subject areas, e.g. RSA Office Practice, RSA Secretarial Duties, A level Business Studies, RSA Background to Business, O and A level business studies, RSA Background to Business, O and A level sociology, and several others.

This trend reflects the widespread use of visual means to communicate with a mass audience, particularly now that computer graphics have made the techniques so much quicker and simpler. For example, we now take it for granted that election results on television are not just reeled off by a newsreader but are instantly translated into bar charts. The written or spoken word is often ignored or misunderstood, whereas picture messages can be taken in 'at a glance'. They can be effectively used to convey:

Immediacy: The saying goes that one picture is worth a thousand words. A press picture or TV film vividly conveys the essence of an event.

Impact: International road signs and danger signals cross language barriers.

Image: Symbols and logos help develop a corporate image which can be used on products and stationery, and in advertising.

(Source: British Telecommunications plc)

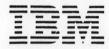

(Source: IBM United Kingdom Limited)

(Source: W.H. Smith and Son Limited)

● Visual humour can add impact and memorability.

(Source: Dalgety U.K. Limited. The Flour Grader Device is a registered trade mark of Spillers Limited.)

Information:
● Attractive presentation seizes and holds attention.
● The message of the written and spoken word is reinforced.
● Complex information is quickly and efficiently conveyed.

DANGER

This chapter is concerned with conveying statistical information by means of charts and diagrams. The use of logos in letterheads and publicity material is covered in Chapters 4 and 13. The use of audio-visual aids is outlined in Chapter 9.

B. ESSENTIAL PRINCIPLES

The main use of graphics in business information is to convey statistical information. Endless columns of numbers are indigestible and time-consuming to read and absorb. The same data presented graphically will be easier to understand and to remember. **Charts** can inform you at a glance about the past, present and possible future. Annual company reports now usually include a variety of charts, and many companies also produce a simplified largely visual version for employees. Local authorities distribute leaflets to householders explaining details of income and expenditure in diagrammatic form.

Exam questions on this topic are of two types:

(a) Those which give you a set of figures and ask you to reproduce them in visual form. Sometimes you will be told what sort of diagram to draw, and sometimes you will have to choose an 'appropriate' format.

(b) Those which ask you to interpret statistical information given diagrammatically, e.g. a line graph showing the incidence of fatalities and serious injuries in road accidents before and after the introduction of seat belts. Sometimes you may also be asked to apply your interpretation to support an argument, e.g. in writing a letter to the press in favour or against the compulsory wearing of rear seat belts.

(Some particularly demanding questions may ask you to draw a diagram, interpret it, and perhaps to argue a case as well.)

Candidates with only a shaky grasp of mathematics will obviously find type (b) easier than type (a). Provided they can extract the gist of the information from the diagram, they should be able to write an intelligent interpretation. However, employers and examiners are now demanding higher levels of numeracy, so it is essential that innumerate candidates make every effort to tackle this topic. The calculations and drawing involved are relatively simple.

You are usually asked to be 'reasonably' rather than 100% accurate, and you are not expected to produce multicoloured artwork to a professional standard. You should remember to equip yourself with the following items: a ruler, a calculator, a protractor, a compass, a fine point pen, a sharp pencil and a rubber. (Graph paper is usually supplied.)

An effective diagram should be:

● **Attractive:** it should be designed to grip the reader's interest.
● **Clear:** it should not be cluttered up with too many words or figures, and all labelling or text should be placed horizontally.
● **Simple:** you should avoid crowding too much complex information in one diagram.
● **Accurate:** unless the instructions make it clear that you are allowed to approximate, you should be as accurate as possible. If you are short of time it is better to complete a rough version than to half-complete an accurate version.

Note: You are unlikely to be expected to draw or interpret more than a few basic types of diagram in a communication exam. If you need to know about more specialised diagrams you should consult the reading list at the end of this chapter.

The list below shows how various forms of data are best presented.

What you want to show	What to use
1. Full and accurate numerical information. Detailed comparisons of figures	Tables
2. Trends in continuous information over a period of time, e.g. total sales 1980–1986	Simple line graph
Comparison of trends between two or more variables over a period of time, e.g. sales of different items 1980–1986	Multiple line graph
3. Comparison between totals over the same period of time, e.g. total sales January–March	Simple bar chart
Comparison between two or more discrete items over the same period of time, e.g. total sales of X and Y January to March	Multiple bar chart
Comparison between proportions of the total made up by two or more discrete items over the same period of time, or at a fixed point in time, e.g. comparative sales of items X, Y and Z, January–March, or during one month	Percentage bar chart
4. How a total is divided up between its component parts. Contrasts between the component parts of a total	Pie or cake chart
5. Procedure or instructions in a logical sequence	Flowchart or algorithm

1. TABLES

Fig. 10.1 Table

LIFE INSURANCE BENEFIT TABLE					
PLAN	A	B	C	D	E
MONTHLY PREMIUM	£10.00	£15.00	£20.00	£25.00	£30.00
AGE NEXT BIRTHDAY	LIFE COVER				
MALE / FEMALE	£	£	£	£	£
19–30 / 19–34	20,000	33,900	40,000	—	—
31–35 / 35–39	11,400	21,200	30,900	40,600	50,000
36–40 / 40–44	7,300	13,400	19,500	25,600	31,800
41–45 / 45–49	4,600	8,400	12,200	15,900	19,700
46–50 / 50–54	3,000	5,400	7,800	10,200	12,600
51–55 / 55–59	2,100	3,700	5,300	7,000	8,600
56–60 / 60–64	1,600	2,700	3,900	5,000	6,200
61–66 / 65–66	1,300	2,100	2,900	3,800	4,600
CASH-BACK BONUS	£1,800	£2,700	£3,600	£4,500	£5,400

Note how the addition of dividing lines clarifies this table.

The totals expressed in a **table** serve as summaries of the detailed information given in the columns and lead the reader to a systematic analysis under appropriate headings (see Fig. 10.1).

Questions including tables either ask you to interpret the figures or to reproduce them in a more effective visual format, e.g. as a graph or a pie chart.

Remember:
- Title and caption
- Headings in logical order
- Do not repeat symbols: £

	£
320 not	£320
245	£245

2. LINE GRAPHS

Line graphs consist of a number of points plotted then joined by a line. They show how changes in one quantity are related to changes in another quantity and often show a pattern of change over time, e.g. a patient's temperature graph, sales figures during a firm's financial year, a movement in share prices. The one quantity (e.g. temperature, sales or price) is presented in relation to another quantity (usually time). Time is usually shown across the bottom on the horizontal axis. The individual points are plotted and joined together by straight, not curved, lines.

Before drawing the trend lines draw your grid and decide your title.

Fig. 10.2 Basic grid for graphs

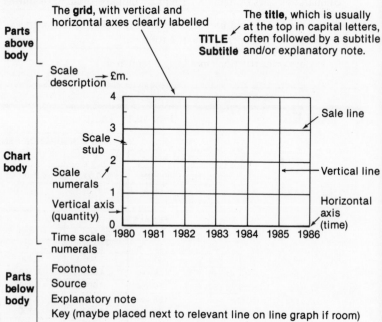

Note that the same type of grid is used for drawing bar charts.

164

Simple and multiple line graphs

Line graphs can be simple (Fig. 10.3) or multiple (Fig. 10.4).

Fig. 10.3 Simple line graph

Avoid cumbersome use of 000,000s by stating £m. in scale caption

Begin quantity scale at zero

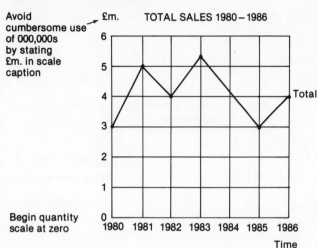

Fig. 10.4 Multiple line graph

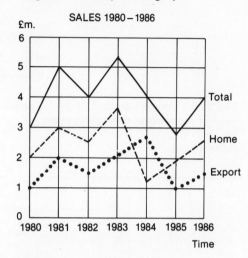

Differentiate lines by using two or more of the following devices, identified in a key.

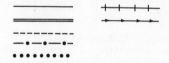

Advantages of line graphs	
	● A large number of values can be plotted in a compact space to give a visual comparison.
	● The movement of the lines show clearly the pattern and extent of change from week to week, month to month, year to year, and they can show gradual changes and trends which could not be shown in a bar chart.

Problems	
	● The impression given depends on the scales used − inappropriate scales are misleading.
	● They only show relative not absolute changes.

3. BAR CHARTS

Bar charts are also drawn from a series of figures or values plotted against a vertical and a horizontal axis. They emphasise the actual quantity and simple fixed values of subjects within a time period. Because they are so versatile they are widely used in company reports to emphasise different points of comparison. For example, a basic table like that below can be converted into several charts as shown in Figs 10.5 to 10.8.

Sales turnover and net profit before and after tax for Emex plc 1984–1986

	Sales turnover (£m.)	Net profit before tax (£m.)	Net profit after tax (£m.)
1984	25	4	2.5
1985	40	9	4.5
1986	32	6	3

Fig. 10.5 Simple bar chart showing sales turnover over three years

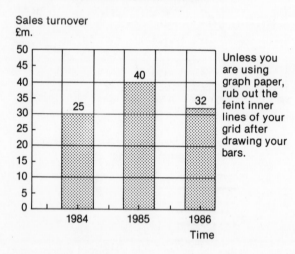

Unless you are using graph paper, rub out the feint inner lines of your grid after drawing your bars.

Fig. 10.6 Multiple bar chart showing the years separately

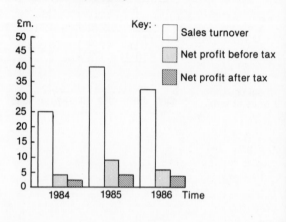

Fig. 10.7 Multiple bar chart showing the variables separately

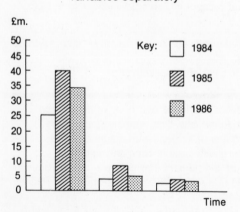

Fig. 10.8 Component and compound bar chart showing breakdown of sales

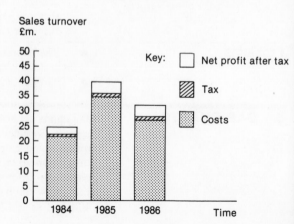

The three variables shown in Figs 10.6 to 10.9 could then be shown simultaneously, distinguished by means of colour, shading or hatching.

The data in the following table are shown in Fig. 10.9 in percentage rather than absolute terms.

Emex plc percentage of sales

	Cost (%)	Tax (%)	Net profit after tax (%)
1984	88	4	8
1985	84	6	10
1986	83	8	9

Fig. 10.9 Percentage bar chart showing net profit as percentage of sales

Percentage of sales

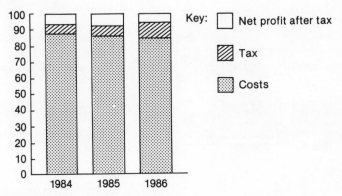

Advantages of bar charts	● They are easy to produce.
	● The separate bars clearly illustrate distinct units.
	● They can be turned on their sides which makes them easier to read.
	● On both vertical and horizontal bar charts two or more items can be shown side by side and within bars.
Problems	● It is difficult to read values accurately if the scale is small.
	● Only a limited amount of data can be shown – multiple bar charts are often overcrowded.
	● Changes over a period are shown less clearly than on a graph.

Remember:
● Bars should be exactly the same width.
● Labelling should be inside or above (for vertical charts) or at the ends (for horizontal charts).
● Extra clarity is achieved by marking the totals on top of the bars.

4. PIE AND CAKE CHARTS

A *pie chart* consists of a circle which represents a total subdivided into segments proportional to percentages of that total. It is a more graphic and attractive way of showing values than a single percentage bar, but harder to draw. If your exam is one which demands accuracy you will need a compass for drawing the circle and a protractor for measuring the segments. (There are special circular protractors for drawing pie charts.) Sometimes you may be given the circles ready drawn. A cake chart gives an extra dimension representing the total.

How to calculate a pie chart

1. Convert figures into percentages

2. Convert percentages into degrees (A circle has 360 degrees, therefore 1 per cent = 3.6 degrees)

Sales	£		%	Degrees
Product A	20,000 ...	$\dfrac{20}{200} \times 100 = 10$		$10 \times 3.6 = 36°$
Product B	80,000 ...	$\dfrac{80}{200} \times 100 = 40$		$40 \times 3.6 = 144°$
Product C	36,000 ...	$\dfrac{36}{200} \times 100 = 18$		$18 \times 3.6 = 64.8°$
Product D	64,000 ...	$\dfrac{64}{200} \times 100 = 32$		$32 \times 3.6 = 115.2°$
Total =	200,000			

Fig. 10.10 Pie and cake chart showing sales of four products in 1986

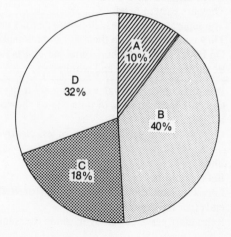
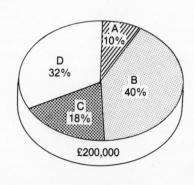

Advantages of pie charts	• A limited amount of information can be vividly conveyed to a general audience.
	• The comparative size of the components of a total is effectively emphasised.
	• Two pie charts of different size can illustrate different totals.

Problems	• Preliminary calculations are cumbersome.
	• It is difficult to differentiate more than four segments without the use of colour.
	• There is no scale to refer to.
	• It is harder to represent small differences in pies than in bars.
	• Changes in totals are less clearly conveyed by two or more pies than by two or more bars.

5. FLOWCHARTS AND ALGORITHMS

These show procedures or instructions in a logical progression, with a definite start and end to the linear sequence. Originally algorithms were designed to help computer programmers by analysing and breaking down an operation into sequential steps by using the binary systems of YES/NO decisions. Electronic equipment such as photocopiers often show algorithmic charts in their instructions to help users to diagnose a fault (see Ch. 5, p. 66).

The symbols on the left used in flowcharts and algorithms are similar to those used in computer programs.

Very complex information can be shown by flowcharts and algorithms. The main difference between the two is that whereas a flowchart usually shows only a *sequence* of steps or operations, an algorithm includes a *breakdown* of the decision-making element, leading to alternative routes at each stage. For an example of an algorithm, see Tutor's answer to Question 2, p. 176.

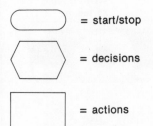

= start/stop

= decisions

= actions

= directions

C. USEFUL APPLIED MATERIALS

Pictograms

Pictorial images are often used to convey a simple message.

Fig. 10.11 Effect of Killit weedkillers

Effect of *Killit* weedkillers
(Source: Mast (Cambridge))

Company annual reports, particularly the simplified graphic versions for employees, are a good source of examples. Information is often conveyed within a witty image of a famous product, as in Fig. 10.12.

Fig. 10.12 Pictorial representation of company results

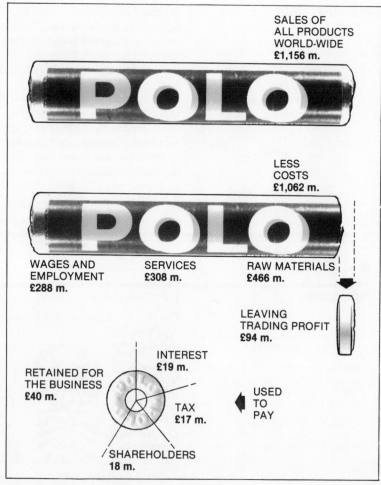

(Source: Rowntree Mackintosh plc, 1984)

Fig. 10.13 Algorithmic presentation of a pension scheme

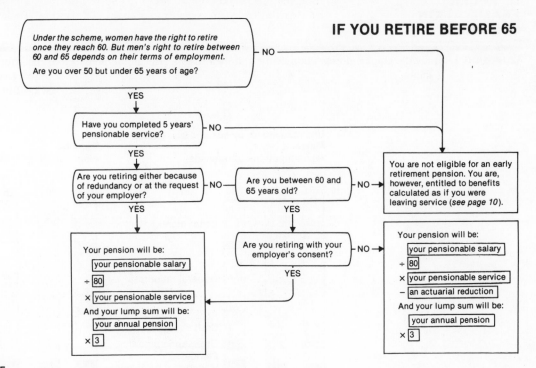

IF YOU RETIRE BEFORE 65

EXAMPLE

If you retire at 62 with your employer's consent, and your pensionable salary is £8,000 and your pensionable service is 30 years

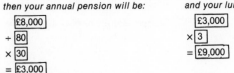

then your annual pension will be:

and your lump sum will be:

This algorithm was designed by Cambridge Communication Ltd, a firm which specialises in the clear presentation of information. It demonstrates how a block of indigestible prose can be 'translated' into a more easily digestible visual format. Here is the relevant extract from the original booklet:

Early Retirement Pensions

A member who has attained age 50 and completed five years' Pensionable Service and who retires before Normal Retirement Age at the request of his employing Institution (or a member who retires on account of redundancy) or a member who has attained age 60 and completed five years' Pensionable Service and who retires with the consent of his employing Institution receives a pension calculated at the rate of 1/80th of his Pensionable Salary for each Year of Pensionable Service up to the date of retirement. If retirement is after age 60 but before Normal Retirement Age but is without the consent of the member's employing Institution then, provided five years' Pensionable Service have been completed, an immediate pension may be granted calculated at the rate of 1/80th of Pensionable Salary for each Year of Pensionable Service but subject to an appropriate actuarial reduction.

In the operation of these provisions all female members will have the right to retire on or after attaining age 60 whereas for a male member this will depend on the terms of his employment or contract of service with his employing Institution.

(Source: Cambridge Communication Ltd.)

D. RECENT
EXAMINATION
QUESTIONS

Question 1 Study the graphic presentation below and then write a critical interpretation of the information it shows.

(10 marks)

(SCOTBEC, 1983)

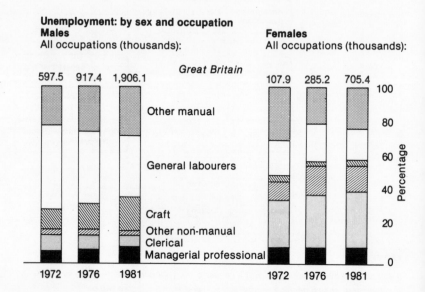

Unemployment: by sex and occupation
Males
All occupations (thousands):

Great Britain

597.5 917.4 1,906.1

Other manual

General labourers

Craft

Other non-manual

Clerical

Managerial professional

1972 1976 1981

Females
All occupations (thousands):

107.9 285.2 705.4

Percentage

1972 1976 1981

Source: Department of Employment

(10 marks)

(SCOTVEC, 1983)

Question 2 The following is a statement of overtime rates for different patterns of working. Convert this into algorithmic form.

(*a*) Overtime worked on a Saturday which ends before midnight will be paid at one and a half times day shift rates.

(*b*) Overtime worked on a Saturday which goes beyond midnight will be paid at one and a half times day shift rates for hours worked up to Saturday midnight and two times day shift rates for hours worked after midnight Saturday until midnight Sunday.

(*c*) Overtime started after midnight Saturday but finishing before midnight Sunday will be paid at two times day shift rates for hours worked PLUS day time rates for subsequent hours until 6 a.m.

(*d*) Rates for overtime worked outside the above hours will be found on Chart 16.

(10 marks)

(SCOTVEC, 1983)

Introduction

For the purposes of this Examination imagine that you are Miss Frances Fulland. You work for Cartland and Co. Ltd, a large store situated at 223–249 High Street, Yorkstone, Bedfordshire YO3 4CZ. The store has 22 buyers, each in charge of a department, and sells fashions, hosiery, toys, china and glassware, household and gardening goods, perfumery, jewellery, lighting and stationery. It also has special displays for periods such as Christmas, Easter and Summer.

You have been working there for about two years but six months ago were promoted from the General Office to be assistant to Mrs Rita Thames, the store's General Manager.

Mrs Thames is extremely busy and often has to rely upon you more than is usual at this stage in your career. This makes the work rewarding and interesting.

Drawing a line graph, pie charts and listing conclusions

SITUATION

Somewhat disturbed by the possibility of confrontation over allocation of floor space between the Toy Department, the Carpet Department and Soft Furnishings which between them occupy the whole of the Top Floor Mrs Thames decided to make herself acquainted with some facts. She took the Monthly Sales Figures for the year 1979–80 for the three Departments and gave you the totals. These were:

Toy Dept.	Jan. £3,000	Feb. £2,000	March £10,000
	Apr. £8,000	May £5,000	June £11,000
	July £8,000	Aug. £9,000	Sept. £7,000
	Oct. £8,000	Nov. £14,000	Dec. £25,000
	Total for the Year £110,000		

Carpet Dept.	Jan. £5,000	Feb. £6,000	March £9,000
	Apr. £8,000	May £8,000	June £5,000
	July £4,000	Aug. £3,000	Sept. £15,000
	Oct. £16,000	Nov. £13,000	Dec. £8,000
	Total for the Year £100,000		

Soft Furnishings	Jan. £2,000	Feb. £3,000	March £10,000
Dept.	Apr. £9,000	May £6,000	June £7,000
	July £4,000	Aug. £3,000	Sept. £8,000
	Oct. £10,000	Nov. £11,000	Dec. £7,000
	Total for the Year £80,000		

ASSIGNMENT

(*a*) On the sheet of graph paper provided plot all three sets of monthly figures superimposing the second and third sets on the first. Draw them so that each set can be clearly identified and compared.

(9 marks)

(*b*) Draw two pie charts one showing the division of sales in September and the other in December.

(6 marks)

(c) Assume that the area occupied by the Departments is normally Toys 25%, Carpets 55% and Soft Furnishings 20%. List the conclusions that Mrs Thames might reasonably draw from the graph and pie charts you have made to support or reject the arguments for more space of the three Department Heads regarding Christmas and Guy Fawkes Week in early November.

(5 marks)

(RSA Communication Skills in Business, Stage II, 1981)

E. OUTLINE AND TUTOR'S ANSWERS
Outline
answer 1

You are presented with two related percentage bar charts. Obviously you are expected to comment first on the totals, but the main concern of the question is your grasp of the proportions of unemployment between the sexes and between the occupations represented.

You will need a ruler for this question to measure the percentages in centimetres. Also, since the percentages are printed on the right-hand side only, you will need to make corresponding marks in the right margin to clarify the male columns.

A *critical* interpretation involves analysis and comment rather than a mere translation of the visual information into words and figures, although you must obviously make factual references to any particularly striking statistics. You are not expected to make exact statistical calculations, but should be reasonably accurate, i.e. totals can be rounded up or down, and percentages can sometimes be translated into proportions, e.g. 32% could be described as 'a third', 27% as 'just over a quarter', etc.

- Total unempt rose from 700,000 – over 2m. in 9 yrs (1972–81)
- male unempt (600,000–2m) × 3; female (100,000–700,000) × 7.
- Male: largest category – gen labs – unempt dropped from 35%–25% slight rise in unempt of craft workers (10%–15%) and managerial/professional (4%–6%)
- Female: largest category = clerical. Unempt constant at 20% with slight rise in mid-70s.
- Undefined categories: 'other' manual and non-manual – unskilled factory workers, cleaners, shopworkers etc. Rise in male unempt from 15–20% matched by fall in female. 'Other non-manual' mainly female – presumably shopworkers etc. rose from 6–10%
- Topical comments – e.g. recession, cuts in building trade.

Tutor's answer 1

Total unemployment, which had been rising gradually from 1972 to 1976, rose steeply from 1976 to 1981 as the recession deepened, and has since risen to 3 million. Male unemployment trebled, from 600,000 in 1972 to nearly 2 million in 1981; while female unemployment rose sevenfold, from 100,000 to 700,000. (Since many women do not register, these figures are an underestimate of female unemployment.)

The largest category of men unemployed was general labourers, partly due to the slowdown of spending on building and roads. Unemployment of general labourers dropped as a proportion of the total from 35 to 25% over the 9 years, but the numbers rose from about 200,000 to 500,000.

Another large category is 'other manual', which presumably includes unskilled factory workers, where male unemployment rose from 15 to 20% of the total. This rise is mirrored by a corresponding fall in female 'other manual' unemployment.

There was a slight rise in unemployment among craftsmen from 10 to 15% of the total, again reflecting the slowdown in the construction industry; while the number of managers and professional men out of work nearly doubled.

Among females, the largest single occupation is clerical work, where although unemployment dropped from a quarter of the total in 1976 to 20% in 1981, the number of unemployed clerical workers doubled from 70,000 in 1976 to 140,000 in 1981. Unemployment in this sector will continue to rise because of new office technology.

'Other non-manual' female workers, presumably including shop assistants and other service sector workers, also suffered from the recession, with numbers out of work rising from 15,000 (7% of 110,000) in 1976 to 70,000 (10% of 700,000) in 1981.

Tutor's answer 2

This question asks you to show different rates of pay for different overtime periods. An algorithm is asked for which breaks down the information logically into a decision-making path, so that employees can pick out the information which applies to their particular situation, and clearly see the rates of pay which relate to the overtime they work.

The two main problems here are organising the information into Yes/No stages and arranging the boxes into an A4 size page. The rough draft shows the first attempt in which the information appears rather cramped. The final version is clearer and more attractively presented. The first version would probably pass, but the final version would gain much higher marks.

Rough draft

HOURLY RATES OF PAY FOR OVERTIME WORKING

Final version

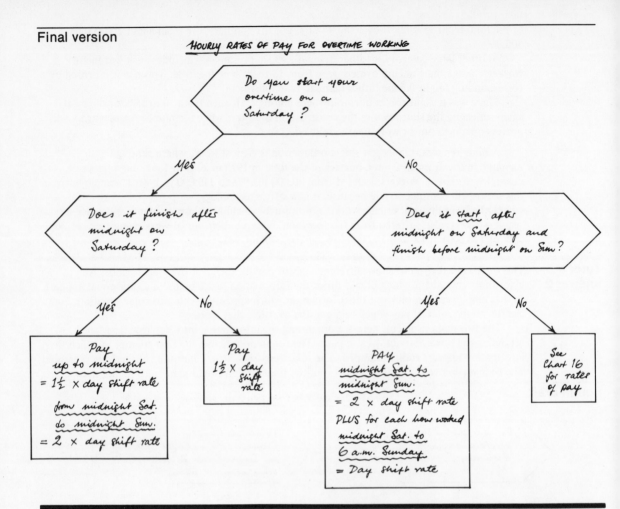

HOURLY RATES OF PAY FOR OVERTIME WORKING

Do you start your overtime on a Saturday?

Yes → Does it finish after midnight on Saturday?

Yes → Pay up to midnight = 1½ × day shift rate
from midnight Sat. to midnight Sun. = 2 × day shift rate

No → Pay 1½ × day shift rate

No → Does it start after midnight on Saturday and finish before midnight on Sun?

Yes → PAY midnight Sat. to midnight Sun. = 2 × day shift rate
PLUS for each hour worked midnight Sat. to 6 a.m. Sunday = Day shift rate

No → See Chart 16 for rates of pay

Tutor's answer 3

This question not only asks you to interpret the figures but also requires you to draw a line graph and two pie charts. The calculations for these need to be accurate. The graph paper will be supplied but you will need a compass, protractor and ruler.

(a) The line graph

1. The vertical axis will represent the sales figures in £; remember that time is always shown along the horizontal axis so you need to show the 12 months across the bottom line.
2. Work out the lowest and highest sales figures — £2,000 and £25,000 — and the appropriate divisions on the graph paper. Your vertical axis will thus have 25 divisions, each £1,000 being represented by one small square on the graph paper.
3. Now decide how you will distinguish between the three lines: perhaps a solid line for toys, a dotted line for carpets, and a broken line for soft furnishings. Colour is not usually favoured by examiners particularly as they already use green and red for marking.
4. Plot the lines one by one, making the points and joining the first line up before plotting the second.
5. Label the line graph with a title at the top.

(b) The pie charts
A calculator will speed up calculations, making the conversions of the sales figures into percentages and then into degrees much easier.

1. Work out the total sales for September and December 1979:

	September	December
Toys	7,000	25,000
Soft furnishings	15,000	8,000
Carpets	8,000	7,000
	30,000	40,000

Therefore 30 = 100% = 360° for the September pie chart
40 = 100% = 360° for the December pie chart

2. Now calculate the proportions as percentages:

September	December
Toys $7/30 \times 100\% = 23.3\%$	$25/40 \times 100\% = 62.5\%$
Carpets $15/30 \times 100\% = 50\%$	$8/40 \times 100\% = 20\%$
Soft furnishings $8/30 \times 100\% = 26.7\%$	$7/40 \times 100\% = 17.5\%$

3. Now multiply the percentages by 3.6 as 1% = 3.6°:

September	December
Toys $23.3 \times 3.6 = 83.9°$	$62.5 \times 3.6 = 225$
Carpets $50 \times 3.6 = 180°$	$20 \times 3.6 = 72°$
Soft furnishings $26.7 \times 3.6 = 96.1°$	$17.5 \times 3.6 = 63°$

4. Now draw the charts, shading each area distinctively. Label the sections with horizontal labelling and insert a title.

(c) The summary
The summary of the conclusions shown by the line graph and the pie charts should outline the major features to support the allocation of space. You have only about 80 words so there is no need to go into detail.

Tutor's model answer 3

(a)

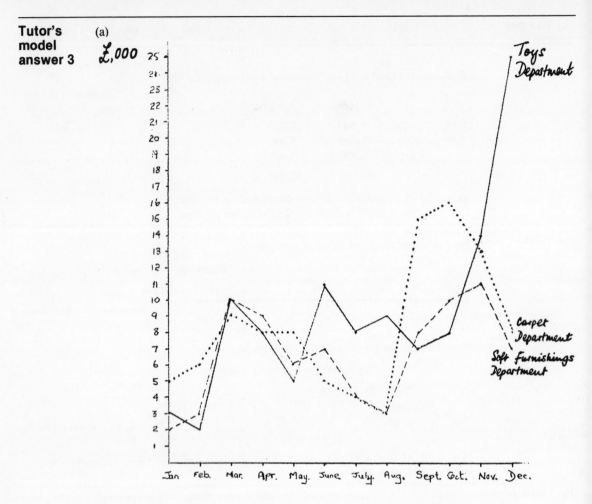

(b)

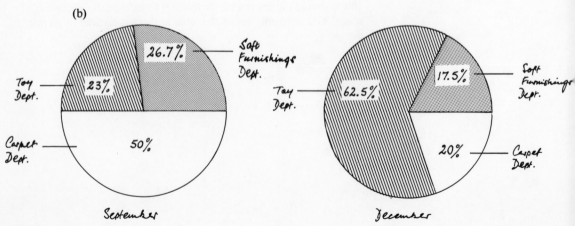

(c) The Toy Department sales figures would seem to justify the allocation of increased floor space for the Toy Department for Guy Fawkes week in early November as the line graph shows toy sales accelerating throughout November and December.

     The Toy Department sales figures, as shown in the second pie chart, account for 62% of total December sales so Mrs Thames might well conclude that this supported the application by the Head of the Toy Department for over half the total floor space during the Christmas period until January, when toy sales start to fall and the sales of the other two departments show an increase.

F. A STEP FURTHER

You should study and compare as many examples as possible of graphics in company reports, rate demand leaflets, bank brochures, and other easily obtainable material.

General books

People and Communication, Evans D W. Pitman 1984. The second edition includes a chapter on visual communication.
Mastering Business Communication, Woolcott L A and Unwin W R. Macmillan 1983.
The Business of Communicating, Stanton N. Pan 1982.

Specialist books

Do-it-yourself Graphic Design, Laing John. Ebury Press 1984. A thorough guide to all aspects of design of visual communication.
The Language of Graphics, Booth-Clibborn, Edward and Baroni, Daniele. Thames and Hudson 1980. A fascinating book about the use and meaning of graphics.
The Illustrated Guide to Employee Reports, Davenport, Jenny *et al*. Industrial Society 1984.

Films

Choosing & Using Charts, Video Arts.

Chapter 11   Forms and questionnaires

A. GETTING STARTED

Both forms and questionnaires are simplified short-cut means of conveying, gathering and processing routine information. You will all have had to fill in forms of some sort, and most of you will at some time or another have answered a questionnaire. It is unlikely that you have ever thought about forms except as pieces of paper on which you enter basic facts like your name, address, National Insurance number, etc. Filling in forms is a routine chore, whereas answering a questionnaire can be quite interesting and amusing, particularly if you are going through it with another person or a group of people, comparing and discussing your answers.

The most obvious difference between them is that forms are inescapable, whereas questionnaires are usually voluntary. If you want to apply for a job or a course, or turn your front room into a beauty salon, or insure a motorcycle, you expect to fill in a form. Indeed it would be much more tedious and taxing to have to put the same information in a letter. On the other hand, if you are approached by a market researcher armed with a clipboard and lists of questions about what newspaper you read, how many bottles of perfume/aftershave you have bought this year, what brands you prefer, etc. you can always refuse to co-operate.

In order to be able to answer examination questions on these topics you will need to think critically about forms and questionnaires. What are their purpose? What is the point of this or that question and is it clearly put? Are the questions well displayed, and is there enough room on the page for your answers? The standard textbooks give only brief guidance, so it is essential to look at a selection of actual examples, deciding what faults you need to avoid and what features you need to copy.

B. ESSENTIAL PRINCIPLES

1. FORMS

Design

Forms are devised in order to obtain specific information in a logical order, often from a wide variety of people. It is important that a form is well designed and simply written so that the form-filler can understand what is required. Otherwise the information will be inaccurate and man-hours will be wasted sending back a further request for details.

In exams you will probably be asked to design a simple form or reply slip/card to obtain information from a limited and specified number of people. You will be unable to use illustrations or coloured background tints, common devices to make forms more attractive and clear. However, you *can* use:

- capitals and different sizes of printed lettering to make the headings of different sections stand out;
- underlining;
- answer boxes;
- space to aid clarity;
- diagrams and algorithms.

Before starting to design the form, think:

- Why is the form being used?
- What information is needed?
- What questions will provide the answers required?
- What is the best order in which to arrange the questions?
- How easy will the information be to analyse?

Some general guidelines for form design are:

1. Explain clearly at the beginning how to complete the form. Keep the instructions to a minimum.
2. Use short sentences in clear simple language; avoid 'officialese' and complicated grammar with a lot of clauses.
3. Use the active not the passive, e.g. *not: if further information is required it may be obtained from* ... *but: if you need more information you should contact* ...
4. Ask questions in a logical sequence.
5. Leave enough room for answers of more than one word.
6. Invite positive rather than negative responses, e.g. circling the appropriate answer rather than deleting what does not apply.
7. Avoid mixing different instructions such as deleting, circling, ticking boxes: devise one system for indicating answers.
8. Use the reader-friendly 'you' where possible.
9. Put the answer space near the ends of the questions in unjustified layout, e.g.

. . . . ?☐

. . . . ? ☐

. . . . ? ☐

This may look untidy, but is quicker to complete than justified
layout, e.g.

. . . . ?. . . .☐

. . . . ?. . . . .☐

. . . . ?. . . . .☐

---

2. QUESTIONNAIRES

Questionnaires provide the most efficient means of obtaining information
and opinions from a number of people in a standardised form which is
easy to analyse and assess. Computers have simplified and speeded up the
analysis of results, and this has led to an increase in the use of
questionnaires and to the standardisation of their format. Their most
obvious and widespread uses are in market research for products and
services, and in surveys of public opinion on political issues.

Large-scale surveys are usually conducted by interviewers who take
the respondents through the questions and fill in the answers for them.
This ensures a more complete and accurate response than relying on the
respondent to answer the questions in private and return the form or wait
for it to be collected later. It also cuts out jokey or cranky answers.

Questionnaires can be aimed at a **selected group** of respondents, e.g.
all clerical staff in a firm, regular passengers on a local bus service,
members of a professional association, retailers of a particular make of
car; or at a **selected locality**, e.g. all residents in a housing estate; or at a
selected group in one or more localities, e.g. middle-income women
between 40 and 60 in two typical Midland towns; or at a **random sample**,
e.g. 700 voters in a parliamentary constituency during a by-election.

You will not be expected to answer questions about the principles
and theory of marketing and sampling in a communication exam, but
you should have a broad idea of the background and context, and also be
clear about your intended respondents. Otherwise you might ask
unnecessary or irrelevant questions, e.g. it would be pointless and
offensive to ask car retailers for their age and sex, but it might be
relevant to a survey of bus passengers. The retailers would expect to give
their names, but the bus passengers would not − and would be highly
suspicious if asked to do so. A questionnaire about leisure facilities in a
particular town (and this is a favourite exam topic) should make it clear
whether it applies only to residents of the town, or to people who come
into town from surrounding areas. A clear idea of the context and
purpose of the survey − who is conducting it and why − will also help
you to narrow down your questions, e.g. if you run a sports hall, you
would not necessarily need to know how often a 19-year-old male bank
clerk goes to the cinema, unless you had a particular reason. Students
asked to choose their own topics for college assignments tend to get
carried away and ask too many unrelated questions.

Another common fault is to neglect the practicalities. How is the questionnaire to be circulated to the sample? What should respondents do with their completed forms? If you rely on them handing them in or posting them, you are likely to get a very low response, so it is usually advisable to make arrangements for collection by a specified date and spell them out either in your introduction or at the bottom of the form.

Below are some examples of the sort of task you might get in exams.

- A survey of employee opinion on the staff canteen, Flexitime, the content of the staff magazine, etc. to enable management to cater for preferences and predict responses, and to ensure that initiatives or changes are appropriate and popular.

- A survey of college students' travel arrangements, or opinions on catering and common-room provision, sports and leisure facilities, etc. to identify needs and preferences, e.g. more motorcycle spaces, better vending machines, the likely demand for jazz ballet.

- A media survey, e.g. a questionnaire about the television viewing habits and preferences of 16–17-year-olds, to provide background material for a course on media studies.

Structure of questionnaire	The **structure** usually falls into three sections:
1. An explanatory introduction with instructions	A typically unsatisfactory opening would be: *This questionnaire is to find out students' opinions about vending machines in the college.* You should start by explaining the reason for the questionnaire and who is conducting it. e.g. *The Students' Union has received a number of requests for vending machines outside the canteen and in the common-rooms. Before making a formal approach to the college authorities, we need to assess current use and likely demand. This questionnaire has been devised by A2 Communications students, and will be circulated and collected by Communication lecturers during the week beginning April 23.* Please tick appropriate boxes or write in the spaces provided.
2. Relevant personal details	These will vary according to the context and purpose, e.g. age, sex, job, course, department, etc. Question marks are not usually needed in this section:

Age	Boxes for age-groups	*Not:* What is your age?
Sex	Male/female	*Not (for obvious reasons):* Sex?
Job title	. . . .	

3. The questions	There are four types of question.

1. *Dichotomous*, i.e. those seeking Yes/No answers:
   Have you bought any hot drinks from a college vending machine during the past month?   Yes☐   No☐

2. *Multi-choice*, i.e. those consisting of a list of items to be ticked:
Which of the following hot drinks have you bought during the past month?

Coffee	☐
Tea	☐
Chocolate	☐
Soup	☐

This sort of combined question is more economical than a series of separate follow-up questions, though it needs careful planning. It could be followed by a matching question about cold drinks.

3. *Semantic differential*, i.e. those which ask for ratings or preferences:
What is your opinion of the quality of the hot drinks?

Good	☐
Average	☐
Poor	☐

You may wish to distinguish between different hot drinks, in which case the simple question above would be replaced by a more detailed version:

How would you rate the quality of the hot drinks?

	Good	Average	Poor
Coffee	☐	☐	☐
Tea	☐	☐	☐
Chocolate	☐	☐	☐
Soup	☐	☐	☐

(A combined question of this type is more economical than a series of separate follow-up questions for each drink, but again needs careful planning. If you also want to ask about the consumption of, and opinions on, cold drinks, make sure you frame a matching simple or combined question.)

4. *Open-ended questions*, i.e. those which invite comment or reasons for a preceding answer:

State briefly what additional items you would like to be able to buy from college vending machines . . . .

Another common device is to put a box marked *other* at the end of a list of items to be ticked, followed by the instruction; *If other, please state* . . . Or: *If your answer to QX was 'no', please give your reason. Sometimes there is an additional section allowing for open-ended comment.*

Rules for writing a questionnaire

Writing questionnaires is much more complicated than might at first appear, so try to stick to the following rules:

1. Be clear about your purpose. Do not try to cover too many topics or ask too many questions, or your respondents will lose patience.

2. Arrange questions in a logical order, and deal with one topic at a time. For example, if some of your questions are only relevant to car owners, you must identify them early on. Some answers may make the next question irrelevant, so you must indicate which questions can be skipped:

Do you own a car?   Yes ☐ No ☐
If your answer is No, go straight to Question 7.

3. Do not 'prompt' respondents into giving what they think is the 'right' answer by feeding them 'loaded' questions, e.g:

    Do you agree that the compulsory
    wearing of seat belts saves lives?   Yes ☐ No ☐ Not sure ☐

    This should be reworded as:
    Do you approve of the
    compulsory wearing of seat belts?   Yes ☐ No ☐ Not sure ☐

4. Do not wrap up two questions in one:
    Do you prefer to go to discos in town or in the village?   Yes/No

    This should be:
    Where do you usually prefer
    to go to discos?   In town ☐ In your village ☐

5. Try to make the style of your questions consistent and self-contained by starting with *what, how, why* and *how*, and ending with question marks:

    How do you usually travel to work?   Car ☐
    Bus ☐
    Cycle ☐

    etc.

    Not:
    Do you usually travel to work by   Car? ☐ Bus? ☐ Cycle? ☐

    Questionnaires are a minefield for candidates with a weak grasp of language and grammar, e.g:

    In your personal opinion, would you say that you yourself like
    different music compared with people of around the same age you
    know, or the same kind of music?   Different ☐ Same ☐ Sometimes ☐

Layout of questionnaire

Questionnaire design is a highly professional job, particularly now the answers are usually checked by computer. Your version will usually be handwritten within a time-limit, so you must decide on a pattern which is quick and clear, even if it is not perfect. If you have time, it is well worth while blocking out a rough draft, because the most common mistake is to underestimate the amount of space needed. Take advantage of the lined paper, and use a ruler for the downward lines, but do not agonise over details of spacing, or spend all your time drawing perfect rows of boxes; Although a high proportion of marks (about 40%) can be gained on layout, the examiners will be even more concerned with the relevance and wording of your questions.

It is usually easier and tidier to write your questions on the left and place your boxes on the right, as in most of the examples shown above. However, you should not push all your boxes to the extreme right of the page. It may look neater, but research has shown that respondents often tick the wrong box if if is placed too far away from the question and key words. The main thing is to be consistent, so decide quickly if you are going to split long questions on to more than one line on the left, or use the whole width of the page with the row of boxes underneath the question, e.g.

How often do you buy hot drinks from the vending machine ?

Once a week	*More than Once a week*	*Once a month*	*More than once a month*	*Once a term*
☐	☐	☐	☐	☐

Finally, it is important to remember that you may be asked to write a report linked to a real or imaginary questionnaire, so you must be able to present the results as tables or diagrams. (See Ch. 7 and Ch. 10.)

C. USEFUL APPLIED MATERIALS

Fig. 11.1   An example of modern form design

Motorcycle and Moped Insurance Quotation Request
(please write clearly)

ABOUT YOURSELF
Mr/Mrs/Ms   Initials   Surname

Address

Telephone No.

Date of Birth   Occupation

Type of motorcycle licence held   Provisional   Full UK   International

Date UK driving test passed   How long have you been resident in the UK?   years

How long in total have you been riding a motorcycle?   years

ABOUT THE MACHINE
Make and Model

cc   Is it pedal assisted?   Yes   No

Value of machine £   Is a sidecar attached? Yes   No   If 'yes' to nearside   or offside

ABOUT ALL DRIVERS
Within the last 5 years have you or any person who will drive the vehicle:

(a) been convicted of any motoring offence (or is prosecution pending) other than parking?   Yes   No

(b) been involved in a motoring loss or accident?   Yes   No

(c) have you or any person who will drive the machine any physical defect or infirmity?   Yes   No

If the answer to any of the above is 'YES' please give full details overleaf.

If anyone other than yourself is likely to drive please provide date of birth, type of licence held, length of UK residence and date test passed.

ABOUT THE COVER
Please indicate cover required   Comprehensive   Third party Only   Third party Fire and Theft

DISCOUNTS AVAILABLE
How many years No Claim Discount will you have earned on a motorcycle at commencement?   years

Have you a RAC/ACU, STEP (intermediate or advanced course) or IAM proficiency certificate? Yes   No

(Source: Endsleigh Insurance Services Ltd)

Fig. 11.2   A city council survey of parking provision and needs

---

BUSINESS SURVEY

This survey is part of the City Council's investigations into the possibility of introducing park and ride services to overcome current parking problems in the city centre. Recently you may have read about the proposals in the local press or attended one of the public meetings.

We would now like to know your own requirements for car parking. Please answer all the questions on the attached form, writing clearly in the spaces provided and ticking the appropriate boxes. If you have any difficulties, our representative will be happy to help you when he calls to collect the form in a few days time.

Thank you for your co-operation

G.G. Jones
City Engineer & Surveyor

1. What is the nature of your business? ....

   ....

2. What is the address of your business? ....

   ....

3. How many staff do you employ at this address (including yourself)?

   full time .... Part time ....

4. How many vehicles are kept here each day by you or members of your staff:

   – on-street outside your business (all day) ....

   – on-street outside your business (part of the day) ....

   – on-street elsewhere ....

   – in your private car park ....

   – in public car parks ....

   – other (specify) ....

5. How many of these vehicles are generally used by you or your staff in the course of your daily

   business? ....

6. How many parking spaces do you provide off-street for your clients/customers/

   deliveries? ....

7. Is there other land on the premises which could also be used for parking for visitors?

                                    Yes☐   No☐   Don't know☐

8. If yes, approximately how many extra parking spaces would be provided? ....

9. Where do your customers/clients/delivery vehicles usually park at present?

on-street ☐   public car park ☐   elsewhere/don't know ☐

private car park provided for them

10. How long do your visitors stay on average?

– customers/clients:
    a few minutes ☐   30–60 minutes ☐
    more than 60 minutes ☐   not applicable ☐

– deliveries:
    a few minutes ☐   30–60 minutes ☐
    more than 60 minutes ☐   not applicable ☐

11. If you wish to make any general comments on parking please write them below.

....
....
....

(Source: Cambridge City Council)

D. RECENT EXAMINATION QUESTIONS

Question 1 You work at Philips and Jones plc as private secretary to Mr G Anderson, the Chief Office Administrator, among whose responsibilities is ensuring that adequate administration services are provided for the 150 staff, including mail, typing services, filing and photocopying. Yesterday Mr Anderson has this to say to you:

'Something will obviously have to be done about the photocopier in the print room – it's broken down again. That's five times in the last fortnight! Staff are always ready to complain when this happens but I'm convinced the breakdowns are caused by people not using it properly. I knew we would have this problem when it was agreed to allow staff free access to the wretched machine – people putting the paper in wrongly or being very clumsy using the controls. They don't seem to realise an expensive machine needs careful handling. Apart from this, they don't know how to get the best out of the machine – not printing on both sides of the paper or reducing two A4 sheets on to one. And it's alarming to see how many copies have been thrown away in the waste bin! I've discussed the matter with senior staff and they agree that something has to be done – the present problems will take the whole of tomorrow to sort out – and this situation is affecting the general efficiency of the company. It's very inconvenient and frustrating for those who do use the machine properly. I want to send something out to each member of staff today, explaining the situation and getting some information from them – how often they use it, how many copies they make in an average week, whether they would like some basic training, etc. – in fact, any information that may help us to sort the matter out. They may, in fact, want all copying done by a trained operator who can be in absolute control of the machine. If I can have their replies by 15 July, I'll be able to work something out to put to the next senior staff meeting.'

(a) Prepare a suitable communication (using about 200 words) for Mr Anderson.
(answered in Ch. 5, Q3, p. 72)   (20 marks)

(b) Prepare a reply form to accompany (a) for staff to complete. This should provide Mr Anderson with the kind of information he requires.

(15 marks)

(LCCI PSC, 1984)   (Total: 35 marks)

Question 2 You have been asked to research the feasibility of introducing a Flexitime system in your firm. At present office hours are 9.00 to 5.00. The instructions given to you are:

(a) to devise a short questionnaire of up to 10 questions to find out if such a system, changing time and routine would be welcomed.

(b) to write an explanatory memorandum to be attached to the questionnaire.

E. OUTLINE AND TUTOR'S ANSWERS
Tutor's answer 1
(b)

This reply-form may seem simple to devise but you need to cater for three different types of question: those requiring straightforward Yes/No answers, those designed to obtain numerical information on how much the photocopier is used and how many copies have been done, and one which is open-ended, i.e. asking for users' comments/suggestions for improvements. Give a choice of answers for frequency and quantity, so making the question easier to complete and to analyse.

Photocopying

The next senior staff meeting will discuss ways to improve the photocopying service and your views are important in considering proposals to increase efficiency.

We should be grateful if you would answer the questions below, ticking the boxes where appropriate.

Please return the form to G. Anderson, chief office administrator, before 15 July.

1. Name ....

2. Department ....

3. How often do you use the photocopier?

    Every ☐   2–4 times ☐   Once a ☐   Once a ☐   Once a ☐   Less than ☐
    day   weekly   week   fortnight   month   once a
                                                                                         month

4. How many copies on   0–50 ☐   50–100 ☐   101–500 ☐   501–1,000 ☐   1,000+ ☐
    average to you make
    per week?

5. Would you like some basic training in how to use   Yes ☐   No ☐
    the photocopier most effectively?

6. Would you like all photocopying to be done by a   Yes ☐   No ☐
    trained operator instead of the present
    self-access system?

(You could put Yes/No, inviting deletion of one alternative)

7. Please give any other suggestions you have for improving the photocopying service:

    ....
    ....
    ....
    ....

Outline answer 2

Flexitime has become much more widespread recently, and is a favourite topic with examiners. The question gives very little background information about how Flexitime is operated, and its advantages and disadvantages, or the usual reactions and results. It assumes that you have covered these aspects in other subject areas, and are able to apply them to a communication task. So you should not launch straight into the questionnaire; you should first clear your mind by jotting down some key facts and relating them to the question. This will be useful preparation for the accompanying memo, which in this case, takes the place of the usual introduction/explanation at the top of the questions.

Your **notes** might look something like this:

Usual scheme = division of 8-hr working day (minus breaks) into compulsory ´core-time' (say 10−12 a.m. and 2−4 p.m.) and Flexitime (8−10 a.m. and 4−6 p.m.). Employees settle times with section heads. Hours totalled over period of one month. Credit (extra hours worked) and debit (extra hours off work) carried over to next month, within set maximum.

Advantages:
- Convenience − adjustment of work/home routine (suits women employees); rush-hour travel avoided; more freedom for outside appointments, e.g. doctor/dentist, so fewer excuses.
- Morale/efficiency − allowance made for differences between people at their best early or late in day; more trust and co-operation, better motivation.

Disadvantages
- Possible complications for colleagues who need to work closely together.
- Careful supervision needed by section heads to avoid abuse.
- Longer total day means higher heating and lighting costs.

Reactions/results: Usually positive − employees welcome choice and flexibility. Higher morale/efficiency. 40% choose usually earlier start, 30% later, 20% stay the same, 10% vary.

Application to firm: Present working day starts and finishes early so Flexitime will mean longer afternoon for factory and clerical staff. Presumably managers already have different hours. High proportion of women employees (60%) − therefore scheme would get positive response and help recruitment.

Of course you will not have time to use all this in your answer, but most of it should at least have flashed through your mind. Maybe it would be a good idea to indicate in your memo that you are enclosing a fuller explanation. In this case it would probably be easier to write the memo before the questionnaire.

Tutor's answer 2

Part (b) The memo

MEMORANDUM

From: Personnel Officer
To: All staff

Date: 12 June 19. .

Subject: FLEXIBLE WORKING HOURS

As you may be aware, several local companies are now operating a system of Flexitime, which has been generally welcomed by employees. It has been suggested that we would benefit from a more flexible working week, and that this would help overcome current shortages of secretarial and clerical staff.

In order to help us decide whether to introduce Flexitime, and if so, to make the most appropriate and convenient arrangements, I should be grateful if you would complete the enclosed questionnaire and hand it to your supervisor by 19 June. Although you may wish to consult your colleagues, your answers will be treated in the strictest confidence.

A detailed description of Flexitime and how it might operate in our company is attached for your information. Please note that the introduction of Flexitime would mean that the office would open at 8.00 a.m. and close at 6 p.m. Lunch breaks could be shortened to half an hour, or extended to 1½ hours.

T.H.W.

Part (a) The questionnaire

FLEXITIME QUESTIONNAIRE

Department: ....

Job title: ....

Age: 16–20   20–30   30–40   40–50   Over 50
              ☐   ☐   ☐   ☐   ☐

Sex: Male/Female

1. How long have you worked for the firm?   1–5 years ☐   5–15 years ☐   Over 15 years ☐

2. Are you in favour of the introduction of
   Flexitime?   Yes ☐   No ☐   Don't know ☐

3. Would you personally want to change to
   Flexitime?   Yes ☐   No ☐   Don't know ☐

4. If answer to question 3 was Yes, please state:
   (a) when you would usually like to start work;   Earlier ☐   Later ☐   Same ☐

   (b) when you would usually take your lunch
       break;   12–12.30 ☐   12–1 ☐   12.30–1 ☐

                                                                       1–1.30 ☐   1–2 ☐

   (c) when you would usually like to finish work.   Earlier ☐   Later ☐   Same ☐

5. What are your reasons for wishing to make the
   above change/s?   Domestic   Travel/
                                                  arrangements ☐   transport ☐

   (You may tick more than one box)   Shopping/   Other ☐
                                                  appointments ☐

If *other*, please state: ....

Please comment below on what effects youn think Flexitime will have on your own work, and the work of your section.

....
....
....

Thank you for your co-operation in completing this questionnaire. Please give it to your section head by 19 June. The results will be circulated during the week beginning 8 July.

T. Watson.

E. NOTES ON ANSWER

- The use of the opening 'please state' in question 4 of the questionnaire avoids the need for question marks.
- The boxes could have been listed one below the other down the right-hand side, e.g. in question 4(c).

Earlier	☐
Later	☐
Same	☐

- The statistical results of this questionnaire would be best presented as tables or diagrams in a report (see Ch. 10).

F. A STEP FURTHER

The Plain English Story, Martin Cutts and Chrissie Maher. Plain English Campaign 1986. Contains many instructive and amusing examples.
Effective Communication, Eyre E C. W.H. Allen 1979. Chapter 16 shows other types of Form, e.g. invoices.
Communication in Business, Little P. Pitman Chapter 11.
Marketing Research (2nd edn), Proctor T and Stone M. Macdonald & Evans 1982.

Chapter 12

Job applications and interviews

A. GETTING STARTED

Preparation for job applications and interviews is usually an essential component of the communication part of business studies or secretarial courses, even those courses which include personnel or general management subjects. Most candidates, even those already employed, will benefit from practice in writing a curriculam vitae (C.V.) and a letter of application, and from rehearsing interviews – preferably on video.

Moreover, the analysis of the recruitment from the employer's point of view will give you further insight into the expectations of potential employers, and so help you to prepare for what is often regarded as an ordeal – the job interview. It should also make you aware of the other sorts of interviews you might experience during your careers, e.g. performance appraisal.

In this chapter we concentrate on those aspects of the subject most likely to crop up in exams. Questions usually take the form of writing a letter applying for a post, writing a reference or drafting a newspaper advertisement. You may sometimes be asked to comment on some aspect of interviews, or to report on one or more candidates on a short list.

B. ESSENTIAL PRINCIPLES

The centre-piece of the job application process is, of course, the interview itself. It might be compared to a one-act play which might be a hit or a flop. Before the 'performance', both parties will have gone through several stages of preparation. The interview*ee* will have assessed his strengths and weaknesses, found out as much as possible about the organisation and the post, anticipated possible questions and responses, decided what to wear, worried about how to walk and sit and what to do with his hands. He may even have had a rehearsal, or at least practised in front of the mirror. The interview*er* will have thought about the type of person needed, discussed the post with colleagues, framed some essential questions, decided who will be present, who will ask what, what room to use and how to arrange the furniture.

Both parties will also have contributed to the script. The interviewee will have filled in an application form and/or written a letter of application and a c.v., studied the Job Description, and perhaps written to his referees. The interviewer will have checked the Job Description and Job Specification, perhaps have amended them or written new versions; read the application form and/or letter of application and c.v., usually have read one or two referees' letters, drawn up a list of questions, and prepared an interview assessment form. After the interview he might

Fig. 12.1   Applying for a job

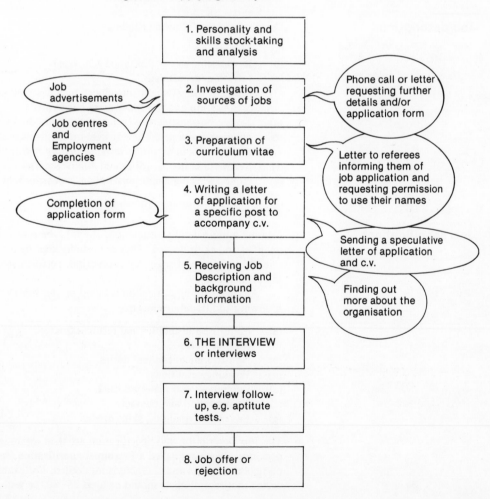

have to write letters to the successful and unsuccessful applicants. (See also *Exam Guide to Office Practice and Secretarial Administration*).

Now we consider the **documents** used in the recruitment and job application process, in the usual order of preparation and writing.

---

1. Job Descriptions and Job Specifications

You are unlikely to be asked to write either of these documents in an exam. However, in order to be able to answer general questions you need to know why they are written, what they contain, and the distinction between the two.

Before a new vacancy is advertised management will have to decide on the status of the post and duties required. The job is then defined and the duties listed in a **Job Description** which serves two functions:

- To inform candidates about the organisation, department, status and role of the post, and the duties/responsibilities;
- To provide the employee with a legally binding record of his role and duties.

Job descriptions

Usually have the following headings:

(a) **Title of job**.
(b) **Responsible to** ... (Specified Manager)
(c) **Location/department**.
(d) **Scope of job**. (Usually introduced by a description of the organisation and the department concerned.)
(e) **Duties/responsibilities**. (A list of the main duties/responsibilities entailed in the job. The last item on the list is usually a 'catch-all' such as: *any other duties as requested by X from time to time*.)
(f) **Responsible for** ... (Specified Junior Staff).
(g) **Hours/working conditions/holidays/pension scheme, etc.**

(A full Job Description is shown in Fig. 12.7.)

Job specifications

Contain a more detailed account of the job, the results expected, and the qualities and skills needed. They are usually kept by management and referred to in case of selection, promotion, performance appraisal and job evaluation.

A typical Job Specification is based on the Job Description, with the following additional headings:

(a) **Major responsibilities and results expected**.
(b) **Routine duties**.
(c) **Non-routine occasional duties**.
(d) **Working conditions**.
(e) **Equipment and materials used**
(f) **Co-operation and contacts**.
(g) **Education, qualities, skills needed**.

The Job Description and Specification are then expanded into another personnel document called a **Personnel Specification**, spelling out the particular qualities and characteristics needed. For example, you might decide that receptionists should be aged 25–40, be well groomed, have clear speaking voices and be non-smokers. The Personnel Specification is then used as a guide for job advertisements in order to attract suitable applicants and deter unsuitable applicants. (See Fig. 12.7.)

2. Job advertisements	The object of advertising a vacancy is to attract a small number of well-qualified candidates quickly and cheaply. An advertisement which attracts hundreds of unsuitable replies is wasteful. In order to hit the right targets it should be placed in the appropriate media, include all necessary detail, and be displayed and written in an attractive positive way.
(a) The media	Manual posts are usually filled by advertising in the local press, but if there is a shortage of particular skills they may also be advertised in the popular national papers and the trade press. Junior office staff are also usually recruited locally, while higher-grade posts such as personal secretaries are often advertised locally and/or in the quality national press, e.g. the Thursday 'Crème de la Crème' page in *The Times*. General middle-management posts appear in the local press and a wide range of national papers, e.g. The *Daily Mail* and The *Daily Telegraph*. Senior and/or specialised posts are carefully placed in the quality papers and professional magazines and/or referred to specialised employment agencies or recruitment consultants.
	Many jobs are never formally advertised. Applicants get to hear of vacancies through agencies, friends and relatives or through the 'grapevine'.
(b) Content	The advertisement is a potted version of the Job Specification and Person Specification, so usually contains most of the following:

1. **Job title**. Sometimes an organisation will list several vacancies in one advertisement.
2. **Type of employer and location**. Small employers often use enticing phrases such as 'Busy estate agents' or 'Well-established financial consultancy' rather than announcing their names at the outset.
3. **Outline Job Description**. The amount of detail will depend on the nature of the post and the need to eliminate casual enquiries.
4. **Qualifications, experience, skills required**. The details will depend on how wide or narrow a range of applicants will be considered. For example, a quality restaurant seeking a chef must make it clear that it is looking for a *haute cuisine* background and a magic touch with fillet of sole, whereas a fast-food chain will be seeking an applicant who can produce a hamburger in record time. Relevant academic requirements should be specified, as well as essential skills such as the ability to drive, operate a computer, etc. and desirable skills such as foreign languages. For example, if you need receptionists with O level English language and the ability to exchange routine greetings and give basic instructions in German, this should be indicated.

If there is a desired age range it must be specified, as well as any other essential physical characteristics such as minimum height, good eyesight, etc. (Remember that it is against the law to specify

197

sex or race; hence all those rather ridiculous-sounding advertisements for 'Handypersons'.)

5. **Working conditions**. The wage or salary may be specified, or broadly indicated, e.g. 'Good wage' or 'Salary negotiable', or not even mentioned. The same applies to hours of work and fringe benefits.

6. **Training and promotion prospects**. Research has shown that inclusion of this item attracts a larger number of suitable candidates, and projects a good image.

7. **How, where and by when to apply**. Name, address and/or telephone number, indicating whether to send a curriculum vitae and letter of application, or to request an application form and further details.

(c)   Presentation and style

Fig. 12.2   A brief and simple statement

> GRADUATE SECRETARY/PA
>
> Required for Director of executive recruitment/advertising agency. Accurate typing, pleasant telephone manner. Apply with c.v. to: Jim Morton, Morton Mack Consultancy, 34 Swindale Wharf, St Judes Dock, Napier Lane, London SE1 3BC

Fig. 12.3   A more detailed description

> GRADUATE SECRETARY/PA £7.500
>
> Senior partner in busy Recruitment Company/Advertising Agency is looking for a highly motivated PA able to work flexibly and efficiently under pressure, and use initiative. Fast accurate typing and word processing, pleasant telephone manner and good communication skills essential. Experience in Personnel or Advertising would be an advantage.
>
> We are a young expanding company able to offer a stimulating and responsible career. Our bright new offices are situated in a converted warehouse with glorious views of the Thames. Please write for further details to:
> Jim Morton,
> Morton Mack Consultancy,
> 34 Swindale Wharf,
> Napier Lane,
> LONDON SE1 3BC
> Or telephone 01 245 7376 for further details

Note that this version invites candidates to obtain the 'Further details', i.e. the Job Description, before deciding whether or not to apply.

Fig. 12.4   An individual off-beat approach

> GRADUATES,
> WE DARE YOU TO ADMIT YOU CAN TYPE!
>
> For the graduate who regrets ever taking a secretarial course, here's a unique career opportunity we bet you've never thought of.
>
> We're a lively and busy recruitment company with a sister advertising agency and we're offering a strong-minded and analytical graduate the first step on the route to a fascinating, responsible and highly remunerative career. It's only fair to state clearly that we want to make use of your typing and organising skills in the short term, but we need more than a secretary.
>
> You will revel in the moody splendour of our Thameside offices near historic Tower Bridge. Prepare yourself for unreasonable workloads (if you're bored it's your fault). Cast off your shackles and do an exciting job for a change.
>
> Call Jim Morton to talk it over on 01 245 7376 or send me a c.v. at:
> Morton Mack Consultancy, 34 Swindale Wharf, St Judes Dock, Napier Lane, LONDON SE1 3BC

The cost of placing a job advertisement is high, averaging £350 for a 9-cm bold display box in the national quality press, and £50 in the local press. So you need to pack as much relevant information as possible into a small space, and make your display stand out among all the surrounding boxes. The examiners will not expect you to write to size, so take plenty of space, draw a large box, and block the words in pencil. When you are satisfied with the spacing and wording, you can either rub out the pencil underneath or do a fair copy on a fresh sheet.

As shown in Figs 12.2, 12.3 and 12.4 job advertisements can be written in three different styles.

3. Curriculum vitae (c.v.)

A c.v. should give a potential employer a brief factual summary of the main events of your life so far. Until recently the usual convention has been to follow chronological order. A better, more modern approach is to start at the present and work backwards. An employer first wants to know about you most recent qualifications and experience, not how many O levels you passed, or when you started your paper-round.

C.v.s are used in answer to advertisements inviting you to apply in writing, and for any approach you might make on your own initiative. Your potted biography should be divided into sections and **typed**. Avoid the first person and colourful detail; these should be reserved for your covering letter of application.

Fig. 12.5 A sample c.v.

```
                        CURRICULUM VITAE

   NAME:  Mary Louise Thompson        MARITAL STATUS:  Single

   SEX:  Female                       AGE:  23

   NATIONALITY:  British              DATE OF BIRTH:  14 April 1962

   HOME ADDRESS:  12 Minster Street   WORK ADDRESS:  Sunway Travel
                  Hillston                          East Street
                  Beds. BH5 9HJ                     Bedford BT2 3JR
                  Tel. 0362 758                     Tel. 0234 6540


   EDUCATION                          QUALIFICATIONS

   1979 - 1982   Luton College of     HND in Business and Finance
                 Higher Education     Business Education Council (BTEC)
                 Bradwell Street      Course included:
                 Luton LK5 9QT        Personnel
                                      Marketing
                                      Business Communication
                                      Quantitative Methods (computing)
                                      Accountancy
```

| 1974 - 1979 | Bellview School
Luton LP6 7BT | 'A' levels
English (c)   French (B)
7 'O' levels including English
Language and Mathematics
RSA I Typing |

WORK EXPERIENCE

1984 - 1986	Sunway Travel East Street Bedford BT2 3JR	Assistant Manager
1983 - 1984	Sunway Travel Bristol Road Birmingham TR4 7BM	Sales Assistant
1982 - 1983	Anglo-Balkan Tours Bedford Road Luton LX8 6TR	Courier

ADDITIONAL INFORMATION

School tennis captain

Secretary, Bedford Anglo-Greek Society

Clean driving licence

INTERESTS

Tennis - participation in tournaments

Travel - especially driving in remote areas

Folk Music - specialising in Balkan countries

REFEREES

Mr. N.P. Jolly
Area Manager
Sunway Travel
Bedford BT2 3JR

Mrs. T.R. PHillips
Department of Management & Business Studies
Luton College of Higher Education
Luton LK5 9QT

4. Letters of application

The letter enclosed with the c.v. should include four sections:

1. An opening statement expressing interest in the post (use the precise job title), how and where you learned of the vacancy (give the name and date of the newspaper) and the receipt of the Job Description (if it has been sent to you).

2. A paragraph or two saying why you are attracted to the post. Avoid expressing the most obvious reasons in stock phrases, e.g. 'I am interested in hotel management because I enjoy meeting people.' Try to say something slightly but not absurdly different, e.g. 'Hotel reception work appeals to me because it offers the chance to meet people from all over the world, and to give them a friendly and favourable impression of Britain.'

3. A paragraph or two showing what qualities and experience you will be able to apply to the post. The common mistake here is to repeat basic information included on your c.v. and/or application form such as examination results, typing speed, etc. You must expand on these bare facts, e.g. how your O level Spanish has blossomed into useful fluency after a 3-month holiday job in a bar in Marbella, or that you have recently learned how to operate a word processor.

4. A final paragraph indicating availability for interview and what notice you need to give.

Far too many applications letters are flat and predictable. Remember that your letter will have to stand out among hundreds of others, so try not to use safe standard language – remember that this is your opportunity to show a glimpse of individuality and character, and the ability to express yourself correctly and fluently. Don't be too modest and negative, e.g. 'The only weekend job I've done is serving in a paper shop.' Make the most of your talents and experiences, e.g. 'During my weekend job serving in a paper shop I often had to take responsibility for twenty teenage deliverers.' At the other extreme, be careful not to sound aggressive or conceited, e.g. 'As you can see from my c.v. I have exactly the sort of qualities and experience you are looking for.' Be tactfully confident. 'I would welcome the opportunity to deal directly with clients and visitors, and feel that my experience has prepared me to take on more responsibility.' (See tutor's answer on p. 209.)

INTERVIEWS

The interview is a form of oral communication which is usually approached by examining bodies as a distinct subject area together with all the documentation involved. However, it is important to refer to and remember our comments in Chapter 8 on the skills and sensitivity required for effective speaking and listening, both one-to-one and in groups.

An interview can be defined as a structured conversation with the general purpose of exchanging information, and a specific purpose, e.g. to solve a problem, elicit information, fill a post/get a job. The length of the interview, the way in which it is conducted, and whether it involved two or more people will depend on its specific purpose. A counselling interview should be one-to-one, informal and open-ended, whereas a disciplinary interview may involve more than two people and will probably be short and sharp. Selection interviews will vary according to the post and the custom of the organisation.

This chapter is mainly concerned with the selection interview because it is the most likely topic of specific questions in all but a few higher-level professional exams. However. you should also be aware of some of the other forms of interview which often take place within organisations:

- Performance appraisal
- Promotion/reward
- Grievance
- Disciplinary
- Dismissal
- Termination
- Counselling

(see booklist on p. 210)

A range of communication skills is needed if the interviewer is to achieve all the objects of any of these forms of interview − skills which are often sadly lacking. There has been an increasing emphasis in recent years on training managers in interview techniques and preparation. The most important aspects of interviewing are summarised below.

(a) Structure

The interviewer needs a clear sense of purpose, and should put the questions in a logical order in order to draw out the necessary information. Most interviews start with a few low-key friendly exchanges, move into a sequence of increasingly specific questions, and end with an invitation to the interviewee to ask any final questions before the final thank-you courtesies. If there are two or more interviewers it is essential for them to decide their various roles beforehand and apportion the questions and responses.

(b) Balance

The great majority of interviews should be seen as two-way forms of oral communication. The actual proportion of time each party spends speaking or listening will depend on the purpose of the interview, but both parties should be aware of the need to be good listeners as well as effective speakers. Interviewers should not hog the show by sticking rigidly to a prepared list of questions, asking long-winded questions or by constantly interrupting; interviewees need to strike a balance between modestly saying too little, and boastfully − or nervously − talking too much.

(c) Atmosphere

The character of the room, the arrangement of furniture and props, and the appearance, choice of dress, age and sex of the parties involved will all have an effect on the atmosphere. Interviewees − especially job applicants − will have spent anxious hours imagining the scene; whereas interviewers often lack the imagination and foresight to avoid tactless mistakes like placing the interviewee's chair at an awkward angle, or forgetting to stop incoming phone calls.

(d) Procedure/manner

The purpose of the interview will usually determine the way it is conducted. Most interviews will fall into one of three broad categories:

- *Standardised*: following a predictable sequence of questions, often based on a form or questionnaire.
- *Individualised*: with the interviewer using a wide range of questions designed to lead to an 'in-depth' exploration of the problem or job application.
- *Stress*: where the interviewer will be deliberately aggressive and unpredictable in order to test the interviewee's confidence and competence. (Such techniques are only used in very particular cases.)

Skilled interviewers will vary their manner of questioning according to the purpose and procedure of the interview. There are five broad types of question:

1. *Closed/direct* questions, inviting short factual answers, e.g. 'When did you pass your driving test?'
2. *Yes/no* questions, e.g. 'Have you been to Glasgow?'
3. *Leading/loaded* questions, inviting agreement, e.g. 'Don't you find it rather hot in here?' 'Isn't that a dreadful book?'
4. *Probing/follow-up* questions to winkle out further information, e.g. 'How would you deal with complicated telephone calls in Spanish from our Madrid office?'
5. *Open-ended* questions, allowing the interviewee to expand on his knowledge/experience, and express opinions/ideas, e.g. 'Tell me about your year in Peru.'

These general principles apply to a wide range of interviews and should equip you to answer general questions such as 'Why do so many interviews fail to achieve their purpose?' Here we are concerned with the particular characteristics of the selection interview.

THE SELECTION INTERVIEW

Most examinees will have consulted a careers officer at some stage, and so be familiar with the usual practical advice given to candidates for interview. The purpose of this chapter is to prepare you for likely exam questions on interviews and job applications, rather than give detailed advice on 'how to succeed at interview'. We therefore look at selection interviews as part of recruitment policy and procedure, with the emphasis on the role of the interviewer rather than the interviewee.

The process of short-listing and interviewing candidates is all too often rather 'hit or miss'. The British National Institute of Industrial Psychology (BNIIP) recommend an assessment procedure based on a **seven-point plan:**

1. *Personal/physical*: age? sex? appearance? speech? health? physical suitability?
2. *Education/qualifications/attainments/experience*
3. *General intelligence*: lively mind? sensible and interesting responses?
4. *Special aptitudes*: verbal and/or numerical skills? manual dexterity?
5. *Interests*: practical? sporting? artistic? intellectual? solitary/social?

6. *Disposition*: manner? maturity? emotional/psychological characteristics?
7. *Circumstances*: marital status? family situation? housing? transport?

This list, which now has many variations and refinements, usually provides the basis for the assessment form completed after the interview. Of course the assessment of these points will not usually be based on the interview alone, but will draw on information in application forms, c.v.s, and letters of application. The attention paid to letters from referees varies to a surprising degree. They might be read before the short listing, or before the interview; or, in some cases, not until after the interview, when they are consulted as confirmation − or otherwise − of the interviewer's own impressions.

Job applicants approaching interviews often ask careers advisers what to expect. The Roehampton Institute has drawn up the following list of twenty likely questions:

A **Employers expect candidates to have some knowledge of the area of work they are seeking to enter.**
1. Has the candidate read the literature we sent him/her?
2. Has he/she read beyond what we fed him/her?
3. Has he/she bothered to talk to people already working in the field?
4. Has he/she any relevant experience, e.g. through holiday/weekend work?
5. Has he/she discussed his suitability for this post with a careers adviser?

B **Employers need reassurance that a candidate will respond well to their methods of training and is up to the daily intellectual demands of the job.**
1. What is the candidates's academic track record?
2. Are his/her examination results adequate evidence of high general intelligence?
3. Can he/she pick his way through complex data and arguments?
4. Can he/she make decisions and how does he reach them?
5. Is he/she numerate?

C **Employers need reassurance that the candidate has personal qualities appropriate to the job and also likely to make him/her a congenial colleague.**
1. How effectively has he/she communicated with us on paper and in interview?
2. What social skills has he/she demonstrated in the selection procedure?
3. Can he/she assert him/herself and still carry others with him/her?
4. How varied are his/her personal interests and what do they tell us about him/her?
5. Do we like him/her as a person?

D **Employers need to anticipate what contribution the candidate is likely to make in the organisation, as well as any problems he may generate.**
1. Has he/she ties outside work that may limit mobility?
2. What motivates this person − money, influence, self-fulfilment?
3. Could he/she meet the emotional demands of responsibility?
4. Will some of his personal goals conflict with those of the organisation?
5. Is he/she self-motivating, or will he/she need to be driven?

This rather intimidating list might give the (wrong) impression that interviewers know exactly who/what they want and are rigorously objective in their search for the right person/people, and in their final choice/s. What usually happens is that their preconceived picture of the ideal candidate, but after the interview the subjective question C5 might outweigh all the other questions put together. Interviews are largely a matter of interpersonal 'chemistry'. Non-verbal communication is of particular importance here, because the outcome of interviews may often depend on a first impression of manner, voice, gestures and style of dress.

C. USEFUL APPLIED MATERIALS

Addenbrookes Hospital
Hills Road

ACCOUNTANCY ASSISTANT

This post would suit someone looking for a career in accounting. Candidates should have a good general education and must be interested in figure work. Salary will start at £4,897 p.a. rising by annual increments to a maximum of £5,925 p.a. Postholder will work a 37 hour 5 day week. Closing date 22 January 1985. For application form and Job Description write to: The Regional Personnel Division, Hills Road, Cambridge, Tel: Cambridge 45151 Ext. 7350

Fig. 12.6   Job advertisement with job description

EAST ANGLIAN REGIONAL HEALTH AUTHORITY

JOB DESCRIPTION
Accountancy Assistant
Higher Clerical Officer
£4,897 per annum rising by annual increments to a maximum of £5,925 per annum.

The District treasurer's Department is a compact team of 12 staff involved in the provision of financial management information. The Department is divided into two sections each complementary to the other.
The Financial Management section deals with Budgetary control and the preparation of annual Cost Statements whilst the Financial Planning Section deals with the financial assessment of projected developments and is involved in assessing the feasibility of incentive bonus schemes.

Details of Job
(a)   General assistance with the provision of financial management information, budgetary control statements on a monthly basis.
(b)   Assisting in the collection of statistical information for costing and budgetary control purposes.
(c)   Assisting in the preparation of annual cost accounts and involvement in subsequent cost investigation.
(d)   Any other duties relative to the above which may be assigned from time to time.

Working Relationships
The section is supervised by a Senior Administrative Assistant to whom the Accountancy Assistant will be responsible. The Senior Administrative Assistant is accountable to the Principal Management Accountant.

Career Prospects
Financial assistance is available to staff in this grade who wish to pursue a recognised course of study. In order to give staff wider experience in the Department it is anticipated that rotation within the two sections of Financial Planning and Financial Management will be available.

(Source: Cambridge Evening News)

Fig. 12.7   A personnel specification

1 Secretary/Course administrator – This job is one which is divided equally between secretarial duties for a management and training adviser, and the administration of courses in a particular field.

1 *Physical*	Essential:	Good health record
		Clear, pleasant telephone voice
	Desirable:	Over 20, under 30

2 *Attainments*	Essential:	O level (or equivalent) English language
		Typing — 40 wpm
	Desirable:	A level English
		Shorthand or speedwriting — 80 wpm
		Previous experience of training department; course administration
3 *Abilities*	Essential:	Good layout of typing
		Above average at spelling
4 *Disposition*	Essential:	Able to work without direction
		Able to work with others
		Flexisble
	Desirable:	Sense of humour
		Lively
5 *Circumstances*	Essential:	Reasonable and reliable travel to office
	Desirable:	Living locally
		Telephone at home
		Willing to be away from home occasionally

(Source: BACIE; Interviewing in 26 steps)

D. RECENT EXAMINATION QUESTIONS

Question 1 The Royal Edinburgh Hotel, Kirk Terrace, Dumfries has been seeking to establish a reputation for high standards of service and food. It has achieved a great deal in this and is anxious to use every means of publicising the fact. As one of these means they have decided to use staff advertising to carry this message.

Due to the discovery of irregularities, which led to the Hotel suffering substantial losses, certain of the staff have just been dismissed. The Hotel is faced with having to find a Hotel Butcher, Baker, Head Waiter and Housekeeper quickly.

These are all permanent positions with good salaries, meals while on duty, accommodation if required, free clothing for the Butcher and Baker, and all positions give access to a pension scheme.

The Personnel Manager, Jim Fallon, wants replies sent to him and, if anyone wants further information, they are to be referred to him at Dumfries 4333. The telephone area code is 89. He does not want enquirers dealt with by anyone other than himself so that he can deal tactfully with questions about what has happened to make such a large number of important staff leave at the one time.

Draft an appropriate advertisement.

(10 marks)

(Scottish Higher National Diploma in Secretarial Studies, 1985)

Question 2 A question which involves the close reading of a Job Description (which provides a model example) and the writing of a letter of application.

In response to an advertisement placed in *The Daily Courier*, you recently applied for details of the post of Personal Assistant to the Personnel Manager of Prestige Office Furniture Limited, 14 Lennox Road, Middleton, Midshire ML6 4AQ. In addition to receiving the forms of application you were also sent the following job description for the appointment:

JOB DESCRIPTION

Title:	Personal Assistant to Personnel Manager.
Department:	Personnel.
Function:	To assist the Personnel Manager in the discharge of his duties by providing administrative/secretarial support; to maintain effective communication with the Personnel Manager and all members of staff and people in contact with his office; to supervise the work of three junior clerical/typewriting staff.
Hours of Work:	8.50 a.m. −5.20 p.m. Mondays −Fridays (1 hour lunch) 37½ hours weekly, plus overtime as required.
Accountable To:	Personnel Manager.
Responsible For:	1 shorthand typist;
	1 audio copy typist;
	1 clerical assistant.
Authority Over:	3 staff members as indicated above.

Duties/Responsibilities:

1. Work within company rules, regulations and procedures.
2. Assist the Personnel Manager in all aspects of his work, utilising appropriate administrative/secretarial skills.
3. Maintain the efficient operation of the Personnel Manager's office and its systems.
4. Act on behalf of the Personnel Manager in his absence as required.
5. Supervise the work of three junior staff in the Personnel Manager's office so as to maintain efficient standards of work and productive staff relations.
6. Coordinate and attend meetings and conferences and take minutes, notes, etc. as required.
7. Receive visitors and company personnel and maintain a favourable company image.
8. Employ initiative, resourcefulness and discretion in contacts with all company personnel and people outside the organisation.

You were asked in a covering letter sent with the details of the appointment to submit your application to the Personnel Manager, Mr G.A. Johnson, quoting reference PM/PA 26.

Compose a suitable letter of application to support your application for the above post. The body of your letter should comprise between 300 and 350 words.

(RSA DPA, 1980) (20 marks)

E. TUTOR'S ANSWERS

Tutor's answer 1

The challenge here is to project a positive image to allay suspicion in the trade. You can assume that the advertisement will appear under an appropriate classified heading and will only be read by specialists, so do not try to invent salaries or other details not included in the question.

Remember that up to half the marks for this sort of question will be for clarity of layout, but with less than 20 minutes you cannot afford to fuss too much over details of design. Write extra clearly and make the lines on the paper work to your advantage for a logo and capital letters. Block it out in pencil until you are satisfied with the layout, then go over it in ink (preferably using the sort of pen which can produce both thin and thick lines) and rub out the pencil. A typical display advertisement of this type will usually be reduced to a 3−5 inch double-column space in the local newspaper, but you should do a larger version.

The growing reputation of the Royal Edinburgh Hotel, Dumfries, as one of Scotland's premier hotels has led to a reorganization of staffing.

We are therefore able to offer the following vacancies:

HOTEL BUTCHER
HOTEL BAKER
HEAD WAITER
HOUSEKEEPER

All positions offer a rewarding job in an elegant hotel renowned for high standards of food and service. Excellent working conditions including meals while on duty and accomodation if required. Free clothing is provided for the Hotel Butcher and Baker. Good salaries for experienced applicants.

Full pension scheme.

For further information please contact:

JIM FALTON,
THE ROYAL EDINBURGH HOTEL,
KIRK TERRACE,
DUMFRIES.

Tel. Dumfries (89) 4333

Tutor's answer 2

In real life such a post is unlikely to be offered as a first job to a newly qualified applicant, so you could imagine yourself as having had at least two years' relevant experience since completing your course. This is the approach adopted in the tutor's answer. Alternatively, and equally correctly, you could write as a DPA candidate seeking a first post, making the best of any work experience you might have had. In either case you should indicate why you are particularly interested in personnel work, and try to relate your experience and aptitudes to the duties listed in the Job Description. Remember that the prospective employer might know little about the DPA course, so you could devote at least a paragraph to the syllabus and your results/anticipated results.

> 15 West Road,
> Middleton,
> Midshire MJ5 2KA
> Tel. 072 6481
>
> The Personnel Manager,
> Prestige Office Furniture Ltd,
> 14 Lennox Road,
> Middleton,
> Midshire ML6 4AQ
>
> Dear Mr Jones,
>
> <u>Personal Assistant to the Personnel Manager</u>
>
> Thank you for sending me the Job Description of the post of personal assistant to the personnel manager. I enclose my completed application form and curriculum vitae.
>
> Personnel work particularly attracts me because of the range and variety it offers, and the opportunity it provides to meet people from all departments of the company. In my present job as personal secretary to the training officer of Addpress Engineering I assist in the arrangement of day-release further education courses for junior clerical staff and the monitoring of their progress. My work often involves attendance at meetings with the personnel department, which have given me some insight into staff recruitment and industrial relations. I would welcome the chance to extend my interest in these areas.
>
> My experience covers most of the duties and responsibilities outlined in the Job Description, and I am used to taking charge of the office in my boss's absence. I am not directly responsible for any junior staff, but have to work closely with the general office and the typing pool. The area of work which would be new to me is receiving visitors and company personnel. I would very much look forward to this aspect of the post, since I enjoy meeting new people and learning about different aspects of management.
>
> The Diploma for Personal Assistants course gave me an excellent secretarial training, and an invaluable knowledge of related topics. The subjects I most enjoyed were the Personnel and Functional Aspects of Administration and Communication in which I obtained distinctions. The DPA entitles me to exemption from part of the Stage 1 examination for membership of the Institute of Personnel Management. I have recently attended a training course on the use of computers and word processors which has proved very useful.
>
> My present job is interesting and enjoyable, but since it holds little prospect of promotion in the near future I am keen to move to a post which carries more responsibility and extends my range.
>
> I should be pleased to attend an interview at any time convenient to you, and were I to be offered the post, I would need to give one month's notice to my present employers.
>
> Yours sincerely,
>
> Jane Roberts (Miss)
>
> Enc. c.v.

F. A STEP FURTHER

Many candidates will already have had first-hand experience of job applications and interviews and will be able to share their experiences with other students. All students should write a professionally presented c.v. and keep it up to date. Some of those who already have, or have had jobs, may have kept a copy of their application letter or their letter of acceptance/rejection. Such raw material is easy to collect and share among a class.

The press contains thousands of job advertisements each day, and it is interesting to compare the way different newspapers are used to attract different ranges of applicants. Some papers devote each day of the week to a distinct specialism, e.g. *The Times* advertises legal posts on Tuesdays, secretarial on Thursdays.

Recruitment brochures, application forms and Job Descriptions are available on request from firms advertising vacancies. Careers offices are well stocked with useful books, leaflets and company literature, and often provide interview training either to individuals or groups.

General books

People and Communication, Evans D W. Pitman 1984.
Mastering Business Communication, Woolcott L A and Unwin W R. Macmillan 1983. Chapter 8 provides a clear and concise survey of interviews.

Information and advice on job applications and interviews can be found in:

Successful Job Hunting, Miller R C I. Blackwell 1983.
Coping with Interviews, Higham M. New Opportunities Press 1981.
University of Edinburgh Student Guide to Jobhunting Applications and Interviews. AGCAS Careers information booklet 1983.
(See also *Which*? magazine Oct. 1985. Consumers' Association.)

For useful summaries of the topic from the management point of view see:
Human Resources Management, Graham H T. Macdonald & Evans 1983.
Interviewing in 26 Steps (reprinted annually). BACIE Booklet.
Selection Interviewing (reprinted annually). The Industrial Society.

Films

Manhunt (selection). Video Arts.
How Am I Doing? (appraisal). Video Arts.
I'd Like a Word with you (disciplinary). Video Arts.
Hilarious dramatisations of interviews starring John Cleese. All have accompanying booklets which can be ordered separately.

Chapter 13

Public relations and publicity

A. GETTING STARTED

Several examining bodies are increasingly fond of setting written tasks associated with public relations (or PR, as it is generally known). This is a welcome trend, since it gives students an insight into an important area of modern communication techniques, and opens up a range of less conventional written tasks.

Not that such questions are a soft option – often they are summaries or essays in painless disguise. Writing a press release is just as exacting an exercise in organisation of material and conciseness of language as a conventional précis.

This chapter deals with the main forms of PR and publicity writing set as exam questions: leaflets, press releases and articles. Related topics are covered in Chapter 5 (House Magazines) and Chapters 3 and 7.

It is a specialist subject, so students interested in the background should refer to the bibliography at the end of this chapter. But a few comments might serve to set the broad context.

Public relations is a very wide and loose term for any form of planned communication between an organisation and its public or publics – including its own employees. Although PR is often regarded with suspicion, it is most noticeable when it fails.

Professional public relations officers (PROs) consider themselves as much misunderstood. They have a reputation as smooth talkers with lavish expense accounts whose function is to whitewash the truth and sell the company image by laying on 'junkets' and softening up journalists with gin and tonic.

Of course this sort of thing goes on, particularly where PR overlaps with advertising and sales promotion, but journalists regard such antics with cynicism, and an organisation that overdoes the candy floss while neglecting the substance soon gets the brush-off. To promote a serious factual image many organisations call their PRO an information officer or press officer. Large PR departments may have both a chief PRO/information officer and a press officer who writes routine press releases and answers press enquiries.

By whatever name, it is a growing profession, largely due to the spread of instant mass communication and its appetite for news. Local government, trade unions and charities such as Oxfam have all become aware of the importance of PR and are employing professionals to put their case across. There are also specialist PR consultants who take on client organisations which do not have an 'in house' officer.

B. ESSENTIAL PRINCIPLES

Impact

The first thing to remember when writing any form of publicity material is that, unlike most reports and business letters, the reader may choose whether or not to read it. So it has to capture the attention straight away. For example, essential information about something the public needs to know, such as the arrrangements for refuse collection over Christmas (see Fig. 13.1), should not be buried in a **leaflet** written in official language and presented in blocks of tiny type. Those who do not throw it away might lose it or be irritated by the effect of disentangling the contents. Imaginative PR creates goodwill and co-operation by putting people in the picture ...

Fig. 13.1   The front page of a seasonal council leaflet

(Source: Cambridge City Council)

... thus making them more inclined to read the message and co-operate with the instructions on the centre pages.

Press releases should also announce themselves clearly and boldly:

COUNCIL TELLS PUBLIC ABOUT CHRISTMAS
REFUSE COLLECTIONS

120,000 new-style leaflets will be delivered this week to every household in the city ...

Although journalists are trained to look for 'news value' in even the most amateur efforts, they might be less attracted to the story if it opened like this:

Christmas Refuse Collections.

In order to inform residents of arrangements to maintain an acceptable standard of refuse collection over the coming holiday period, the City Council ...

Articles are more of a challenge because there is no 'captive audience'; even pieces written by specialists for specialists and published in specialist publications may not be read until the end of a busy week. They need a tempting headline and a sharply focused opening:

DUSTMEN GET THE CHRISTMAS SPIRIT

The message for the festive season is 'Don't rubbish your dustman'. The City Council is sending out 120,000 eye-catching leaflets this week ...

The same story makes less impact presented like this:

CHRISTMAS REFUSE COLLECTIONS.

At a meeting today of the City Council's Public Health Committee, arrangements were approved for refuse collection over the Christmas period, and leaflets will be distributed to every household.

Target Audience

The key to successful PR writing is to know your readership. Is your **leaflet** aimed at a wide public or at a specific group of knowledgeable and intrested people, e.g. members of a particular profession? Is your **press release** aimed at local newspapers, national newspapers or specialist publications? If it is aiming for all three at once it will probably fail on all fronts − you may need three different versions of different length emphasising different angles and details. Is your **article** aimed at a local or national readership? Expert or amateur? Of high or low reading ability?

The examiners try to vary the imaginary media and audience for these questions, so you must sample a wide range of real examples. Get into the habit of picking up leaflets wherever they are offered and testing them for presentation and clarity. Make sure your communication lecturer gets hold of some press releases – local newspapers are only too happy to get rid of them.

Browse in newsagents, comparing the style of various papers and magazines, and looking out for pieces of between 300 and 500 words on likely topics. Get hold of some company house magazines and track down short articles of general interest. Be more critical of the stories you read in your own newspaper or any magazine you regularly buy – do not just look for content; look for structure and style. Decide which journalists you particularly like, and why. Then try to copy their technique.

Now we consider these three forms of communication in more detail.

1. LEAFLETS

(a) Layout

Being asked to 'design' a leaflet in an exam paper is a rather unreal and cramping exercise. You know that in reality you would have different typefaces, several colours, photographs, etc. Luckily the examiners know this too and do not expect fancy artwork. But they *do* expect your answer to look something like a real leaflet, so even if there are no explicit instructions on layout it is acceptable to ignore margins and to write on both sides of the paper unless instructed otherwise.

You can use a new sheet for each page of your leaflet, numbering the pages and indicating where any illustrations should be placed. A more radical but easier method is to fold your paper into two or three. You then have an outside cover for announcing the contents in capitals and for names, addresses and telephone numbers, and inside pages for details which can be divided into blocks or columns. (This method is easier on unlined paper.)

Fig. 13.2 Paper folded into two or three

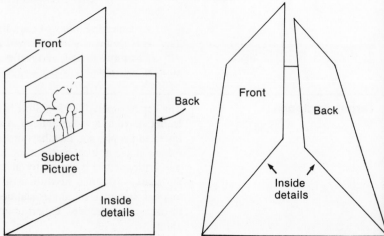

(b) Content

Most exam questions assume a maximum length of 200–300 words. You may be given very little background, leaving you scope for invention, or you may be given more information than can be included in the leaflet.

Suppose you have been asked to draft a leaflet on insulation grants to be distributed through libraries and ticket offices. What will people want to know?

- Who is entitled.
- How much can be claimed.
- How and where to apply.

Now decide on the order in which the information should be presented, how much detail to include, and roughly how many words it will take. Then split it up into two or three sections corresponding to the shape you have chosen. Use plenty of headings and indentations marked by bullet points, dashes or asterisks. Sometimes *questions* make effective headings, e.g.

Who can get a grant?

- Owner-occupiers.
- Private tenants.
- Council tenants.
- Landlords.

(c) Style

The first essential is **clarity,** so keep your sentences short and simple. If you are publicising an event or service do not use exclamation marks or over-enthusiastic adjectives like 'fantastic' which sound like advertising. If you are issuing advice or official information avoid grey bureaucratic language – your tone should sound crisp but friendly.

Do not use note-form – write in complete sentences, and remember that grammatical and spelling mistakes will stick out more embarrassingly than in other forms of writing.

(**Brochures** are longer than leaflets and produced as booklets. You are unlikely to be asked to write more than a brief extract from this type of publicity information.)

2. PRESS RELEASES

90% of the thousands of press releases sent out each day are thrown straight into editors' wastepaper baskets, 10% get 'spiked' for possible use, but only about 5% get used. Most offerings simply have no news value; many are really advertising 'puffs' posing as news – especially those produced by PR agencies; while others may be interesting in themselves but lack the appropriate angle for that particular audience.

Although journalists are very cynical about press releases they will also admit that their job would be much harder without them. Local newspapers rely on that newsworthy 5% for much of their copy, especially the business page. The free weeklies consist almost entirely of advertisements and items taken straight from press releases. The trade and technical press always needs information about new products and services. Television looks for unusual pictures of gadgets, events, personalities, etc, and radio needs a constant supply of interviewees. The different types of press release/news release are described below.

Fig. 13.3 Types of press release/news release

1. *Those that just give information*

   Examples

   - About new products or changes to existing products.

     New packet soup flavour. Addition of croutons to tomato soup.

   - About a new service or change in existing services.

     Advice bureau for small businesses. Saturday opening of banks.

   - About new orders for goods or services.

     Bulk order of boots for policemen. Advertising agency gets important new account.

   - About people – promotions, transfers, retirements, achievements.

     New managing director of company. Top Apprentice of Year award.

   - About events.

     Announcement of theatre production. Charity fund-raising gala.

   - About changes in policy, take-overs, mergers, etc.

     Price reduction of home computer. UK company taken over by multinational.

2. *Those which also seek to persuade*

   Examples

   - Stressing need for/advantages of product or service.

     Special scissors for left-handers. Convenience of Saturday bank opening for family shopping trips.

   - Linking product, service, advice, to topical circumstances.

     Boom in ice-cream sales during heat-wave. Anti-drinking and driving campaign over Christmas.

   - Presenting one side of a case in dispute, conflict, negotiations.

     Reasons for sacking/resignation of Managing Director. Union's reasons for calling strike.

   - About reports, statistics, surveys.

     Summary of enquiry on Sunday trading. Consumer survey on beer consumption.

   - Summaries of speeches.

     National Farmers' Union President on butter prices.

Once you've decided what type is required, try to imagine yourself as a budding PRO and the examiners as editors. Their mark-scheme will be broadly divided under the following headings: **news value, awareness of audience and angle, structure and content, style, presentation and format.**

(a) News value

Your story has of course been invented by the examiners, but there is usually some scope to improve on it by adding one or two plausible details. For example, your new factory/office-block/hotel might have some original or even controversial feature, or be designed by a famous architect. Your export order may have been won against fierce international competition or there may be something unusual or unlikely about it worth stressing in the opening paragraph, e.g. when a British company recently landed an order from Italy for pasta! If your event is rather old hat, e.g. a sponsored run, try to include something that would provide an unusual photograph. Link your new product to an expert celebrity, e.g. thermal underwear worn by an Arctic explorer; or find an unexpected application for it, e.g. video equipment used to train football referees. Or use a topical angle, e.g. a 'flu epidemic would be a good time to publicise paper tissues. Such points could be illustrated by relevant pithy quotes.

Remember that editors are allergic to giving free space to anything that smacks of advertising. If a man were to walk from Land's End to John o' Groats in the same pair of socks without wearing a hole in them, that might just merit a mention for the trade name of the socks.

Some questions give you a set of notes in random order. The test here is to spot the newsworthy aspects of the story and put them at the beginning of your story.

(b) Audience and angle

A local newspaper uses the following illustration: If an electronics company wants to announce a new device which automatically counts the number of peas going into a packet, this could well be of interest to trade and technical journals in the field of food packing and electronics, but would in itself be of little concern to the readers of a national paper. Even the firm's local paper would mainly want to know if the device would lead to taking on extra employees, extending the factory, and promoting local managers; or it might be more interested in the background to the research carried out by local engineers. Photographs of key personnel could be attached to the press release.

(c) Structure and content

A press release is essentially a news story, so it should be designed to fit the same basic shape as a newspaper report. Your object is to present it in a form that can be published with the minimum of cuts and alterations. It is better to keep it short, leaving the journalists to make their own additions, than to write far more than they need and risk losing those points you are most anxious to see in print.

You should build your release in 'pyramid' form, with the peak opening paragraph supported by paragraphs of further details in descending order of importance. This convention makes for ease and speed of editing; when subeditors are in a hurry, they simply cut from the bottom up. So it is safer to use the concluding paragraphs for such details as the technical specifications of the product, a potted history of the organisation, quotations from speeches, information about the way a survey was conducted, etc. (See examples in Section C).

Central paragraphs should also be short and self-contained, so that they can be cut out without ruining the sense and flow.

Into this mould you then pour the content of your story, with the points arranged in a way that brings out what journalists call the **five 'W's:**

- *What* is happening/being done or said.
- *Who* is doing/saying it.
- *Where* it is happening/being done or said.
- *When* it is happening/being done or said.
- *Why* it is happening/has happened.

What, Who, Where, When should always be in your first two paragraphs, though not necessarily in that order. Why follows naturally as part of the following explanation/background. Question 3 on p. 232 provides an example of how a typical five 'W's opening might unfold:

– Anderson Enterprises . . .	*Who*
– are opening a new £x. . . factory . . .	*What*
– on the Clydebank Business Park . . .	*Where*
– on September 23.	*When*
– This expansion is the result of increased demand by	*Why*
the building industry for prefabricated windows.	

You may then develop the story by reporting how the expansion will bring extra jobs; then how £x. . . investment in new machinery will speed up production.

Over the top of your story you write a **title**. Do not try to think up a witty headline – leave that to the subeditors. Your object is to state clearly what the story is about. It will pack more punch if it contains a verb, e.g. 'SOUTHWICH FIRM WINS £X,000 SOFT DRINK ORDER FROM NIGERIA' rather than 'LOCAL FIRM'S BIG EXPORT ORDER'. Headings are usually one-sentence summaries of the first paragraph.

(d) Style and tone

An inviting opening paragraph, known to journalists as an 'intro' or 'lead', is crucial. If the opening is uninformative, long-winded or just plain dull, an editor might push your offering straight on to the reject pile. An examiner will plough dutifully through the rest, but will mark you down from the outset, and be less receptive to your perfect format and brilliant quotes.

The 'intro' is the hardest part to get right because you have to give the gist of the mesage quickly, without overloading your opening sentences with too many points. Two or three short sentences are better than one rambling sentence of epic length.

Turn to the exam question shown in Ch. 1, p. 2, and suppose that you had been asked to write a news release about the Eastview Shrub event for the local press. This does not work:

'Following its successful Dutch bulb festival last year, Eastview Nurseries are planning a Shrub Week as part of National Shrub Week, with demonstrations, special offers, competitions and free gifts, to be opened by Mr Ted Eden on July 21, and including other attractions during the rest of the week.'

Nor does this:

'Glanton residents will be delighted to hear that Eastview Nurseries are holding a Shrub Spectacular from July 21–28, with lots of free gifts and special offers. We promise you fun for all the family, and the chance to meet the famous TV personality Ted Eden!'

This does:

'TV gardening expert Ted Eden will open a Shrub Week at Eastview Nurseries on Saturday July 21. The event is part of a National Shrub Week, and many new varieties will be on show for the first time. There will be a full programme of demonstrations by specialist staff, as well as competitions for local enthusiasts.'

The first version is flat and vague, the second sounds like a cross between an invitation and an advertisement, whereas the third contains useful and tempting information.

Press releases need a crisp lean style with short sentences and paragraphs. The journalists will add whatever extra colour or detail is needed to suit the particular publication. The tone should be positive but strictly factual. There are seven main rules:

1. Paragraphs should not exceed a maximum of fifty words or contain more than four sentences. Sentences should not exceed twenty-five words.
2. Vary the length of your sentences and paragraphs. This adds bounce and urgency, and helps with editing. Some paragraphs may consist of only one sentence.
3. Use strong verbs like *win* and *start* rather than weaker equivalents, and prefer the active to the passive, e.g:

    'X won the contract' rather than 'The contract was given to X.'
    'Work on the road will start on May 2' rather than 'Work will be commencing next week.'

4. Be precise. Avoid vague terms like 'many' (how many?), 'various' (which?), 'better' (in what way?), 'soon' (when?). If the question itself is vague, invent plausible details.
5. Avoid boastful claims that cannot be specified, like 'record-breaking' (what record?), 'unique' (in what respect?), 'revolutionary' (how?).
6. Avoid using too many adjectives which sing the praises of your product/scheme/event, like 'exciting', 'luxurious', 'exotic'.
7. Never address the press directly, e.g. 'You are invited to attend the opening', or 'We are sure you will be impressed by our new range of designs.' And never use exclamation marks!

Quotations

It is often a good idea to quote a comment or explanation from someone directly involved in the story provided it adds something new. Do not use quotes as a means of inserting ecstatic platitudes from the boss, e.g. 'Mr David X, managing director of X & Y, said, "The company is extremely proud of our exciting new range of fabrics … blah, blah, blah, etc."' Use him to advance the story, e.g. 'Mr David X, managing director of X & Y, said, "The new range of fabrics is specially designed to appeal to the teenage market."' And/or you could quote someone with a different angle, e.g. the designer, or a pop star, or a representative of the workforce/trade union welcoming the ectra jobs involved.

(e) Presentation and format

Your press release will make a more favourable impression if it looks professional. Large organisations and PR agencies have special headed paper which is distinct from their stationery used for letters. There is wide variation in appearance and layout, and, unfortunately, in standards. Figure 13.4 demonstrates all the ingredients of a thoroughly professional format.

Fig. 13.4   Structure and layout of a press release

NEWS FROM: NAME OF ORGANISATION.
                              Address.
                              Telephone and Telex.   LOGO

PRESS RELEASE. For Immediate Release.   January 21
(Or: Embargoed until 10 pm January 23.)

> HEADING. BRIEF IDENTIFICATION OF STORY.

> *Intro*:   Gist of story.
> *What?*   Product/contract/service; or event/campaign.
> *Who?*   Organisation/individual.
> *When and Where?*   Date and place.

> *Why?*   What is new or different. Advantages/progress;
>   or problem/issue.

> *How?*   Applications/users/markets.
>   Campaign/measures/action.

– more –

> *Details*: Prices/materials/specifications.
>   Participants/arrangements.

> *Further details*: Suppliers/sources.
>   Potted history/background.

– ends –

For further information contact: Writer's name
                                 and role.
                                 Telephone. Ext.
                              or: Name, address,
                                 telephone no. of
                                 other source.

Enc.

Press releases/News releases should follow standard newspaper conventions so that, after subediting, they can be sent straight to the printers.

1. Use one side of the paper only.
2. Use double-spacing between lines, and leave two clear lines between paragraphs. Even though this makes handwritten exam answers look very spread-out and gappy, it shows that you know the drill.
3. The name of the organisation should be boldly displayed at the top, with the address and telephone number either directly underneath it or at the bottom of the page.
4. *Embargoes* are only used for 'hot' news stories, to ensure impact through simultaneous coverage. They often coincide with the time of a press conference.
5. Capital letters should be used for proper nouns only, e.g. Jones, India, Bombay. Do not use capitals for job titles; put managing director, not Managing Director, and never write company or product names entirely in capitals except in headings, e.g. Lloyds, not LLOYDS.
6. Only use the full name and role for the first mention; thereafter use an abbreviated form, e.g. Anderson Enterprises Ltd; then simply Anderson's: Mrs Joan Anderson, managing director of Anderson's; then simply 'Mrs Anderson'.
7. Sets of initials should not be punctuated, e.g. BBC not B.B.C.
8. Do not underline anything in the text because this is the standard instruction for the printer to use italics.
9. Numbers of one to nine should be in words; 10 onwards in figures.
10. Dates are shown in reverse to letter style, e.g. June 26.
11. *Continuations*. If there is more than one page, write 'More' or 'Continued' in the bottom right-hand corner. At the top left of the following page write a key phrase, e.g. Shrub Week − 2. It is still usual to write 'Ends' after the last paragraph, though not strictly necessary.
12. Quotation marks should only be used for direct quotes.
13. If you are enclosing a photograph, write a suitable caption, not on the back of it but separate and attached to it, e.g. 'The hardy Fuschia Grandifloria is one of the new varieties which will be on show for the first time at the Eastview Shrub Week on July 21'.
14. Remember to include the contact's name and telephone number at the bottom.

(See also *Public Relations*, by F. Jefkins.)

3. ARTICLES

Once you have grasped the structure and style of press releases you will find articles much easier to write, because you can follow a similar approach, adding appropriate variations on the background, with comments, opinions and conclusions, e.g. a new product or service may have wide implications for consumers, a new office or factory may arouse local debate over the site.

(a) Types of articles

The examiners will nearly always tell you what sort of publication and readership you are writing for, but if there is no specific guidance write as for the readers of a mid-market newspaper such as the *Daily Mail* or a popular magazine, and make this clear to the examiners. You will usually be given a maximum word length; if not, aim at about 350.

You are unlikely to be asked to write a learned piece for *The Times* at one extreme, or a racy item for the *Sun* at the other. Nor should you be set technical articles based on specialist material outside your range. The list below includes some of the most commonly set topics and publications, with tips on structure and style.

General interest articles for newspapers and magazines

Some exams set general topics calling for argument and opinion – known to journalists as 'think-pieces'. Likely topics include: careers advice and job-hunting, provision for youth activities, some aspect of the mass media, the changing role of the secretary, etc. These are really short essays in disguise, but call for a very different approach. You should first decide on your angle, i.e. whether you are going to be provocative, or amusing, or enthusiastic. You might link the subject to a real or imaginary topical event, issue or person – known to journalists as a 'peg' – on which to 'hang' our article or report.

Instead of a title as for an essay, or a straight heading as for a press release, you need a punchy **headline** which gives an indication of what the story is about and arouses the readers' curiosity, e.g.

'BUT I WANT TO BE A BRAIN SURGEON'
'SHORTHAND GETS THE BIRD'

Do not waste your first 10 minutes groping for a good headline; get on with the story and hope for inspiration when you have finished, possibly by using one of your quotes.

Then instead of starting with a statement of the argument as in an essay, you might start with a challenging or amusing incident, observation, quote or question, e.g.

'I went into the interview hoping to be a brain surgeon', said 15-year-old Kevin, 'but I came out thinking perhaps it would be easier to be a careers teacher.'

'How many secretaries end up wishing they'd never learned shorthand?'

After a lively, sharply focussed opening, you should then broaden out and discuss more general aspects of the subject, perhaps brightening it by following up the 'lead' topic and/or by adding a further illustration, quote or question. The final paragraph should come to some definite conclusion, or point the way forward. It should not be flat or repetitive.

If you are asked to write for a local paper, bring in some 'human interest' and colour based on your knowledge of where you live and what your neighbours would be interested to read about.

Advertising features and articles for the trade press

Newspapers often publish sections which are paid for by commercial interests and consist of publicity articles surrounded by advertisements devoted to particular industries or services. For example, a local newspaper might print an article on a new hotel and invite advertising from firms which have supplied it with carpets, lighting, kitchen equipment, etc. The trade press will often take complete articles as well as press releases. The content should be strictly factual, and the style plain and functional.

Articles for house magazines

Large organisations often distribute two types of publication; an up-market quarterly glossy for employees, shareholders and customers, containing articles of general interest; and a monthly magazine or newsletter for staff only, containing items of local interest.

Likely topics include:

- An aspect of management policy, e.g. training schemes, the introduction of new technology, canteen arrangements.
- Company activities, e.g. the opening of a new branch, launch of a new product, important contracts and orders.
- Social activities, e.g. an anniversary celebration or a staff outing.
- Personalities, e.g. profiles of people retiring or being promoted.

The style should be simple and fairly chatty in order to appeal to a readership ranging from top management to manual workers. The tone should be positive but not gushing – house magazines can be regarded by employees as hyped-up management propaganda. (See Fig. 13.9.)

(b) Presentation

- Leave equal margins each side of the page, and a clear line between paragraphs.
- Vary the length of your paragraphs. The occasional one-sentence paragraph adds impact.
- Divide material into chunks of about 200 words marked by simple short subheadings, e.g. JOB CENTRES, WORD PROCESSORS, PROMOTION.
- Remember to put a 'by-line' either after the headline or at the end; e.g. 'By Penny Wright'. For house magazines add your job title and/or department.

C. USEFUL APPLIED MATERIALS

Fig. 13.5 An outline Job Description of a PRO from Roget's *Guide to Graduate Employment and Training.*

Projecting and maintaining a desirable image of a business or other organisation and keeping the public informed of developments of general interest. Some typical activities may include:

- Keeping up to date with all internal and external developments which may affect clients' or employers' organisaton.
- Preparing press notices for circulation to newspapers, journals, radio, television, etc.
- Organising visits by press and public to the organisation concerned.
- Arranging exhibitions, press conferences, meetings, discussions, etc. to project organisation's image, foster goodwill and gain publicity.
- Organising works' newspapers, house journals and similar organs to improve internal communications and relations.

- Advising on all aspects of the organisation's contacts with the public and liaising with outside organisations to arouse interest in the client's or employer's organisation.

A publicity campaign

Fig. 13.6 illustrates one stage in a government publicity campaign about loft insulation.

Fig. 13.6   A leaflet publicising a government home insulation scheme

Please remember

* don't do any work before your council says so;
* you must use a loft insulation product on your council's list of materials.

Ask your local council office about a loft insulation grant.

Prepared by the Department of the Environment, the Welsh Office and the
Central Office of Information, 1984
Printed in the UK for HMSO.
Dd 8831246 ENVIJ 0039 NE

Save money on loft insulation.

Grants for 90% of the cost for the elderly and severely disabled on low incomes, and 66% for other people.

Loft insulation could keep you warmer

If your home was built before 1976, and has no loft insulation, or none 30mm thick or more, you could get a grant towards the cost.

If you are elderly or severely disabled, and on a low income, the grant could cover 90% of the cost up to a maximum of £95. For everyone else, the grant is normally two-thirds of the cost, up to a maximum of £69.

You can apply for a grant if you are an occupier or the landlord of the dwelling. If it is unoccupied you may apply if you are entitled to occupy it.

Could you get a 90% grant?

Yes, if–
* you are getting a supplementary pension or allowance, or a rent or rate rebate or rent allowance (together known as housing benefit);

And as well, either–
* you or your wife or husband, or anyone living with you as such, is over retirement age (65 for a man, 60 for a woman)

Or–
* you or your wife or husband, or anyone living with you as such, or one of your dependent children living with you, is receiving a–
* mobility allowance or war pensioners' mobility supplement;
* attendance or constant attendance allowance;
* DHSS private car maintenance allowance;
* three- or four-wheeled vehicle provided by DHSS.

Dependent children include children under 16, or between 16 and 20 who are receiving full-time education other than advanced education, or who qualify for child benefit.

How much will you get?

If the work costs £105 or less, the grant is 90%. That means, say £63 if the bill is £70. If the work costs £106 or more the grant will be £95.

The grant does not cover the whole cost of the work. You will have to pay the rest. If you pay someone to do the work for you, the grant can go towards the cost of labour as well as materials.

How do you apply?

Just fill in an application form which you can get from your local council office. If you are a tenant, you may need to get your landlord's agreement to having the work done.

Don't start work without the go-ahead from the council or you won't get the grant

You won't qualify for a grant if –
* your home was built after 1975;
* a grant has already been paid towards the insulation of your loft;
* your home has had loft insulation 30mm thick or more in any part of the loft(s), excluding extensions, during your occupancy or ownership.

Your council must be satisfied that your home is eligible and will inspect some lofts. They will let you know as soon as possible whether or not you can have a grant. If they do agree, they may ask you to wait until they give you the go-ahead to do the work, depending upon the money then available for grants.

What you have to do

To get a grant you must normally–
* insulate the whole of your loft using a material on your council's approved list of materials;
* lag the cold water tanks and pipes in the loft (if they are not already lagged);
* lag the hot water tank (if it is not already lagged);
* do the work within the time limit the council will give you.

When the work is completed, you have to sign a claim form. If anyone has done the work for you, they must sign it as well. Give the council the bills showing how much it all cost. Then you will get a grant.

In some cases the council MAY pay you the grant before you have to pay the bill. You can also ask them to pay the contractor direct.

(Source: 1984 edition of DOE leaflet "Save Money on Loft Insulation". The information in this leaflet is subject to revision.)

- *Posters* are pinned up in public places to alert people to energy conservation and to inform them that grants are available for loft insulation. The A4 poster design is based on an enlarged version of the leaflet.
- *Leaflets* (Fig. 13.6) are distributed in public libraries, council offices, etc. to provide additional information about the grants and how to apply. Note the use of questions for headings, also the positioning of 'asterisks' and 'bullet points'.
- *Application Forms*, and *brochures* giving installation instructions are provided on request.

The press release at Fig. 13.8 resulted in many news reports – one of which is given in Fig. 13.9. Note the minimal changes needed to adapt the release for a news story. The subject-matter allowed subeditors to have a field day inventing facetious headlines. Some borrowed the words from the press release – a sure sign of success!

Note how the release on p. 227 could be cut from the bottom up, and how it could be adapted for the following publications: the consumer pages of national and local newspapers, the Sheffield media, the trade press, women's magazines, etc.

Fig. 13.7 An excellent press release about a product

Press Information

PRESS EMBARGO — MAY 1st 1984

**KITCHEN DEVILS WIN DESIGN COUNCIL AWARD FOR
THEIR PROFESSIONALS**

Kitchen Devils, now part of Wilkinson Sword Limited, have won a Design council Award for their Sheffield-made range of Professional knives . . . the first such award to be given to a complete range of kitchen cutlery.

HRH The Duke of Edinburgh will make the presentation at a ceremony in London on Tuesday 1st May, 1984.

The Design Council judging panel, chaired by Kenneth Grange CBE, described the range as well engineered, good to look at and highly professional. 'The knives work well practically — the shapes of both blades and handles are excellently thought out.'

Kitchen Devils, already a major force in the domestic kitchen knife market with their best-selling serrated-edge knives, decided four years ago that the time was right to launch a range of British-made knives to compete in the professional sector of the market — a sector previously dominated by foreign imports.

Robert Welch, MBE, a Royal designer for Industry, was commissioned to design the range and exacting attention was given to balance, comfort and function, as well as to the overal aesthetic appeal of the shapes.

Blades for the Kitchen Devils Professionals are made from the finest surgical steel with a carbon content that gives excellent edge retention. The handles, of glass-filled polypropylene, are moulded to the extended tang ensuring maximum hygiene in use and they are 100% dishwasher proof.

The range, which has been extended since the launch in 1981, now includes fourteen items with knives suitable for all culinary uses, a cleaver, fork and steel. Like all Kitchen Devils products, the Professionals carry an unconditional lifetime guarantee.

Kevin Cubbage, Managing Director of Kitchen Devils, intends to continue the original company philosophy of manufacturing and marketing well-designed, high-quality British products which enjoy excellent sales in both the home and overseas markets.

Issued on behalf of: Kitchen Devils Limited Sword House Totteridge Road High Wycombe Bucks HP13 6EJ Tel: (0494) 333000	Press Enquiries: Sheila FitzJones PR Consultancy 15 Fitzroy Road London NW1 8TU Tel: 01-586 9749

(Source: Wilkinson Sword Limited)

Fig. 13.8 An example of a press release about a consumer survey conducted as part of a campaign

---

National Consumer Council

18 Queen Anne's Gate   London SW1H 9AA

Telephone 01- 222 9501

PRESS RELEASE

Embargo: 00.01 hours, December 31, 1982

SURVEY ASKS: WHEN IS A PINT NOT A PINT?

Sixty-five per cent of beer/lager drinkers say they like a head on their beer. But they want it on top of their pint - NOT to count as part of it.

Another 13 per cent prefer their beer without a head.

Only 21 per cent say they are happy for the head to be considered part of their pint.

Releasing these findings from a National Opinion Poll today (New Year's Eve) the National Consumer Council and Scottish Consumer Council said in a joint statement:

'The evidence is overwhelming. People want fair measures. If people are paying the price of a pint of beer, that's exactly what they should get - not nine-tenths of a pint, or less, plus froth.

'It's simple to measure out a pint of beer into lined measuring glasses. Those who like a head on their beer can still have it. But we say they shouldn't have to pay pint-size prices for anything less than a full pint of beer.'

Michael Shanks, the National Consumer Council's Chairman, has written on behalf of the National Consumer Council and the Scottish Consumer Council to Dr. Gerard Vaughan, Minister of Consumer Affairs, urging him to use his powers under the Weights and Measures Act to order that a pint of beer must be a pint of liquid. Previously, say the two Councils, the Government has refused to act, on the grounds that there was no evidence that people were dissatisfied with the present situation.

- more -

But the poll findings show that a majority of beer drinkers <u>are</u>
concerned, say the Councils.

Michael Shanks said: 'Magna Carta laid down that "one measure of wine
shall be throughout our realm; and one measure of ale". But in May
this year, Lord Donaldson and Mr Justice Webster put an end to all
that in the Divisional Court. They ruled that when beer is sold by
brim measure (that is, a glass which holds 20 fluid ounces when
filled to the brim) how much liquid you get depends on local custom
about the head on the beer. So the Great British pint now, by law,
consists of some variable amount of beer up to 20 fluid ounces,
depending on how much head people are used to locally,'

Esme Walker, Chairman of the Scottish Consumer Council, said: 'A
recent Scottish survey showed that the so-called pint of beer may,
in fact, contain as little as 87 per cent of a pint of liquid; the
rest was froth. People can pay six or seven pence, or even more, just
for the froth on the top. That makes it hard to compare beer prices in
different pubs. It also puts publicans who sell exact measures at a
disadvantage, against the rest.'

<u>The poll</u>

The NOP survey was carried out between November 18 and 23 by NOP Market
Research Ltd, and involved interviews with 1,864 people aged 15 and
over, in 180 Parliamentary constituencies. A 'systematic probability
sample' designed to be representative of all adults in Great Britain,
was used.

Sixty-eight per cent of men, compared with 59 per cent of women said th
the head on beer should not count as part of the pint. A further 13
per cent of beer drinkers preferred beer without a head (10 per cent
men, 18 per cent women). Twenty-one per cent were happy for the head
to be part of their pint. Only 2 per cent of beer/lager drinkers
didn't know <u>what</u> they thought.

END

Wendy Toms   01-222 9501 (daytime
Chief Press Officer   December 23)
                        0580-80 312 (daytime and
                                    evenings
                                    December 24
                                    to January 3)

(Source: National Consumer Council)

Fig. 13.9 Resulting news reports.

Bitter protest over froth

There is overwhelming evidence that Britain's beer drinkers are unhappy at the amount of froth that goes into a pint, it is claimed today.

A survey found that 65 per cent of beer and lager drinkers like a head on their brew — but they want the froth counted as topping and not part of the measure.

Only 21 per cent are happy for the head to be considered part of the drink.

'People shouldn't have to pay pint-size prices for anything less than a full pint of beer', says the National Consumer Council and Scottish Consumer Council, which ordered the survey through the National Opinion Poll.

National Consumer Council chairman Michael Shanks is calling for change in the Weights and Measures Act to make a pint of beer mean a pint of liquid.

The council says past Governments have refused to alter the rules because of lack of evidence that people were unhappy with the measures.

'The evidence is overwhelming now. People want fair measures', adds the council.

The Divisional Court ruled earlier this year that the amount of beer or froth depends on local custom when beer is sold in a glass that holds 20 fluid ounces when filled to the brim.

'The great British pint now, by law, consists of some variable amount of beer up to 20 fluid ounces, depending on how much head people are used to locally', says Mr Shanks.

The Scottish Consumer Council says that people could pay six or seven pence, or even more, just for the froth.

The survey, between November 18 and 23, involved 1,846 interviews with people aged 15 and over in 180 Parliamentary constituencies.

(Source: Northampton Chronicle and Echo)

HEADS WE WIN!
When is a pint not a pint?

There is overwhelming evidence that Britain's beer drinkers are unhappy at the amount of froth that goes into a pint, it is claimed today.

A survey found that 65 per cent of beer and lager drinkers like a head on their brew — but they

(Source: Burton Mail Group)

Fig. 13.10 An example of an article from a company newsletter

Just the job

How and why your role is evaluated

Wanda Skinner, Personnel Controller explains the new job evaluation for non-management staff

What is job evaluation? Why do we need it? During October, most of you will have attended one of the presentations on job evaluation given whether by Martin Warner or myself.

Job evaluation is a technique that compares jobs using a set of common criteria in order to determine their relative positions within an organisation.

Widespread use of job evaluation is, in this country, largely a phenomenon of the last 20 years. Few major organisations now expect to operate a salary policy and structure without the firm foundation of job evaluation schemes appropriate to the employee groups involved.

A large number of jobs within Dun & Bradstreet remain ungraded since the original work in 1977; the structure of the organisation has changed dramatically; and job content has changed in some of the jobs that were graded under the 'old' scheme.

These are some of the major reasons for introducing a new job evaluation scheme. It will provide us with:

● a fair and equitable basis for salary structure;
● a more objective method of deciding relativities between jobs;
● a good basis for selection, training and development through concise and accurate job descriptions;
● assistance in the efficient organistion of work.

The company is starting off this process with supervisory, clerical and admin jobs which we have defined as 'non-management'. We have selected an evaluation method which is simple, easily understood, and practical in that it concentrates on the actual tasks performed in the job.

It is based on a classification scheme designed by the Institute of Administrative Management and is used extensively throughout the UK, providing the only standard scheme for office jobs used nationally across many sectors of industry and commerce.

The scheme comprises six grades, coded A to F, ranging from Grade A, which covers the simplest clerical operations, up to Frade F, which covers the supervision of an office section and work requiring professional or specialised knowledge and use of judgement and initiative.

Each grade level is briefly and carefully defined in a way that clearly indicates the differences in skills and responsibilities required at each grade level.

The classification system requires a panel of evaluators with a general knowledge of the organisation in order to fit jobs into appropriate grades. Within D&B, panels have been selected across different divisions and levels of management and non-management to achieve indepth knowledge and experience of the organisation and the jobs within it.

During November, we have asked you to prepare job descriptions for evaluation under the new scheme. As you know, where there are several jobholders with the same job, such as business analysts, an experienced job holder will be selected from ach group of people to write one job description. However, other business analysts will have the opportunity to read through this job description and contribute where appropriate.

Job grading will start towards the end of November and continue throughout December, January into early February. Results will be notified to each individual, detailing: the new grade and other jobs falling within the same grade, the grade above and the grade below. New salary bands will also be published at that time. This will indicate where your job fits in to the organisation. There will be the opportunity to appeal through your line manager if you fedl that your job has not been graded correctly in relation to others.

Full implementation will take place in April. Finally, just a reminder that this exercise does not mean a general salary increase, but no salaries will be reduced!

(Source: Dun and Bradstreet Limited Update 1984)

D. RECENT EXAMINATION QUESTIONS

Question 1 *Producing a leaflet*
This question is part of the complete case study paper shown in Ch. 1, p. 2

Question 2 (a) What are the most important characteristics of an effective press release? (10 marks)
 (b) How can the administrator ensure that the organisation produces effective press releases?
 (15 marks)
 (ICSA, 1984)

**Question 3
Drafting a
Press
Release** Andersen Enterprises is a firm manufacturing prefabricated windows for the building industry. They have recently experienced some financial difficulties which led to problems with deliveries to long established customers, and are aware that those customers who suffered have lost some confidence in their reliability. They have overcome their financial difficulties and are confident that their customers will now have a reliable service from them but they are experiencing some difficulties in the attempts of their salesmen to convey this in a convincing way.

As part of a concerted campaign to overcome this problem, they decide to use the occasion of the opening of a new factory at the Clydebank Business Park in a month's time to obtain publicity which will help in the creation of an image of success and expansion being built upon a new financial health. They do not, however, wish to encourage customers to recall their recent period of financial instability.

The move will create about 70 extra jobs and over £12,500 has been invested in new machinery to ensure high standards of construction and finish in their products.

They want a *Press Release* issued one week before the opening of the factory. Draft a Press Release to meet the above situation.

(10 marks)
(SCOTVEC SHND in Secretarial Studies, 1984)

**Question 4
Writing an
Article** As personal assistant to the Training Manager at Safeguard Insurance Limited, you are closely involved in the company's staff training and development programmes. As part of a plan to improve the induction of new employees into the firm, you have been asked to liaise with the Personnel Manager and to write an article for the next edition of the company's house magazine.

The article is aimed at junior school-leavers joining Safeguard in the July/August period and is to be entitled:

'Making A Good Start — How To Handle Colleagues, Callers and Customers Successfully!'

Compose a suitable article of between 350 and 450 words. (20 marks)
(RSA DPA, 1980)

**Question 5
Writing a
press
release
and an
article** (a) The following information describes a recent experiment in shopping methods. Using ALL the details provided write a **press release** 200–250 words long designed for business editors of national newspapers.

Computerised shopping experiment — involves Fransco Foods and Wallsfoot Borough Council. Postan Street branch library, Wallsfoot, used since May 3rd. Two Fransco staff attend there four mornings a week — use a side room. Wallsfoot Social Services Dept. co-operating — they picked out 60 local folk who find it hard to get about — the old, the sick, the handicapped and mothers with young children. These people all shop at library. Fransco has at Postan Street library a data terminal cash register with memory and Prestel viewdata Fransco price lists — customers order from these. As 'background' — slide projection scenes from Fransco's town centre store — to make customers feel they're in the supermarket. Deliveries free the same day. All very successful. Fransco plans follow up: three KcT 47 microprocessors to connect two branch libraries and Social Services department direct to Fransco's town centre store — up to 700 handpicked 'customers' this time. Their shopping orders go down phone as digital data to supermarket — faster service follows. Overall customer savings — no fares to town centre, shorter trips, avoidance of expensive corner shops, less congestion in supermarket.

(15 marks)

(b) Using SOME of the details from the notes given in Question 1, write an **article** 300–350 words long for the *Wallsfoot Chronicle*, bringing out the 'human interest' features of the computerised shopping experiment. Give the article a title and add your name.

(20 marks)
(RSA DPA, 1983)

E. OUTLINE AND TUTOR'S ANSWERS

Outline answer 1

This would probably be best presented on one sheet folded in half unless instructed otherwise. You are going to need a map, which might be best displayed on the back cover. The front cover should announce the event with a bold picture — maybe a photograph of a bright seasonal shrub. Choose one from the list. The reverse side (inner two pages) should contain all the details. The essentials are given in the question, so all you have to do is invent some details, e.g. about the competitions.

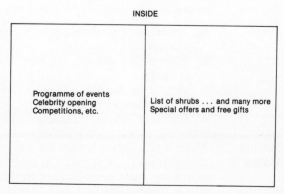

OUTSIDE

EASTVIEW NURSERIES
SHRUB WEEK

photo of Ted Eden

Map

Colour picture of fuschia

Parking, restaurant, and play area

INSIDE

Programme of events
Celebrity opening
Competitions, etc.

List of shrubs . . . and many more
Special offers and free gifts

Outline answer 2

(a) There is not much point in just giving a list of adjectives here; you need several complete sentences with a certain amount of explanation, e.g:

- It must be newsworthy to compete with hundreds of others sent out daily.
- The gist of the story should come across at the beginning.
- It should be well presented, with double spacing and wide margins for editing, and end with name(s) and telephone number(s) for further information.

(b) A more general question probing your background knowledge of PR policy and the practical steps needed to project an appropriate image:

- By the appointment of an in-house PR expert, or a contract with a sympathetic PR firm.
- By encouraging senior managers to supply items likely to be of interest to the press and specialist publications.
- By anticipating adverse publicity and forestalling it with timely and positive information.

Outline answer 3

A good example of a press release to counteract recent bad publicity. You are given more information about the past problems than about the new factory, but for only 10 marks it has got to be a short snappy release of about 150 words with little added detail.

NEW WINDOW FACTORY TO OPEN AT CLYDEBANK BUSINESS PARK

- On May 10 Blank Blank (invent local political celebrity plus name) will open Andersons' new £... factory at Clydebank Business Park.
- Factory will enable Andersons to step up production of its prefab window frames for building industry and improve delivery service.
- 70 new jobs for area of high unemployment.
- Over £12,500 investment in latest machinery for new range of products.
- Quotation from MD or big local building firm (if time.)

Outline answer 4

The examiners complained that most of the answers to this question fell back on empty generalities about smiling your way through everything, rather than offering practical advice on day-to-day problems and challenges. Start on a humorous note − perhaps with an anecdote about a junior who made a mistake because he/she had not been told what to do, then move on to specific points, e.g.

- Correct and friendly telephone procedure. How to cope with angry callers. Give a typical example.
- When to deal with a matter yourself and when to consult a senior, with reference to safeguard.
- How to deal tactfully with the prejudices and idiosyncracies of older people who have worked there a long time.
- Outline of company's induction scheme. Who to go to for advice.

Outline answer 5

Rather a gift question because the article almost writes itself after you have digested the material and written the press release. The story has high news value; there is the novelty of the experiment, and a nice mixture of fashionable 'high-tech' and social interest. The scheme has already been running for a week or so, but you must not make it sound like stale news.

Since it is for the business pages of the national press it obviously comes from Fransco rather than the council, though they may do their own version for local and specialist media. The line to take is 'the human face of commerce'.

The facts have been jumbled up, so the first thing to do is to group them in rough priority order. The passage is about 170 words, so you have to plump it up by about a third. Putting in the missing verbs and articles will use up a lot of your word allowance, so it is fairly tight. You cannot afford to take much over half an hour.

The headline needs to combine the three main ingredients — computerised shopping, the library, and the customers. COMPUTERISED SHOPPING does not tell you enough, nor does it sound very new.

HANDPICKED CUSTOMERS SHOP BY COMPUTER IN PUBLIC LIBRARY

- Fransco's experiment with computerised shopping in Wallsfoot library.
- Customers chosen by Social Services.
- How orders are made. Deliveries.
- Staffing, slide projection.
- Success, plan for expansion.
- Quote from Social Services. (More effective than having Fransco praising its own scheme)
- Quote from customer.

The article is a contrasting exercise. You have 100 more words to play with and you do not have to use all the facts, which allows scope for some invention. Try to imagine yourself arriving at this rather odd scene with a photographer, and remember that your readers will be interested in the local angle and the characters involved.

So the last point in your release could come first. You could focus on a group of customers or an individual. An alternative lead would be the oddity of seeing the familiar library transformed into a 'supermarket' — but without the trolleys and checkout queues.

Next explain the system and describe the customers choosing groceries from the screen. Then fill in the background — why Wallsfoot was chosen, the reaction of Social Services, and perhaps the librarian.

Finally, you need some sort of up-beat pay-off — perhaps check up on a delivery.

PENSIONERS BUY BAKED BEANS FROM LIBRARY SHELVES

- Group of pensioners taken to library by Social Services to do shopping.
- Focus on pensioner. What does she buy? Quote.
- Describe how system works — advantages.
- Reaction of Social Services. Librarian?
- Plan for expansion.
- Follow-up with pensioner at home.

Tutor's answer 5

FRANSCO FOODS **plc**, Brandon House, Westway, London W12 4PL
Telephone: Telex:

NEWS FROM FRANSCO FOODS   May 10 1983

HANDPICKED CUSTOMERS SHOP BY COMPUTER IN PUBLIC LIBRARY

A unique experiment in computerised shopping has been running since May the 3rd at a branch

library in Wallsfoot for customers who find it difficult to get about. The Wallsfoot Social

Services Department has selected 60 local housebound people, including the elderly, disabled, and mothers with young children, to order their groceries from a TV screen.

The customers choose their purchases from price lists displayed on Prestel viewdata. Their orders are fed into a data terminal cash register with memory and go down the phone as digital data to the supermarket. Deliveries are made the same day free of charge.

A side room of the library is staffed by two shop assistants four mornings a week. A real shopping atmosphere is created by slide projections of scenes from the main city centre store.

The scheme has been so successful that Fransco plans to expand it by using three KcT 47 microprocessors to connect two branch libraries and the Social Services Department direct to their main store. This would cater for up to 700 handicapped customers.

Director of Wallsfoot Social Services Joan Grant is enthusiastic. 'We welcome this ingenious experiment. People who find shopping difficult can save time on journeys to the town centre and avoid the crowds and checkout queues. They also save money on fares and high prices in the corner shops. We now have a long waiting list of potential customers who are looking forward to joining the scheme.'

For further information contact:

Michael Crown
Customer Services Manager
Tel. 01 245 8266
　　　ext. 570

Joan Grant,
Wallsfoot County Council,
Wallsfoot.

Tel. 321 7834
　　ext. 351

The enclosed photograph shows Fransco customer services manager Michael Crown demonstrating the Prestel price list to 78-year-old Mrs Hilda Gray of 32 Chester Road, Wallsfoot.

The article
for the *Wallsfoot Chronicle*

PENSIONERS BUY BAKED BEANS FROM LIBRARY SHELVES

by Penny Wright

Every Wednesday morning twelve elderly residents of Manton House are taken by Council minibus to do their weekly shopping – in the local library. A large side room of the Postan Street Branch library has been turned into a supermarket. The usual rows of books have turned into constantly changing shopping scenes, and customers are served by shop assistants instead of librarians.

The day's price lists are shown on a Prestel screen which is changed by the press of a button, so the customers can sit in comfort and take their pick. Their orders are then fed into a computer cash register with a telephone hotline to the supermarket.

SHOPPING BASKET

78-year-old Mrs Hilda Gray spotted peach slices among the Special Offers and ordered two cans with a packet of sponge fingers to go with them. 'It's my favourite sweet', said Mrs Gray, who suffers from arthritis. 'I know it's fattening, but at my age you might as well spoil yourself.' She filled up her 'shopping basket' with sausages, baked beans, half a dozen oranges and a bottle of sherry – 'to keep out the cold'. Then she and her friends went through to the fiction department to change their library books.

MORE CUSTOMERS

The Wallsfoot library 'supermarket' is the first to be tried by Fransco, who hope to extend this scheme to other cities in the Midlands and the North-West. Customer services manager Michael Crown told me that Wallsfoot had been chosen for their experiment because of the enthusiastic response from Wallsfoot County Council.

Social Services Director Joan Grant hopes that more local people will benefit from the scheme, particularly mothers with young children who find it an expensive struggle to get into town with prams and pushchairs. Fransco has plans to add another 600 customers by an extended link-up between Social Services and branch libraries.

Deliveries are made the same day free of charge, so by 5.30 Mrs Gray was enjoying her tea of sausages and baked beans. She was already looking forward to next Wednesday. 'I fancy a chicken pie – and an Agatha Christie.'

F. A STEP FURTHER

Since PR writing is scantily dealt with in the general communication textbooks, it is essential to look at as much material as you can lay your hands on.

Leaflets can be picked up easily at railway and bus stations, public libraries, local council offices, Citizens' Advice Bureaux, etc. Some are obligingly delivered or sent by post by public services such as the Gas and Electricity Boards, the GPO, local authorities, etc.

Press releases can be supplied by your local newspaper. Send a request and a stamped addressed envelope to the business editor. Or look up PR firms in the Yellow Pages and ask them for samples; if they fail to respond they are guilty of not practising what they preach.

Articles are published in abundance every day, so make a collection of 300−500-word pieces from newspapers, magazines, company publications and the trade press. A useful **general textbook** which includes this topic:

Mastering Business Communication, Woolcott L A and Unwin W R. Macmillan 1983, pp. 72−6, 240−1.

Useful specialist books

Public Relations, Jefkins, F. Macdonald & Evans 1980, pp. 1−12, 32−45, 81−98, 118−26.

Advertising Writing, Jefkins, F.

Effective Press Relations, Jefkins, F.

The author has wide experience in commerce and industry, and his books are comprehensive, informative and well presented. Essential reading for any student with PR aspirations.

Using the Media, MacShane D. Pluto Press 1983, pp. 69−97, 187−92. The author is a professional journalist dedicated to passing on his expertise to trade unions and pressure groups. The chapter on press releases is exceptionally clear and stimulating.

Editing and Design, Evans H. Heinemann 1984. Volume I (*Newsman's English*). The ex-editor of the *Sunday Times* has written an encyclopaedia for journalists, with well-chosen examples of style and layout.

Index